NUMBER 77

Yale French Studies

Reading the Archive: On Texts and Institutions

Yale French Studies

E. S. Burt and Janie Vanpée, *Special editors for this issue*
Liliane Greene, *Managing editor*
Editorial board: Ora Avni (Chair), Peter Brooks,
   Shoshana Felman, Richard E. Goodkin, Denis Hollier,
   Christopher Miller, Antonia Mulvihill, Charles Porter,
   Allan Stoekl, Brigitte Szymanek, Helen Williams
Staff: Lauren Doyle-McCombs
Editorial office: 315 William L. Harkness Hall.
Mailing address: 2504A-Yale Station,
   New Haven, Connecticut 06520.
Sales and subscription office:
   Yale University Press, 92A Yale Station
   New Haven, Connecticut 06520
Published twice annually by Yale University Press.

Designed by James J. Johnson and set in Trump Medieval
by The Composing Room of Michigan, Inc.
Printed in the United States of America by the Vail-
Ballou Press, Binghamton, N.Y.

ISSN 0044-0078
ISBN for this issue 0-300-04540-9

E. S. BURT AND JANIE VANPÉE

Editors' Preface

The authors of the articles that follow do not raise their questions about institutions chiefly on empirical grounds. They recognize that established educational institutions, to take the example most often discussed, may fail in their task of preserving and transmitting past knowledge intact, or, alternatively, may act forcefully to exclude certain modes of knowledge from the curriculum there where some success at transmitting a tradition can be said to occur. Denunciations of, and pragmatic prescriptions to remedy these empirical failures are not, however, their chief concern. They tend to see it as a constitutive problem of educational institutions that their space is not exclusively a space of pure knowledge, a library where disincarnate beings pursue abstract research, nor yet exclusively of power and action, where agents of the state publicly profess state doctrine, confer degrees and titles, or, sometime double agents, surreptitiously preach subversive doctrines in the classroom. It is one consequence of the fact that the space of the university is constructed by a double and conflictual obligation—the charge to preserve and transmit a body of knowledge to the public, and the charge to translate the public space, the authorizing system, into knowledge—that failures to live up to one or the other of these obligations can always be discerned. It is another consequence that an empirical critique, be it from the right or the left, can always be recuperated by the university as made at its behest and in keeping with the obligations that define it. Be it because empirical analysis fulfills the office of disclosure, of making knowledge public in the name of an ideal inadequately realized by a determinate institution, be it because such analysis can be summoned by the university to render an account of the system of legitimation on which it calls, and thus to translate into systematic

1

knowledge the ideal of the interpretative community it serves, empirical critique does not stand outside the conceptual space of the university but always analyzes in the name of a model university whose concept it does not question. The articles that follow have assumed the implications of the insight that the space of the university is not limited to the determinate space enclosed by gray walls, but is at least in part an ideal construct. While their attention to empirical evidence is great, their analyses are not chiefly empirical.

This does not mean, however, that the authors of the following pieces are engaged in abstract and a-political speculation or that they seek to construct a model for all institutions. The search for such a model would imply, they suggest, a belief in the possibility of a final harmony to be achieved between system of knowledge and system of legitimation toward the accomplishment of which ideal all determinate institutions should strive. If the authors of these articles are concerned with analyzing the foundations of the university, it is for very different reasons and with a very different model in mind. The target of their critique is the concept of the university itself. In asking the question of the university, one has not only to ask about determinate institutions, but also about the determination of its concept: is the university, for example, a historically defined concept? Does its claim to universality, to the systematic comprehension and transmission of the totality of human knowledge, not imply a teleological fiction that has been discredited, a finality whose time has passed? Over and over these articles make use of the tools of reading put at their disposal in the past two decades to ask whether the model of the university is not through and through an ideological space, a shopworn or ruined concept. Work on the discrepancies between the constative and performative dimensions of language, sign and meaning, grammar and figure; analyses of a hybrid genre like autobiography whose truth claims are undecidably those of fiction and those of history, or of political theories suspended between making promises and giving theoretical knowledge of the structure of promises; critiques of authority, of aesthetic ideology, of the dream of a universal language—all inform these articles in their critique of the concept of the university, its compartmentalization and professionalism, its carefully delineated fields of study, its systematicity, etc.

Some might think that the authors of these pieces are arrogantly claiming to inhabit the position of the disinterested observer, the scientist "outside" the ideological space criticized, in whose foundations they discern gaps, conflicts of indeterminate outcome, an undecidability that the ideologues within the university fail to see, deny, or cover over. Were these authors claiming the position of the scientist viewing an autonomous object, were they claiming no engagement within the university, some irritation at a contradiction apparent in the position of university professors daring to question the ideology of the university might be justifiable. Were it furthermore the case that these authors were recommending nihilism, suggesting that, because the concept of the university is discredited, one should therefore dismantle all universities, something more than irritation would be in order. Disinterest is not the claim, nor nihilism the object of these pieces, however.

On the contrary. The noncorrespondence between the university as theoretical and as pragmatic space, the open question as to whether it is a space of knowledge or a space of power and legitimation, is seen to provide a chance and a responsibility. The gaps that open in the very foundations of the university only lie "outside" it, if one refuses the obligation under which we are placed by the university to know even such gaps as may be constitutive of it. The contesting of the university as ideology only appears as a contradictory nihilism if one neglects the equally weighty obligation accepted by these articles to transform pragmatically the site of the university, to displace its conflicts, to translate its question—as one translates from one language into another—across the lines of its disciplines. The discrepancies that place the university at odds with itself, send it "outside" itself as determinate concept, appear "within" its fields of study as an occasion to undo its most confining myths. Each of these articles seizes the undecidability of the university—fictional construct or empirical set of walls?—as an occasion, as a chance for displacement, for discovery, for the inaugurating of a study. If they tend to propose, either directly or indirectly, fields and methods of study disrespectful of the lines dividing disciplines, if they tend sometimes to propose as worthy of study fields for which diplomas have not hitherto been awarded, or to suggest that in some fields no titles of competency are, or ought to be, awarded, these are the effects of a displacement of the institutional space, as of the critique of its ideology. In a word, the engagement of the critic of the university with the question of the university is felt to provide a chance and a responsibility.

The strategies taken in the articles that follow are very different.

Some take on the larger structures of the university, the academy, the archive, and analyze and make their displacements with those structures in view. Others reread founding texts, texts from which orthodox schools, whole theories of politics or education, have been derived, and seek in them signs of an unresolvable conflict between their function as inaugurating texts, and the knowledge they provide of that function. Others, construing the undecidability of language as having something to say about the undecidability of the institutional space, read the texts most subversive of and reflective on language, namely poetic texts, in the light of language's capacity to subvert the ideological spaces it sets up. The difference in strategies ought not to be passed over too quickly, since strategic positioning in a conflictual field where inside and outside are problematic must be a crucial question. To this question, the articles themselves must speak, however. It is enough, in a general introduction, to suggest it to have a bearing on displacement and translation, that is, the problem at the heart of these pieces.

I. Instituting Acts

JACQUES DERRIDA

Sendoffs*

"Coups d'envoi" was published in *Collège International de Philosophie: Sciences, Interscience, Arts*, as part of a "Rapport présenté à M. Jean-Pierre Chevènement, Ministre d'Etat, Ministre de la Recherche et de l'Industrie, par François Châtelet, Jacques Derrida, Jean-Pierre Faye, Dominique Lecourt," dated 30 September 1982, 105–55. Portions of the report, including "Coups d'envoi," were also reprinted in a booklet titled *Extraits d'un rapport pour le Collège International de Philosophie*, prepared by the College in the Fall of 1983, and parts of "Coups d'envoi" were excerpted as "Légitimité de la philosophie," in *T.E.L. (Temps Economie Littérature)* 8 (25 November 1982): 1,7.

Châtelet, Derrida, Faye, and Lecourt made up a French government "mission" charged with investigating the possibilities and conditions of an International College of Philosophy. The idea for such an institution had grown in some measure out of the militant struggles of the Groupe de Recherches sur l'Enseignement Philosophique (GREPH, founded in 1974) and the Etats Généraux de la Philosophie (1979)—in which Derrida had played a major part—against the attempts made by conservative governments to eliminate or restrict the teaching of philosophy in French schools. A year after François Mitterand's election as president and the victory of a Socialist parliamentary majority in May 1981, the mission was formally created by Jean-Pierre Chevènement, the new Minister of Research and Industry. On 18 May 1982, Derrida circulated on behalf of the mission an open letter to interested parties worldwide, citing Chevènement's instructions and inviting potential participants in the College to identify themselves and to propose research and projects (the

* "Sendoffs" is printed in advance here with the permissions of Jacques Derrida and the Harvard University Press.—*Editors' note.*

YFS 77, *Reading the Archive: On Texts and Institutions,* ed. E. S. Burt and Janie Vanpée, © 1990 by Yale University.

letter was widely disseminated; see, for instance, *La Quinzaine Littéraire* 374 [1–15 July 1982]: 29, and *Substance* 35 [1982]: 80–81). Four months later, after extensive consultations and evaluation of the more than 750 replies to the open letter, the mission recommended the establishment of the College as an autonomous but state-funded teaching and research institution, aimed principally at encouraging and organizing work on (quasi-) philosophical themes or objects not sufficiently studied in existing institutions. Their report, a somewhat technical government document, outlined in its first hundred pages the mission's collective recommendations for the definition, the regulating idea, and the constitution of the College. This was followed by four individual "projections," one by each of the four philosophers, "Coups d'envoi" being Derrida's contribution.

The College was officially founded in Paris on 10 October 1983 and began operating that semester, with Derrida as its first director, followed by Jean-François Lyotard, Miguel Abensour, and others. Today it offers, free and open to the public, without prerequisites, a wide range of courses and research programs, as well as frequent colloquia and lectures, by scholars in its six "intersections": philosophy/science, philosophy/art and literature, philosophy/politics, philosophy/psychoanalysis, philosophy/internationalities, and philosophy/philosophy. It is directed by an Assemblée Collégiale, the current president of which is Philippe Lacoue-Labarthe. Its work, particularly the work of its seminars, is documented in a regular series of *Cahiers*. Requests for schedules and other information can be addressed to the College at: 1, rue Descartes, 75005 Paris.

Helpful discussions of the College in English can be found in Steven Ungar, "Philosophy after Philosophy: Debate and Reform in France Since 1968," *Enclitic* 8, nos. 1–2 (1984): 13–26, especially the appendix on the College; and in Vincent Leitch, "Research and Education at the Crossroads: A Report on the Collège International de Philosophie," *Substance* 50 (1986): 101–14.

Work in English by Derrida concerning the College includes: "The Principle of Reason: The University in the Eyes of its Pupils," trans. Catherine Porter and Edward P. Morris, *Diacritics* 13, no. 3 (Fall 1983): 3–20; "On Colleges and Philosophy," discussion with Geoff Bennington, *ICA Documents* 5 (1986): 66–71; and the interview with Imre Salusinzky in *Criticism in Society* (New York and London: Methuen, 1987), 8–24 especially 14–18. In French, see: "Philosophe au collège," interview with Jean-Luc Thébaud, *Libération* 692 (11 August 1983): 15–16; "Popularités: du droit à la philosophie du droit," in Jean-Claude Beaune et al., *Les Sauvages dans la cité* (Seyssel: Champ Vallon, 1985), 12–19; and "Cinquante-deux aphorismes pour un avant-propos," in *Psyché* (Paris: Galilée, 1987), 509–18.

These and other texts related to the College, including "Sendoffs," will appear, along with the rest of Derrida's work on the institutions and teaching of philosophy, in Jacques Derrida, *Institutions of Philosophy*, edited by Deborah Esch and Thomas Keenan, forthcoming in 1990 from Harvard University Press.   —The Editors

FOREWORD

I.

The propositions advanced in this chapter claim, certainly, a certain coherence. But it will be neither the coherence of a *system*—even less that of a philosophical *doctrine*—nor even that of a *program*, in the technical and institutional sense we give this word in our Report.

What is called a *philosophical system* constitutes in fact a certain type of coherence or continuous cohesion, a form of *ontological* ordering that has appeared historically, and, we can even say, as linked to the essence of the history of philosophy. In the form of *doctrine*, the system has always linked philosophy to its discourses and its pedagogical institutions. But every consistent discourse, organized or simply gathered together with itself, does not necessarily have the form of a system (perhaps it is even destined to break with this form from the moment it addresses itself to the other). Since the College will be directed toward making the *systemic* idea or project (in general) *one of its themes*, one of the problems to be considered, and since, correlatively, the College should never neglect the questions of teaching, pedagogy, education, doctrinal effects, and all their sociopolitical aims [*finalités*], etc., it could not be a question of imposing the form of a "system" on this research, this history, this "thought." For this very reason, however, the nonsystemic coordination we are going to propose will have nothing of the rhapsodic or the empirical about it either.

Nor will it sketch out a *program*. First, because everything will not be undertaken there in the form of a prescription, with its "objectives" and its end-oriented [*finalisée*] production. Furthermore because, without being necessarily kept there, several research groups—called "programs" in the first part (called "The Regulating Idea") of this Report—will eventually be able to cooperate, communicate, try to cross with, confront, and translate each other there, *but above all without ever renouncing their most precise specificity, their autonomy, and their internal necessity.*

II.

These propositions claim a demonstrative value, a demonstrativity both intraphilosophical and with regard to certain singular borders of philosophy. But this demonstrativity cannot be constantly *exhibited as such* here. This is in keeping with the limits of such a Report, whether it is a matter of the material limits of this chapter or, especially, of those that come with the genre, with the *aim* [*finalité*] or with the *destination* of such a text, with the very nature of the *mission* assigned to it. There is nothing fortuitous in this, for the values of *aim*, of *destination*, like the entire semantics of the mission (placing, emitting, missive, missile, sendoff [*envoi*], etc.), will form one of the essential foci of my propositions or "projections." Referring implicitly but without dissimulation to other work (my own included), drawing directly or indirectly on the lessons of all the discussions in which the Mission has engaged over the course of the last months, I will try to limit myself to practical or technical *conclusions* concerning the research to be instituted in the College, to what in any case seems to me as though it should be given priority. *But the necessity of these conclusions should be capable of imposing itself on the basis of other premises.* My rule here will be: project the necessity of certain research, but always in such a way that one could be convinced of it on the basis of other perspectives or other premises about which nothing will be said, and even without any general "perspective" or "premise" other than the intrinsic merit of such research. The non-systematic unity of this "projection" or "setting into perspective," the possibility of coordination which it might present should thus be considered here only as a *supplementary interest*, a *premium* to which one might attribute all the values one wishes (philosophical, aesthetic, economic, reason, poem, painting, history, etc.).

Contenting myself often with naming or titling, with situating some *"topoi,"* I naturally have to leave implicit both the reference to a great deal of work, French and foreign, and the essentials of an analysis of the philosophical, technoscientific, poietic, etc., "fields." We will retain only some indices of these macro- or micro-analyses, which we practice constantly and which orient our approach here: those which have guided us in the definition of the College, its project, its regulating idea, its constitution; those which have been spectacularly confirmed in the course of the Mission; those which have helped us discover or better situate new orientations; and finally all those which have taken the form of commitments or of research projects (we attach them to this Report and we will refer to them at the right moment).[1] But we neither could nor should have gone beyond this in the course of this Mission. It was not a question for us of drawing a map of French or world philosophy, for example, nor of proposing a general interpretation of it, even if complete abstention or reserve on this matter was impossible. We strove for this, however, for obvious reasons which are recalled in the first part of the Report. Without proposing any sectioning or cartography of the philosophical terrain, we have made use of many works which could have helped us do so, whether we cite them or not. That is the case, notably, with the recent Report by Maurice Godelier and his collaborators.[2]

We were only able to take account of it at the end of our Mission, but the "upshot" and the recommendations we encountered there were already known to us, at least partially (concerning philosophy, for example). Although the objects of these two Reports are very different, certain convergences appeared to me remarkable and encouraging. We should nevertheless, for obvious reasons, limit ourselves to this general reference, and presume that our reader will be aware of the "Godelier Report."

---

1. At the end of every chapter of this "projection," I will multiply the numbered references to the contributions addressed to us during the course of the Mission. All of these documents will be collected as we have indicated, and attached to the final Report. They have extremely diverse forms and functions (letters of support, advice, suggestions, offers of participation or association, very elaborate projects). They have been addressed by individuals (teachers, researchers, students, artists, experts or practitioners), by groups or institutions, from France and abroad. Without picking and choosing from among the different types of correspondence [envoi] in my references, I have allowed myself to be guided simply by a classically thematic principle. Of course, it could not be rigorous, given the intersections to which we have appealed from the outset. Certain references will have to appear several times. Nonetheless, it seemed useful to constitute this kind of thematic index, however approximate. It might help the first readers of the Report to form an image of the ensemble of contributions and exchanges to which the Mission has given space. Its interest and scope will be more obvious, and the consultation of the adjoined Dossier may be facilitated. Especially, beyond this first reading, and if the College is created, such an instrument could be indispensable when the time comes to make our first initiatives and it is necessary to make contact again with all our correspondents. [In the absence of the supporting documents, these notes have been deleted from the translation. —Eds.]

2. Maurice Godelier, Les Sciences de l'homme et la société (Paris: Documentation française, 1982), 2 vols.—Trans.

III.

Let us recall once and for all: for reasons already stated in the first part of the Report, we will too often be making use of words that we would like to see received without assurance and without tranquility. For it is without assurance and without tranquility that I will speak, for example, of proposals for *research*, properly *philosophical, scientific, theoretico-practical, poietic*, etc., research, or research on a *theme*, or *problematics*, or *field*. Now it is understood: all these words remain for the moment inevitable, but they are for the College titles of problems and problematic titles, including the values of title and of problem: the laws and the procedures of *legitimation*, the *production of titles and of legitimate problems*, these are also what the College will study, analyse, transform all the time, notably in its own space. The concept of *legitimation* itself, which has become so useful and so "legitimate" in so many sociological discourses (sociology of research and teaching institutions, sociology of the arts and culture, etc.), should not remain out of range of this questioning. How has it been constructed? What are its presuppositions and its limits? What is sociology today, the aim and strategy of its "usage"?, etc. We will return to these questions. What we have provisionally and within quotation marks called "thinking," in the first part, should mark the style and the site of such an approach. It proceeds to the limits "on the subject" of all these current values, called "philosophy," "science," "art," "research," "technique," "theory," "practice," "problem," "law," "legitimacy," "title," etc. These precautions are not purely formal. Evidently they do not concern only the vocabulary in which one generally speaks of research and teaching institutions. We will not be able to avoid this lexicon, but we will give it, for anyone who wants to hear, a certain interrogative inflection: what are these things we're talking about—"philosophy", "science," "interscience," "art," "technique," "culture," "production," "theory," "research," etc.? What is an "object," a "theme," a "problem," a "problematic"? How to think the question "what is" concerning them?

These forms of interrogation will assign to the College its greatest and most permanent opening, which it must never suture with the assurance of a body of knowledge, a doctrine or a dogma. Whatever the abstract generality of this axiom, we believe it is necessary to inscribe it in the very charter of the institution, as a sort of founding contract. That will not prevent—on the contrary—further analysis of the values of *contract*, of *foundation*, and of *institution*.

IV.

Despite the measureless unfolding and the infinite reflection in which these preliminaries might seem to engage, the concrete propositions I will present in this chapter are strictly delimitable: *a four year sendoff*. During the *first four years* of the College, a large number of activities—*we are not saying all the activities*—can be coordinated in a supple and mobile fashion, without ever being constrained by some general and authoritarian planning. *Without being kept there and without renouncing its most precise specificity*, each of the research groups I am going to define will be able to refer to a general and common theme. We could call it a "title," "category," "regulating idea," "problematic," or "working hypothesis." Its unity would be only *presumed*, according to different modes, and it will assure, at least during this initial period, a common reference, a principle of *general translation or of possible transfer(ence)* for the exchanges, debates, cooperations, transversal or oblique communications.

V.

Despite these limits, the propositions that follow will traverse an immense and differentiated terrain. But it goes without saying that this territory does not have to be covered or saturated by the College's research. Conforming to the style proper to this institution, that of *pathbreaking [frayage]* or trailblazing *[fléchage]*, it will be a matter only of *provoking new research* and of selecting *inaugural incursions*. I will not return to what was laid out in the first part, namely the necessity of interrogating and displacing in this respect the ontological encyclopedic model by which the philosophical concept of the *universitas* has been guided for the last two centuries.

DESTINATIONS

Without all this amounting either to *giving the word* or to saying everything *in a word*, from now on I will make all of these proposals converge toward their most simple, most economical, and most for-

malizable statement, namely the category or the theme of DESTINA-
TION.

What does this mean?

For reasons announced in the Foreword, I will dispense with the
exercise (which would otherwise be necessary) destined to show that
it is not a matter here either of a theme or a category. The philosophical or "thinking" history of the theme, the *thesis* or the *ka-*
tegoreuein, would make it clear that the meaning of destination
won't allow itself to be subordinated to them. But this is not the place
for that development. Let's speak in a more indeterminate fashion of a
scheme of destination, and content ourselves with a single question,
in its elementary unfolding: What of destination? What does "to
destine" mean? What is "to destine?" What happens to the question
"what is?" when it is measured against that of destination? And what
happens to it with the multiplicity of idioms?

Let's not unfold this problematic in its most easily identifiable
dimensions yet (destination and destiny, all the problems of the end
and thus of limits or of confines, ethical or political aim, teleology—
natural or not—, the destination of life, of man, of history, the problem of eschatology (utopian, religious, revolutionary, etc.), that of the
constitution and the structure of the sender/receiver system, and
thus of the dispatch or sendoff and the message (in all its forms and in
all its substances—linguistic or not, semiotic or not), emission, the
mission, the missile, transmission in all its forms, telecommunication and all its techniques, economic distribution and all its conditions (producing, giving, receiving, exchanging), the dispensation of
knowledge and what we now call the "orientation" ["*finalisation*"] of
research or of techno-science, etc.).

Let's content ourselves for the moment with situating the strategic force of this question schematically, with situating what constitutes, it seems to me, its most unavoidable philosophical necessity
as well as its performing and performative value as a "lever." The word
"strategy" does not necessarily imply calculation or warlike strat-
agem, but the question of calculation, including its modern polemo-
logical aspect (the new concepts of war, strategy and game theory,
weapons production, military techno-science, the economy of military industrial complexes, relations between the armed forces and
research in all domains, etc.), should be included in this problematic

network and accordingly be fully welcomed in the College. We will return to this.

The "lever," then: having been gathered and identified in these still "classical" forms (destination and end of philosophy, of metaphysics or of onto-theology, eschatological or teleological closure), the problematic of the limits of the philosophical as such seems to have arrived at a very singular point.

On the one hand, the modern sciences ("human or social sciences," "life sciences" and "natural sciences") are continuing or beginning again to adjust themselves to the problems we have just redirected toward that of destination (aim, limits, teleology of systems). And their irreducibly philosophical dimension is often there, at the moment when philosophy returns, whether or not we want it, whether or not we hold on to the representation of a post- or extra-philosophical scientificity.

On the other hand—and above all—the recourse to a thought of the *sendoff*, of *dispensation* or the *gift* of being, signals today one of the most singular and, it seems to me, most powerful—in any case one of the last—attempts to "think" the history and structure of onto-theology, even the history of being in general. However we interpret them, and whatever credit we grant this thought or this discourse, we should pause before this marker: the "destinal" significations (sending or sendoff, dispensation, destiny of being, *Schickung, Schicksal, Gabe,* "*es gibt Sein,*" "*es gibt Zeit,*" etc.) do not seem to belong to the *within* of onto-theological philosophemes any longer, without being "metaphors" or empirical or derived concepts either. There is a sense here which is thus not reducible to what the sciences can and should determine of it, whether it is a matter of the empirical sciences, the natural or life sciences, so-called animal or human societies, techniques of communication, linguistics, semiotics, etc. Another thought of the "sendoff" thus seems necessary to the unfolding of the "great questions" of philosophy and of science, of truth, of meaning, of reference, of objectivity, of history.

Let us emphasize the very visible reference which has just been made to the Heideggerian *path,* and not simply to one or another of its scholastic effects. It seems clear enough that the meditation on the history of being, after the existential analytic, opens the question of the ontological difference onto what it always seems to have "presupposed"—in a sense not purely logical—implicated, enveloped, namely a *thought of the sendoff,* of *dispensation,* and of the *gift* (note, by the way, that it's a matter here of another great text on the gift, which should be read in—very complex—connection with Mauss's "Essai sur le don,"[3] that is to say with an enormous corpus of French ethnology and sociology over the last six or seven decades, in its scientific but also in its politicohistorical dimensions; no doubt we would have to encounter and analyze, in the course of that trajectory, the *Collège de Sociologie*[4] whose title was often recalled during this Mission). The thought of the gift and the sendoff, the thought of "destining" *before* the constitution of the sentence or of the logical structure "X give or sends Y to Z," Y being an *object* (thing, sign, message) between two *"subjects,"* the sender or the emitter and the receiver or receptor (ego, conscious or unconscious, Unconscious), *before* this subject/object constitution and in order to take account of it, etc. The same necessity appears, even if in another manner, *mutatis mutandis,* for what I have tried to demonstrate under the heading of *différance* as sendoff, differentiation, delay, relay, delegation, teleand trans-ference, trace and writing in general, destination and undecidability, etc. These indices should naturally be multiplied; for obvious reasons, I limit myself to the most schematic ones and, openly, to what is closest to me. If I hold to declaring these limits and this proximity, it is, contrary to what one might be tempted to think, in order to lift the limits, to distance them and to disappropriate them. It is in order to call for critical debate about them, for open disagreements and explications, for other approaches, and in order to avoid the disguised recentering or the hegemony of a problematic, a discourse or a history. These risks should be avoided with thoroughgoing vigilance. The translating, transversal, and transfering coordinations we are proposing will operate without a pyramidal effect, in a lateral, horizontal and nonhierarchial way. The scheme I have just designated, at the limits of the "destinal," seems to me capable of putting into question and displacing precisely the topological principles that have dominated all of onto-theology, invested its space and commanded its traditional forms of univerticality, in philosophical

3. See Marcel Mauss, "Essai sur le don" (1925), in his *Sociologie et anthropologie* (Paris: Presses Universitaires de France, 1980); trans. Ian Connison as *The Gift. Forms and Function of Exchange in Archaic Societies* (New York: Norton, 1967).—Trans.

4. See Denis Hollier, ed., *Le Collège de Sociologie 1937–1939* (Paris: Gallimard, 1979); trans. Betsy Wing, as *The College of Sociology (1937–39)* (Minneapolis: University of Minnesota Press, 1988).—Trans.

discourse as much as in research and teaching institutions. It is already clear that one should not accord this general "schematic" and its entirely presumed unity the status of a new general ontology, and even less that of a transcendental phenomenology, an absolute logic, a theory of theories, dominating once again the encyclopedia and all its theoretico-practical regions. But let's go further: this "schematic" should not even be admitted as a new organon. By one of the singular contracts without which no opening of thought and no research would be possible, the College should consider this "schematic" as itself problematic, as *debatable:* through and through, in a fundamental debate that would certainly assume its deliberately "fundamentalist" dimension, as one sometime says, but would also go so far as to question the motifs of "depth," "foundation," of "reason" [*Grund*] in all of its possible translations—and in particular in relation to the distinction between so-called "fundamental" and so-called "applied" or even "end-oriented" research. It is useless to insist on this here: it is a matter of an essential stake touching on the axiomatic and the very future of the College, and its relations to the State (to States), nationalities, "civil societies." A singular and paradoxical contract, we were saying, as well it might be: a commitment never to leave the terms of the instituting contract out of the question, analysis, even transformation, resting in some dogmatic slumber. Doesn't this transform such a contract into a fiction and the regulating idea of the College into an "as if" (let us act *as if* such a community were possible, *as if* the priority granted to "still not legitimated pathbreakings" could have been the object of a consensus *in fine, as if* a "general translation" could at least have been attempted, beyond the classical systems and the onto-encyclopedic uni-versity whose totalizing model was imposed—even if in its "liberal" variant, that of Schleiermacher and Humboldt—at the moment of the creation of that occidental paradigm, the University of Berlin)? And doesn't this *as if* give such an engagement, and all the legalized contracts it calls for, a touch of the simulacrum? To which we will respond, at least elliptically, this way: on the one hand, far from being absolutely new, this type of singular contract will have characterized *every* philosophical or scientific institution worthy of the name, that is to say, which has decided never to leave anything out of the question, not even its own institutional axiomatic. On the other hand, the reflection on what could link a fictional structure to, for example, such performative utterances, promises, contracts, engagements, founding or instituting acts, will be one of the tasks of the College, and the richness of these implications is inexhaustible. I will say the same for the reflection on the history and the stakes of the concept of the university since the eighteenth century.

In what follows, my only ambition will be to project some hypotheses. Without being bound by them, those responsible for the College in the future might, if they agree with them, also refer to them as *points of order* for a first movement: a broad discussion, a broad introduction which would also be a four-year "translation." Points of order or of pause, rather than of a planned or uni-totalizing organization. Points of pause, *fermata,* if we want to name precisely those signs destined less to mark the measure than to suspend it on a note whose duration may vary. Rhythms, pauses, accents, phases, insistences—it is with these words and these values that I propose to describe, in their diversity, the possibilities and compossibilities of the College, certain of them at least, during the four years of its instauration.

I. Thinking Destination: Ends and Confines for Philosophy, The Sciences, and The Arts

Under this title, whose slight determination is deliberate, it is a question of designating that research called, in a code that no longer fits here, "fundamental." It is indispensable that it be developed broadly, and to the point of questioning the fundamentalist scheme, such as it has so often been able to regulate philosophy's relation to itself and to other regions of the encyclopedia. Even if we had not been convinced of it in advance, our consultations have provided us with an eloquent proof: the demand for this type of research is very marked today, and it is capable of mobilizing great forces and taking original forms. For reasons and following routes that must be analyzed, this "fundamentalist" thought has given in to a sort of intimidation before the sciences, all the sciences but especially the human and social sciences. It can and should find a new legitimacy and cease being somewhat ashamed of itself, as has sometimes been the case over the last two decades. This can happen without regression and without inevitable return to the hegemonic structure we alluded to in the first part of this Report. Furthermore, this movement is underway. The College should permit it to affirm itself in all of its force: to affirm philosophy and the thought of philosophy. It is not only professional philosophers who ask this but also a great number of researchers engaged in their scientific or artistic practices.

In the perspective which is thus opening up here, the first "themes" of this "fundamental" research will be organized around this series: *destination* (destiny, destining, sender/receiver, emitter/transmittor/receptor) and *gift* (giving/receiving, expenditure and debt, production and distribution).

The necessary development of semantic, philological, historical, etc., inquiries will apply itself to the "great questions" of which the following list constitutes only an indication.

How can a thought of "destination" concern philosophy, more precisely its own contour, its relation to a thought which would not yet or no longer be "philosophy" or "metaphysics," nor for that matter "science" or "technics"? What of the limits or the "ends" of philosophy, of metaphysics, of onto-theology? What of their relation to science and technics? This enormous network of questions can, we will say (and this goes for everything we advance here), be unfolded for itself, independently of any reference to the scheme of destination. So why not do without the proposed guiding thread? Response: Why not, in fact, if possible? We ought to be able to try that in the College, which is why I proposed that the "scheme" never become a "program" or an obligatory "theme," even if I am convinced that it is more and something other than one "guiding thread" among others.

In all cases, foci of reflection should be instituted wherever the question of the *end and ends* of the philosophical as such can *take place*, wherever the limit, the borders, or the destination of philosophy is at stake, wherever *there is cause or space* to ask: Philosophy *in view of what? Since and until when? In what and how? By whom and for whom?* Is it *decidable* and within what limits? In fact and by rights, these *topoi* will also be sites of the College's vigilant reflection on itself: on its own aim, on its destination (today and tomorrow) as a *philosophical* site, on what legitimates it and then confers on it its own power of legitimation, on what decides it politics and its economy, on the forces it serves and the forces it makes use of, on its national and international relations with other institutions. *Destination* and *legitimation*, thus, of the College itself: these are not problems to treat secondarily there or to dissociate (in the space of a sociological analysis, for example) from the major interrogations on the essence and the destination of the philosophical. Furthermore, as noted above the concept of "legitimation," so common today, calls for a reelaboration in its construction and its usage. Starting with the "open letter" [of 18 May 1982] through which we made public the object of our Mission and opened a discussion, we have emphasized ways of research whose *legitimacy* has not yet been recognized. It remained to specify, which a simple letter of this type could not do, that the College would not keep itself simply outside any process of legitimation, that is, within the illegitimable. Even were we to want it, this seems absolutely impossible. The most ruthless critique, the implacable analysis of a power of legitimation is always produced in the name of a system of legitimation. It can be declared or implicit, established or in formation, stable or mobile, simple or overdetermined—one cannot not know it, one can at most deny it. This denegation is today the most common thing in the world. Making it a theme, the College will try to avoid this denegation, insofar as this is possible. We already know that the interest in research not currently legitimated will only find its way if, following trajectories ignored by or unknown to any established institutional power, this new research *is already underway and promises a new legitimacy,* until one day, once again . . . and so on. We also know—and who wouldn't want it?—that if the College is created with the resources it requires and, above all, if its vitality and richness are one day what we foresee, then it will become in its turn a legitimating instance that will have obligated many other instances to reckon with it. It is this situation which must be continuously analyzed, today and tomorrow, to avoid exempting the College as an institution from its own analytic work. In order to track without complacency the ruses of legitimating reason, its silences and its narratives, it would be better to begin in the knowledge that we do so from an authorized, that is to say accredited, site; and from one which is accredited to confer accreditations, even if in a form or according to procedures and criteria completely different from—indeed incompatible with—current practices. Not telling (itself) too many stories about its own independence from this or that power of legitimation (dominant forces of society, institutions, university, State, etc.) is perhaps the *first* condition of the greatest possible independence, though that does not preclude looking for others. What we propose is not the utopia of a wild non-institution apart from any social, scientific, philosophical, etc., legitimation. It is a new apparatus, the only one capable of freeing, *in a given situation,* what the current set of apparatuses still inhibits. Not that the College is today the only or even the best form of institution possible in this respect. But to us it appears indispensable to the given set. And it is, moreover, for that reason that the necessity has been able to make itself felt, even as a symptom.

What I have just said about *legitimation* is easily transposed in terms of *orientation*. The ruses of the orientation of research must give rise to a new strategy of analysis. The opposition between end-oriented research and fundamental research has doubtless always been naive and summary. It is today, in all domains, startlingly obvious. We must yet again reelaborate this problematic from the fundamentals up, and that is finally what I propose here, at the same time as I insist on the *topoi* of a "fundamentalist" research-style. Which ones?

A

The questions of metaphysics and of onto-theology everywhere they can be recast: new approaches or connections. The interpretations of the "entire" history of philosophy (teleology, periodization, "epochalization," historical and systematic configurations).

B

The problematic of the *completion or of the limit of philosophy* (teleological or genealogical interpretations, critique, deconstruction, etc.). With the proper names appearing here only as indices, we can thus recommend coordinated and intertwined work on Kant, Hegel, Feuerbach, Kierkegaard, Marx, Comte, Nietzsche, Husserl, the Vienna Circle, Wittgenstein, Russell, Heidegger, etc. There is a great deal of room for original research in these directions, especially if it practices grafting, confrontation, or interference. This is almost never done rigorously and deliberately in France; it would break with homogeneous traditions and with institutions closed in on themselves.

This research would put "major," that is to say already recognized and well-known sites into "configuration." We will recommend later initiatives of another style; they will have in common a concern to analyze—even sometimes to put in question—the processes by which philosophical problematics and traditions become dominant: How and under what conditions are discourses, objects, and philosophical institutions formed? How do they become "philosophical" and how are they recognized as such? Under what conditions do they impose themselves (and on whom?) in order to minoritize or to marginalize other ones?

Each time one of these questions finds an original, interesting, and necessary determination, a *research group* might be created, of greater or lesser dimensions, longer or shorter duration. The example I am going to specify was imposed on me primarily by the *scheme of destination*, but it should be able to be translated, transposed, and multiplied. Research organized into one or many seminars, one or many programs, short-lived or long-term, should be able to correspond to each of the "proper names" just listed and to the movements of thought they represent.

C

Take the example of Heidegger. Around his work and its "problematic" (like those of other thinkers listed), a Program could be organized by the College, then transformed into a relatively independent research center, linked by contract to the College under conditions to be studied. In this case as in others, the College would have the role of provocation and initial organization. In the process which would make the Program into a Research Center, the work would first off be magnetized by these questions about the limits, ends, and destinations of onto-theology. It would treat, among others, each of the following "themes," which are all strongly marked in the Heideggerian text:

• The interpretation of the history of Being. Meaning and truth of Being.
  • Thinking, philosophy, science.
  • Thinking, philosophy, poetry.
  • Technics and metaphysics.
  • The work of art.
  • Language, languages, translation (beginning with the theoretical and practical problems of translating the corpus being considered). Technics and translation (formal and natural languages, problems of metalanguage and translation machines).
  • The political: what, *for example*, of Heidegger's political thought, its relations with his thought in general and with his political engagements on the other hand? (The same questions impose themselves, naturally, for other thinkers.) As for Heidegger, what of his "reception"

in France? What will have been its singular destiny? We would thus follow the history and the course of his "legacy" over the last fifty years, during which it will have, in one way or another, traversed all of French philosophy in an alternation of eclipses and reappearances, different each time and always highly significant, even today. Such research should naturally be coordinated with work that takes a fresh look at this century's history, at the constitution of a thematic of modernity or postmodernity in Germany and elsewhere, and at the analysis of the phenomena of totalitarianism, Nazism, fascism, Stalinism, without limiting itself to these enormities of the twentieth century. There again, we might see the originality of the paths to be broken, the specific necessity which will impose them on the College, especially in the active and intense crossings between all these different research efforts. Although we have proposed the example of Heidegger, such crossings should traverse other problematics, past or contemporary, around the destinal limit of philosophy (Hegel, Feuerbach, Marx, Kierkegaard, Comte, Nietzsche, Husserl, the Vienna Circle, Wittgenstein, Heidegger, the Frankfurt School, etc.) as well as work on the genealogy of these dominant problematics, of their domination itself. In all these efforts, the rigorous distinction between internal and external reading should not be disregarded, but neither should it be treated as a dogma. This problematic, like that of "context" and of contextualization in general, requires a new elaboration.

• The reason of the university. All these "philosophies" carry with them, whether thematically (Hegel, Nietzsche, Heidegger, at least) or implicitly, a discourse on reason which is also a discourse on the university, an evaluation of or a prescription for the destiny of the modern university, its politics (notably in its relations with the State and with the nation), and the organization of relations between philosophical and technoscientific research. The constant reflection of the College on its own mission, its aims or its eventual "orientation," should pass by way of, among other things, an encounter with these thoughts which are all thoughts of the university.

Such research communities exist nowhere, as far as I know, neither in France nor anywhere else. Outside of informal groups and dispersed initiatives, the only organized research depends on narrowly specialized centers, most often incapable of the opening, the mobility, and the intertwined or diagonal approaches we are proposing here. The difficulty for them (and this stems more often from institutional mechanisms than from people) is to *mobilize* this research, which sometimes becomes pure philology, without philosophical ambition, even if it is armed here or there with modern technology; the difficulty is to measure this research against the most serious stakes, today's and tomorrow's. No one should read in these last remarks a will to discredit historicizing attitudes or interest in the past as such, rather the contrary. The paradox is that, in France at least, historical, philological, even "archival" work—despite the premium of positivity which it receives in many institutions—remains very deficient in the domain we have just invoked. In any case, for reasons that the College should analyze, there are enormous and inadmissable delays here—beginning with that of the publication and translation of the fundamental corpus of the twentieth century. Its translation remains largely incomplete, dispersed, heterogeneous. This deficiency is not only serious in itself, but also in what it signifies or entails for philosophical or scientific research. To cite only these examples, we know that this is the situation of the works of Freud, Wittgenstein, and, precisely, Heidegger, which need a complete and, insofar as possible, homogeneous translation, based on the scientific and complete edition of his writings (now underway). In all these tasks, the College could associate its initiatives with those of other research institutions (CNRS and universities).

D

Numerous indications permit us to affirm that such programs and centers would be active and efficacious, that they would attract many researchers and would bring together many specialties—those of philosophers, but also of philologists, historians, poeticians, linguists, logicians, political scientists, and theorists, sociologists, translators, writers, etc. . . . They ought thus to be structured in their own identity and at the same time traversed by all the other axes of research. But this should be able to be said of all the research groups we will be led to determine.

Another indicator, particularly exemplary in this respect, would be that of "women's studies"—even though, at least at first glance, it does not have a direct relation with the preceding example. I consider this relation essential, but without attempting to demonstrate it here I will recall only a few obvious things. The institutional underdevelopment of these studies in our country is scandalous (in comparison, for example, with the United States for the university, and with the richness and force of these "studies" in France outside of public institutions). As the "Godelier Report" recalls, in France there is only one "women's studies" research group accredited by the former government (directed by Hélène Cixous, at the University of Paris VIII). On the other hand, it is too evident that if women's studies should, for this very reason, be developed extensively in the College, they should also expand, without dissolving, into all the other sites of research.

II. Destination and Orientation

The "themes" we will situate under this title should by right not be dissociated from the preceding ones, with which they can cross at many points. But an original inflection will mark their treatment. It will be a matter of reactivating or reactualizing categories said to be classical by adjusting them, if possible, to new objects, putting them to the (transforming or deforming) test of situations which may seem unprecedented or specific. All the themes and problems which organize the great philosophical tradition, from Aristotle to Kant, from Leibniz to Hegel and to Marx, from Nietzsche to Bergson, etc., around *teleology* and *eschatology, ends* and *aims*, will have to be mobilized in directions as numerous and different as modern biology and genetics, biotechnology, biolinguistics, and "biotics." A new reflection on law in relation to the technoscientific mutations of medicine will open as well onto the ethnical and political dimensions of a thought of destination. As for examples, we suggest engaging in very precise research at the intersections of the following paths:

A

The philosophical *implication* of the life sciences. In this "domain" of uncertain frontiers, the richness and the acceleration of "discoveries" *engages* philosophy more than ever in its most essential and most critical questionings. We say "implication" and "engagement" in order to mark the fact that it is doubtless a matter of something other than an epistemological reflection which *follows on* scientific production. Without disputing the necessity of such an epistemology, in this domain and in all others, must we not also take into account the possibility of "philosophical decisions" opening and orienting new scientific spaces? Here it would not necessarily be a matter of spontaneous or dogmatic philosophy, of residues of precritical philosophy in the activity of scientists, but of inaugural philosophico-scientific approaches productive, as such, of new bodies of knowledge. While this possibility can claim a noble history in all domains of scientific theory, it seems particularly rich and promising today in all the spaces which put the life sciences in communication with other sciences and emerging technical mutations (sciences of language, physics, computing, etc.). The dissociation between all these investigations and all these resources, like that between philosophy and these techno-sciences, has to do more often with socioinstitutional effects of the scientific or technical community than with the intrinsic nature of the objects. The College could play a vital role in this regard.

B

The philosophical, ethico-political, and juridical problems posed by new medical technologies. The foundations of a new *general deontology.* Whether it is a matter of demography (in all its dimensions, from the distribution of nutritional resources to birth control worldwide), gerontology (the science of aging in general and not only of "old age"—of which theoretical and institutional developments have a worldwide breadth often disregarded in France), genetic manipulation, the enormous problematic of prostheses and of organ transplants and grafting, biotics (biocomputers with synthetic genes, constitution of "artificial senses"), or euthanasia—each time the philosophical stake is obvious. It is not posed simply in terms of knowledge or of mastery but, demanding in this regard the highest competence, it calls as well for ethical intepretation, for taking sides and decisions. It also supposes putting back into play the whole fundamental axiology concerning the values of the body, the integrity of the living, "subject," "ego," "conscience" or "consciousness," individual and community "responsibility." Linked with these are all the questions of a politics of "health" (society's rights and duties with regard to what we call "health," but also the reelaboration of its very concept)and those of a politics of research in this domain (priorities, orientations, articulations with military-industrial research).

C

Psychiatry and Psychoanalysis. Certainly we will be attentive here to link them to the research we have just situated, to link them to each other, but also to dissociate them in their most jealous and irreducible originality. This said, in both cases, whether it is a matter of knowledge, "theoretical" discourse, technique, or institution, the necessity of a philosophical discussion is widely recognized and called for by the "practitioners" with whom we have been in contact during our consultations, most widely by those—and they are very numerous in every domain of research—who "deal" today with psychoanalysis in one way or another. Whether we interrogate literature or linguistics, history, ethnology or sociology, pedagogy or law, the very axiomatic of research finds itself transformed in every way by it. Let's not insist here on something so obvious. I will only emphasize a point on which the future directors of the College should remain particularly vigilant. This has recently been verified on the occasion of the discussion organized by Maurice Godelier and Gérard Mendel: many psychoanalysts are very concerned to preserve what is in their eyes the irreducible singularity of their discourse and their practice. The majority of psychoanalysts want to maintain the greatest independence with regard to social public health organizations or public research institutions. Whatever one thinks of these very complex problems, with which I prefer not to engage here, it seems to me desirable in any case that the College never consider them "resolved" in any way; in other words, that it maintain a policy of reserve and abstention about them, which does not mean that it not pose them in a theoretical mode, rather the contrary. But it should not seek to determine some social inscription of psychoanalysis, for example by means of some kind of link between the College and a group of analysts or an analytic institution as such. All research contracts will be made with individuals or with groups *interested* in the psychoanalytic problematic, but not with psychoanalysts *as such* (even if they are that in fact and if their work in the College concerns the institution or history of the analytic movement). There is nothing paradoxical in this. The recommendation which I am formulating here, in the interest of everyone and first of all the College, addresses a request often formulated by psychoanalysts. A good number among them have told us that they prefer to work in these conditions rather than in a space which would be reserved for them by statute, in the CNRS, for example, or in other research institutions. Whether wrongly or rightly, they fear being too (theoretically) hemmed in and too (sociopolitically) engaged there, and they prefer more open and more multiple exchanges with philosophers, researchers in the social sciences and it must be strongly emphasized, in the life or "natural" sciences as well, in France and abroad. This international dimension takes on certain particular aspects here to which some of our correspondents have repeatedly drawn our attention.

D

Law and philosophy of law. There is a spectacular deficiency in the French field here, something of which we were convinced at the start of our mission and which has received the most emphatic confirmation. Many philosophers and jurists regret it and propose that a special effort be launched in this domain. This effort might first be undertaken in the directions we have just indicated by taking account of the legal problems posed by certain modern (technical, economic, political, artistic) mutations. The themes of destination, the gift, and thus exchange and debt lend themselves to this in a particularly privileged way. We should not speak only of the "comparative," ethnosociological, and historical approaches this requires, but also of certain less classical ones, for example, those based on "pragmatic" analyses of the structure of juridical utterances. Inversely, we will also study the juridical conditions of the constitution of artworks or of the production and reception (or destination) of works. Not to mention all the possible connections with a political, even theologico-political, problematic. To limit ourselves to a few indicative examples, here are some "modern" provocations to this new philosophico-juridical reflection, accumulated in their apparent diversity: the phenomena of the totalitarian society, new techniques of physical and psychic torture, new conditions of the investment and occupation of space (urbanism, naval and air space, "space research"), the progress of computerization or informatization, the ownership and transfers of technology, the ownership, reproduction and distribution of artworks under new technical conditions and given new materials used in production and archiving. All these transformations in progress call for a thorough reelaboration of the conceptuality and axiomatics of law, international law, public law, and private law. A *new* problematic of human rights is also underway, progressing slowly and laboriously within the major international organizations. It seems that French philosophy has not been terribly interested in this so far. This deficiency is often dissimulated behind the classical eloquence of declarations in favor of human rights. However necessary they are, such declarations no longer take the place of philosophical thought. Such thinking has to measure itself today against a situation without precedent.

E

The police and the army, warfare. Here too, technological muta-tions in progress are profoundly transforming the structures, modes of action, stakes, and aims. Philosophical reflection seems to be keep-ing too great a distance from research already underway on this sub-ject in numerous French and foreign institutes.

The College should make possible confrontations between ex-perts (on the police, different police forces, prison institutions, ar-mies, modern strategy and polemology) and other researchers, es-pecially philosophers. The directions of research are numerous and diverse, as important projects which have come from France and abroad remind us. There is practically no theme evoked by this "pro-jection" that should not, in one way or another, cross with the prob-lematics of the police, the army, and warfare. Warfare in all its figures, which are not metaphors (ideological warfare, economic warfare, broadcast warfare). Biocybernetics, so-called "smart" weapons, and self-guided missiles would here be only the most conspicuous and determined paradigms of a problematic of the "sendoff" or "launch" and of the "destination" in this domain. In fact the field extends to the regions of game theory, the politics of (military-industrial) research, psychoanalysis, semiotics, rhetoric, law, literature, and the "status of women."

III. Languages of Destination, Destinations of Language

"Language"—the word is understood here in its most open sense, beyond the limits of the linguistic and the discursive proper, in their oral or graphic form. The values of "information," "communication," "emission," and "transmission" will be included here, certainly, in *all* their forms, yet they will not exhaust it. That is to say directly that, under the title of "language," the study of all "destinal" sig-nifications or operations (destining, sending, emitting, transmitting, addressing, giving, receiving, etc.) can and should in turn traverse *all* the College's fields of activity. And we have laid down the principle, in the first part of this Report, that this activity would not only be theoretical study but also, connected to it, "creation" and perfor-mance. Referring for convenience to classical categories, let us indi-cate the titles and the principal paths of these intertwined research efforts.

A

Philosophy of language. What can its specificity be, if it is neither simply an epistemology of linguistics nor a linguistics? How is this "specificity" constituted? History and analysis of its problematic and categories in relation to all the forms of *teleology.* What is a sender, a receiver, an emitter, a receptor, a message, etc.? How are their "pragmatic" unity and their conceptual identity constituted? Across all the dimensions of this analysis, (metaphysical, psychosociological, psychoanalytic, technoeconomic), we will encounter the problems of decidability and undecidability. We will recognize them in their logical or semantic forms, in pragmatic paradoxes, or again in the interpretation of "works of art."

B

Linguistics. As with all the "immense domains" which I am naming here, it is a question of signaling what the College's precise angle of approach should be. We will not cover all the territory of linguistic research there, nor will we teach all of Linguistics, even supposing that this could be done anywhere. We will try rather, while providing an "initiation" to linguistic research in its newest directions, to interrogate linguists, during debates with other researchers, philosophers or not, on the subject of philosophy in linguistics and linguistics in philosophy. Not only in terms of the dogmatic presuppositions on each side. Other modes of implication are at least as interesting, as much from the historical as from the systematic point of view. We can interrogate anew, for example, the inscription of philosophical discourse in a natural language and in the "philosophy of language" it tends to entail; we can interrogate the philosophical decisions, assumed or not, of every linguistics. These decisions are not inevitably negative ("epistemological obstacles"), and not necessarily to be confused with the philosophical discourse or reference *exhibited* by linguistics ("Cartesian linguistics," "Rousseauist linguistics," "Herderian," "Humboldtian"). In medieval thought, so neglected by French academic philosophy, these explorations would doubtless be among the most fruitful. But these are only examples.

C

Semiotics. We can transpose here what has just been said about the philosophical stakes of linguistics. The field will be larger since it covers not only linguistic systems but also nonlinguistic sign systems. We will be particularly interested in *intersemiotic* functionings (speech and gesture, formal graphs and natural or ordinary language, works of art with multiple inscriptions: text, painting, music, etc.). The reflection will thus extend—in a nonencyclopedic but incursive mode, let's not forget—to all systems of signals and all codes, from those of genetic information to the necessary problematic of "artificial intellience." We will not consider as secured or guaranteed any of the philosophical axiomatics with which all the research in progress is engaged, beginning with the opposition between the "artificial" and the whole series of its others.

Likewise, we will not be content to sift and orient, at the start, the impressive range of this "field" by reference to questions of "destination." We will leave open, and constantly reopen, the question of knowing whether the thought of language depends on "philosophy," semiotic theory, or linguistic theory, and whether it is limited by their horizon.

D

Pragmatics. Despite everything it can share with a linguistics, a semiotics, a general semantics, or a philosophy of language, pragmatics is developing today, especially outside France, as a relatively original discipline. Whether it concerns enunciation ("speech acts")or a more complex semiotic context (including for example gestural behavior), it seems to me that it is effecting a general redistribution of great consequence today. Besides its own rich results, it entails an essential coimplication of "disciplines" that formerly compartmentalized or protected themselves in the name of their own scientificity. That is why pragmatics seems to me to require a particularly sensitive place in the College, that of a "crossroads" of heavy traffic (philosophy, semantics, linguistics, semiotics, artistic theory and practice, interpretation of juridical performatives). Given the importance of the stakes, given the place that the College should grant to the "performative" dimension (cf., the first part of this Report), and given as well that dispersed work is proliferating today without specific institutional resources (based on Austin's theory of speech acts and its tradition, but sometimes deviating from them to the breaking point), the College should create a site of coordination and, later, a real Research Center which, though outside the College, would remain associated with it. Numerous proposals in this direction, sometimes highly elaborate, have come to us; we foresaw that, and we sought out and called for them.

E

Technology of telecommunications. "Fundamental" reflection on the concepts of "communication" and "long-distance communication," on the no doubt structural and thus irreducible links between *technē* in general and "telecommunications," from its "simple" and "elementary" forms. In other words, the technology of telecommunications is not one technology among others; whence the link between this problematic and that of distance, of oriented spacing and thus of destination. Among all the possible foci of this reflection, let us signal these, which are among the most necessary today (and tomorrow).

1. Aims, structures, and putting into practice of all *modes of archiving*—and thus of communication (philosophical, scientific, artistic, etc.). Since the necessity of this work and these experiments is too obvious with regard to new techniques (microfilm, data banks, telematics, video), I prefer to insist on the *book* (history of writing and history of the book; the model of the book and its effects on the structure of works and discourses, especially philosophical discourses; the technical and political problems of the culture of the book; the crisis and the future of publishing in general, and of scientific, philosophical, or literary publishing in particular; national and international dimensions of the problem—dominant languages and minority cultures, etc.). Of course, these questions can no longer be considered today as annexes in a research institution such as the College. They will thus be treated in all their breadth and acuity, with the special help of experts (experts in the new techniques of archiving and distribution, printers, publishers, librarians, etc.). These initiatives will be coordinated with those which can be undertaken elsewhere (for example in CESTA, CREA, the Ministry of Culture, and the Direction du Livre).[5]

5. CESTA, the Center for the Study of Advanced Systems and Technologies, and CREA, the Center for Research on Autonomous Epistemologies, are both housed in the same buildings as the College, 1–5 Rue Descartes, the former Ecole Polytechnique. The Direction du Livre is a subsection of the French Ministry of Culture that supervises, supports, and studies various aspects of book production and distribution. It is

2. The *mass media*. Philosophical and scientific reflection, theoretical, empirical, and experimental "Mediology." Among the countless tasks required in this domain, the College could first of all privilege the "cultural," artistic, scientific, and philosophical aspects. This will lead it to a much closer analysis of the relations between "media" culture, research, and teaching. Without a "reactive attitude, without "rejection" (which is in any case doomed to powerlessness), faced with the extension of the mass media, the College will pose the "deontological," "ethico-juridical," or "ethico-political" problems associated with such an extension. It will attempt to propose new uses for these technical possibilities (public or private) and will seek to arrange access to them. What goes for the mass media goes as well for other more diverse and less widespread modes of communication, for example the private or "free radio" stations, or for all the techniques of telecommunication. A great deal of work is underway in foreign universities and in other French institutions: the College should associate itself with it while maintaining the originality of its own approach.

3. *Computer science, telematics, robotics, biotechnologies*. In liaison with other research centers, particularly with the whole CESTA network, the College should participate, in its style and with its resources, in the ongoing scientific and philosophical reflection on "orientation," the modes of production and appropriation of new techniques whose spectacular acceleration is transforming the whole of culture and knowledge. This work should, as much as possible, connect technical initiation—the provision of basic proficiency—with philosophical analysis (ethical, juridical, political) of the stakes.

F

Poietics. In what may be a somewhat conventional manner, we choose this term to regroup everything that concerns, in classical terms, theories of art and artistic practices. The title "poietics" at least has the merit of recalling a double dimension: theoretical and necessarily discursive research on the one hand, and experimental, "creative," and performative research on the other.

The College's projects (at least such as they have been interpreted

---

affiliated with the Centre National des Lettres, a semiprivate organization run by both the Direction du Livre and publishers, which supports such activities as the publication of journals and the activity of small presses, etc. —Translators' note.

and represented by our Mission) have elicited spectacular interest in these domains. The research proposals in this domain have been more numerous and more eager than in any other, above all, we must note, on the part of French researchers or artists. We could have expected this. It confirms, among other things, the difficulty these initiatives have in finding a site—and support—in this country's theoretico-institutional topology.

We insist that, whenever possible, the College seek in these domains to associate itself with the numerous initiatives underway in Paris and above all regionally and abroad, whether public (for example, those sponsored or supported by the Ministry of Culture) or private. Privileged attention will be accorded to those which bring "theorists" together with "creators"—who are sometimes one and the same.

Besides all the "great questions" to be reactivated (origin of the work of art, meaning, reference, art and truth, art and national culture, etc.), what all this research will have in common will concern primarily:

- the structures of destination and orientation ("aim of the beautiful," with or "without a concept"): Who produces what? Destined for whom? Theories of reception, "taste," the art market, the phenomena of evaluation, legitimation, distribution, etc;
- the thematic of destination (destiny, law, chance and necessity) within works and on the "production" side;
- the interpretation of works and the philosophy or hermeneutics involved there. Transformation of "art criticism" in the new audiovisual spaces of the press and publishing;
- mutation of the arts (of forms and materials) following scientific and technical advances;
- critique and transformation of the customary classification of the arts.

While the necessity of a different philosophical questioning is perceptible in all the arts, and while it is primarily the "creators" who have insisted on this, the urgency is doubtless most marked in literature or poetry and music. During the last two decades, proliferating work has mobilized great resources (philosophy, human sciences— linguistics, psychoanalysis, etc.—logico-mathematical sciences), generally outside academic institutions or their customary divisions. An entity which we could call "literature and philosophy," for example, while it is practically recognized in foreign universities (especially in the United States), remains contraband in our country. We have received important projects leading in this direction; others, just as new and as necessary, bring together music and philosophy, musicians, music theorists and philosophers in an original way. But without a doubt, analogous attempts might be made with the visual arts, the so-called spatial arts, the theater, the cinema, and television.

IV. Translation, Transfer(ence), Transversality

Under this title we will indicate and recommend all the transferential proceedings which, *as such*, define the precise specificity of an *international* College open first of all to *diagonal* or *transversal* interscientific research. Translations, then, in the triple sense, whose division we borrow for convenience from Jakobson: *intralinguistic* (phenomena of translation—commentary, reformulation, transposition—within the same language), *interlinguistic* (in the common or "proper" sense of the word, says Jakobson: from one language to another), *intersemiotic* (from one semiotic medium to another, for example speech/painting), but translations also in the larger sense of the transfer of a model or paradigm (rhetoric, art, sciences).

Here are some exemplary directions. It is understood that they should cross with other paths situated under other titles and orient themselves according to the general scheme of "destination."

A. "Fundamental" research on language, the multiplicity of languages, and the general problematic of translation. History and theories of translation, in its linguistic, philosophical, religious and political, poetic dimensions. Contemporary problems of state languages and minority languages (extinction and reawakening, participation in the international scientific and philosophical community, domination and appropriation of techno-science by language).

B. Setting up specialized *centers for linguistic training,* for French or foreign researchers, inside the College or in association with it.

C. *The modern technology of translation: theoretical problems.* Translation machines, "artificial intelligences," programming—in a determined language—of data banks and other modes of archiving or communication.

D. *Languages and philosophical discourse.* The role of natural (national) languages in the constitution of the philosophical as such;

history of "philosophical" languages; the political, theologico-political, and pedagogical dimensions: how does a philosophical language become dominant? This work will be coordinated closely with work in the so-called "comparatist" problematic and on the philosophical institution (see below). Each time the question already posed will be recast: that of the processes by which "philosophical objects" are formed and legitimated.

E. *"Comparatism" in philosophy:* an empirical and uncertain title, but research whose necessity admits of no doubt. The urgency, especially in our country, makes itself felt massively, and the testimonies here are numerous and eloquent. Everywhere it has imposed itself, for better or worse, the word "comparatism" has certainly covered approaches that are difficult to delimit, not quite sure of the existence of their object, and even less of their method.

Nevertheless, as is sometimes the case, this fragility or this empiricism has not prevented some work from imposing itself in strange institutional conditions which would justify an entire study. It is doubtful that "comparatism" *as such* has much meaning in philosophy, but the very critique of this vague notion should itself be produced in the course of analyses which are today too underdeveloped in the West, and particularly so in France (we are speaking of philosophical analyses and not only of "culturological" ones). Let us situate this schematically.

a. *On the difference between thought (in general) and philosophy.* On systems of thought which are not necessarily limited to the "philosophical" form as it was born and has developed under this name in the West. All of these "thoughts," if not strictly philosophical, are not necessarily reducible to what, from a philosophical standpoint, we name with categories like "culture," "world view," ethico-religious "system of representations," in the West and elsewhere. Often the attempts to think beyond the philosophical or beyond what links metaphysics to western techno-science bring to light affinities with non-European (African or Far Eastern) thought. Systematic work and exchanges at these frontiers should cross with others which we might entitle:

b. *Philosophical systems and religious systems,* within and outside the West. Renewal of theological research (to link up with the renaissance of religious and theologico-political movements all over the world).

c. *Philosophical systems and mythological systems.*

d. *Philosophy and ethnocentrism. Problematic of ethnophiloso-phy* (a wide and exemplary debate which has developed in Africa starting from the critique, by Paulin Hountondji, of Tempels's *Bantu Philosophy*.[6] This could be developed in relation to the questions posed by a (semantic, linguistic, ethno-culturological) study of the signification attached to gestures and discourses of destination (giving/receiving, emitting, transmitting, sending, addressing, orienting).

e. *Philosophical "transcontinentality."* On the difference (intra-philosophical and intra-European in its manifestations, even if it affects philosophical institutions that are non-European yet constructed on a European model) between philosophical traditions. What does this difference consist in, once it is no longer determined on the basis of objects or "contents" alone, nor simply of national languages, nor finally of doctrinal conflicts? Over the centuries what I propose to call *philosophical continents* have been constituted. This movement has accelerated and its traits have made themselves apparent in the last two centuries. "Continent": the metaphor, if it were simply geographical, would not be rigorous; it is justified to the extent that geographical or geographico-national limits have often surrounded traditional entities and institutional territories (French, German, Anglo-Saxon philosophy, etc.). Today it is just as difficult to get through the "customs" and the "police" of these philosophical traditions as it is to situate their borderline, their essential trait. An analysis (which we cannot undertake here) would show, it seems to me, that these frontiers do not depend strictly on language, nationality, the types of objects privileged as philosophical, rhetoric, the socioinstitutional modalities of the production and reproduction of philosophical discourse (in the educational system and elsewhere), or general historico-political conditions. And yet the accumulation and intrication of all these conditions have engendered these "continental" formations so closed in on themselves. Their effects are multiple and already interesting in themselves. This original quasi-incommunicability does not take the form of a simple opacity, of a

6. See Placide Tempels, *La Philosophie bantoue,* trans. A. Rubbens (Elisabethville: Editions Lovania, 1945); *Bantu Philosophy,* trans. Colin King (Paris: Présence Africaine, 1959). And see Paulin J. Honntondja, *Sur la "philosophie africaine"* (Paris: François Maspero, 1976); *African Philosophy,* trans. Henri Evans with Jonathan Ree (Bloomington: Indiana University Press, 1983), especially chapters 1–3. —Eds.

radical absence of exchange; it is rather the delay and disorder of all the phenomena of translation, the general aggravation of all the misunderstandings. They do not obtain only or essentially between countries or national philosophical communities. To the extent that each of the great traditions is also represented within each national community, the frontiers are reconstituted inside each country, in diverse configurations.

Inversely, following a process which is also interesting, this situation is slowly beginning to evolve. Certain philosophers are more sensitive to it here and there. Movements are beginning to reflect on and transform this "babelization." An urgent, difficult, original task, without a doubt that of philosophy itself today, if some such thing exists and has to affirm itself. It is in any case the first task for an International College of Philosophy, and the most irreplaceable. Even if the College had been created only to this end, its existence would be completely justified.

Starting with its first four years, the College should prepare the following initiatives:

• *Setting up international working groups,* including each time French and foreign researchers. They will work in France (in Paris and as much as possible outside of Paris) and abroad. Competencies will not only be philosophical, but also, for example, linguistic. They will seek the cooperation of other experts, in France and abroad. All of them will work to analyze and transform the situation we have just been describing. They will take initiatives and multiply proposals concerning exchanges, cooperation, meetings, contracts of association, translations, and joint publications, in all the domains of interest to the College. As the College's constant perspective, this thematic and problematic of "intercontinental" difference will be a high priority program during the first years. Everywhere such groups can be constituted, each time according to original modalities, they will be—in (Eastern and Western) Europe and outside Europe, whether it is a matter of philosophy in the strictly occidental sense or (see above) of nonphilosophical "thought."

• *A program of large international colloquia* will be organized as soon as the College is created, as its very inaugural act. It will not be a matter of colloquia in the traditional form (formal juxtaposition of large lectures and panels). Those organized by the College will be the culmination of two or three years of intense work, in France and abroad, with their active preparation entrusted to specialized philosophers. Periods of study in residence toward this end should be the object of agreements and support in France and abroad: study in residence at the College for several foreign philosophers, abroad for as many French philosophers. It seems to me that the first large meetings of this type should concern first of all French and German thought, French and Anglo-Saxon thought. We will make sure that the most diverse currents of thought are represented there. But particular attention will naturally be given to the most alive and the most specific, whether it is dominant in academic institutions or not. And starting with the preparation of these two large colloquia, setting up other groups should give rise to future meetings (Italy, Spain, Latin America, India, the Arab countries, Africa and the countries of the Far East, etc.).

V. The Institutional Orientations of Philosophy (Research and Teaching)

These two are oriented, to begin with, by the problematic of *destination* (constitution of senders and receivers—individual or collective "subjects"—, units and legitimation of messages, structures of transmission and reception, etc.). Research of great breadth will be brought to bear on the history and system of philosophical institutions, whether of teaching or research, French or foreign. On the one hand "theoretical" (much, if not everything, remains to be done in this domain), they will also be largely practical and experimental. They will aim to develop and enrich philosophical research and teaching. The President of the Republic invited this and expressly committed himself to it in his letter of 8 May 1981 to GREPH. This necessity was recalled by the Minister of Research and Industry, in his letter to the Mission of 18 May 1982: "At a time when the government is preparing to extend the study of philosophy in secondary education, it is important that research devoted to this discipline be assured of the conditions and instruments best suited to its scope." And the Minister specified further on that the College should be "inclined to favor innovative initiatives, open to the reception of unprecedented research and pedagogical experiments. . . . "

The reference I make here to the projects and early work of the *Groupe de Recherches sur l'Enseignement Philosophique* (GREPH) and to the *Etats Généraux de la Philosophie* (1979) has only an *indic-*

ative value.[7] Other paths are possible and the College should vigilantly maintain an opening for them.

Everyone who wants to participate in this research should be provided with the means to do so, particularly secondary school teachers, university and lycée students.

In order to give a schematic idea of such research, I will cite the opening of GREPH's "Avant-Projet"[8] in the hope that this group be associated with the College, under conditions that guarantee at once maximum cooperation and strict independence on the part of both.

Preliminary Proposal for the Constitution of a Research Group on Philosophical Education.

Preliminary work has made it clear that it is today both possible and necessary to organize a set of research investigations on what relates philosophy to its teaching. This research, which should have both a critical and a practical bearing, would attempt initially to respond to certain questions. We will define these questions here, under the rubric of a rough anticipation, with reference to common notions which are to be discussed.

1. What is the connection between philosophy and teaching in general? What is teaching in general? What is teaching for philosophy? What is it to teach philosophy? In what way would teaching (a category to be analyzed in the context of the pedagogical, the didactic, the doctrinal, the disciplinary, etc.) be essential to the philosophical operation? How has this essential indissociability of the didacto-philosophical been constituted and differentiated? Is it possible, and under what conditions, to propose a general, critical, and transformative history of this indissociability?

These questions are of great theoretical generality. Obviously they demand elaboration. . . .

In opening up these questions it should be possible—let us say

7. See the collective volume from GREPH called *Qui a peur de la philosophie?* (Paris: Flammarion, 1977) and the proceedings of the June 1979 *Etats Généraux de la Philosophie* (Paris: Flammarion, 1979). Minister Chevènement's letter is quoted in Derrida's "lettre circulaire" of 18 May 1982 (see headnote). English translations of selected texts from GREPH and the Etats Généraux, as well as François Mitterand's May 1981 letter to GREPH, are forthcoming in Derrida's *Institutions of Philosophy.* —Eds.

8. The complete French text can be found in *Qui a peur . . . ?*, 433–37; English translation by Rebecca Comay in *Institutions of Philosophy.* —Eds.

only *for example* and in a very vaguely indicative way—to study not only:

a. models of didactic operations legible, with their rhetoric, their logic, their psychagogy, etc., within written discourses (from Plato's dialogues, for example, through Descartes's *Meditations*, Spinoza's *Ethics*, Hegel's *Encyclopedia* or *Lectures*, etc., up to all the so-called philosophical works of modernity), but also

b. *pedagogical practices* administered according to rules in fixed places, in private or public establishments, since the Sophists, for example, the Scholastic "quaestio" and "disputatio," etc., up to the courses and other pedagogical activities instituted today in colleges, *lycées*, grade schools, universities, etc. What are the forms and norms of these practices? What are the effects aimed at and the effects obtained? Things to be studied here would be, for example: the "dialogue," maieutics, the master-disciple relationship, the question, the interrogation, the test, the examination, the competition, the inspection, publication, the frames and programs of discourse, the dissertation, the presentation, the lesson, the thesis, the procedures of verification and of control, repetition, etc.

These different types of problematics should be articulated together, as rigorously as possible.

2. How is the didactico-philosophical inscribed in the so-called instinctual, historical, political, social, economic fields?

How does it *inscribe itself* there, that is to say how does it operate—and represent (to) itself—its inscription, and how is it inscribed in its very representation? What is the "general logic" and what are the specific modes of this inscription? Of its normalizing normativity and of its normalized normativity? For example, the Academy, the *lycée*, the Sorbonne, preceptorships of every kind, the universities or the royal, imperial, or republican schools of modern times all prescribe, according to determined and differentiated paths, not only a pedagogy which is indissociable from a philosophy, but also, at the same time, a moral and political system that forms at once both the object and the actualized structure of pedagogy. What about this pedagogical effect? How to de-limit it, theoretically and practically?

Once again, these indicative questions remain too general: above all, they are formulated by design according to current representations and thus must be specified, differentiated, criticized, transformed. They could, in fact, lead one to believe that it is essentially, indeed uniquely, a matter of constructing a sort of "critical theory of philosophical doctrinality or disciplinarity," or of reproducing the traditional debate, regularly opened by philosophy, on its "crisis." This "reproduction" will itself be one of the objects of research. . . .

The preceding questions should thus be constantly reworked by these practical motivations. Also, without ever excluding the importance of these problems outside of France, we would first of all insist strongly on the conditions of philosophical teaching "here and now," in today's France. And in its concrete urgency, in the more or less dissimulated violence of its contradictions, the "here and now" would no longer be simply a philosophical object. . . .

1. What are the past and present historical conditions of this teaching system?

What about its power? What forces give it its power? What forces limit it? What about its legislation, its juridical code and its traditional code? Its external and internal norms? Its social and political field? Its relation to other kinds of teaching (historical, literary, aesthetic, religious, scientific, for example), to other institutionalized discursive practices (psychoanalysis in general, so-called training analysis in particular—for example, etc.)? From these different points of view, what is the specificity of the didactico-philosophical operation? Can laws be produced, analyzed, tested on objects such as—but these are only empirically accumulated indications—for example: the role of the Idéologues or of a Victor Cousin, of their philosophy or of their political interventions in the French university; the constitution of the philosophy class; the evolution of the figure of the philosophy professor since the nineteenth century, in the *lycée,* in *khâgne,*[9] in the *écoles normales,* in the university, at the Collège de France; the place of the disciple, the student, the candidate; the history and function of

a. the programs of examinations and of competitions, the form of their tests (the authors present and those excluded, the organization of titles, themes and problems, etc.);

b. the juries of the "inspection générale," the consulting committees, etc.;

c. the forms and norms of evaluation or of sanction (grading, ranking, comments, reports on competitions, examinations, theses, etc.);

d. the so-called research organisms (CNRS, Fondation Thiers[10] etc.);

9. Two years of post-*baccalauréat* preparation for the entrance examination of the humanities section of the Ecoles normales supérieures. —Trans.

10. The Centre National de Recherche Scientifique and the Fondation Thiers, independent though closely linked, provide permanent and part-time positions for researchers, who do not necessarily teach within the framework of these institutions. —Trans.

e. research tools (libraries, selected texts, manuals of the history of philosophy or of general philosophy (their relations with the field of commercial publishing on the one hand, with the authorities responsible for public instruction or national education on the other);

f. the places of work (the topological structure of the class, of the seminar, of the lecture hall, etc.);

g. the recruiting of teachers and their professional hierarchy (the social background and political stances of pupils, students, teachers, etc.).

2. What are the stakes of the struggles within and around philosophical teaching, today, in France?

The analysis of this conflictual field implies an interpretation of philosophy in general, and consequently, taking positions. It thus calls for action.

As far as France is concerned, it will be necessary to connect all this work with a reflection on French philosophy, on its own traditions and institutions, especially on the different currents which have traversed it over the course of this century. A new history of French thought in all its components (those which have dominated it and those which have been marginalized or repressed) ought to orient an analysis of the present situation. We will trace these premises as far back as possible, while insisting on the most recent modernity, on its complex relation to the problematics of philosophy and its limits, to the arts and sciences but also to French sociopolitical history and to the country's ideological movements, as much those of the French right, for example, as those of French socialisms.

Translated by Thomas Pepper
Edited by Deborah Esch and Thomas Keenan

SAMUEL WEBER

The Vaulted Eye: Remarks on Knowledge and Professionalism

> The professional type is the institutional framework in which many
> of our most important social functions are carried on, notably the
> pursuit of science and liberal learning and its practical application
> in medicine, technology, law and teaching. This depends on an
> institutional structure the maintenance of which is not an automat-
> ic consequence of belief in the importance of the functions as such,
> but involves a complex balance of diverse social forces. Certain
> features of this pattern are peculiar to professional activities, but
> others, and not the least important ones, are shared by this field
> with the other most important branches of our occupational
> structure, notably business and bureaucratic administration.[1]

Despite the imprecision of formulation and the inelegance of style for
which he was notorious, Talcott Parsons's assessment of professionalism, made in 1938, can serve even today as a useful reminder
both of the importance of the phenomenon in modern societies and of
its complexity. "The professional type," which, according to Parsons,
provides the framework for "the pursuit and application of science"[2]
is not to be understood essentially in psychological terms; its operation depends not simply on existing "belief in the importance of the
functions," but rather upon "a complex balance of social forces" involving both the professions themselves, and "other . . . branches of
our occupational structure, notably business and bureaucratic administration." In short, an adequate analysis of professionalism
would have to focus upon its relation to "other" forces, of which, as
Parsons observes, "business and bureaucratic administration" are
doubtless the most notable, if not the only ones. Another, no less
pertinent factor that has emerged since the time of Parsons's study
involves technology, and in particular, developments in the stocking

1. Talcott Parsons, "The Professions and Social Structure," *Essays in Sociological
Theory* (Glencoe, Illinois: The Free Press, 1949), 199.
2. Parsons, 185.

YFS 77, *Reading the Archive: On Texts and Institutions*, ed. E. S. Burt and Janie Vanpée,
© 1990 by Yale University.

and retrieval of information that seem destined to bring about significant changes in what Burton Bledstein has aptly called the "culture of professionalism." Before going any further, it may be useful to recall some of the more salient traits that characterize this "culture":

> 1. Modern professionalism presupposes the systematic codification of a body of knowledge held to be relatively autonomous and self-contained. Such knowledge provides the basis for the delimitation of a *field* rendering possible an equally defined and codified form of *practice*.

> 2. The kind of knowledge that informs this practice is held to have universal validity within the confines of the specific field.

> 3. Professional practice distinguishes itself from "business" practices through the claim to a certain disinterest: the professions seek to portray their activities as essentially directed towards fulfilling social (and natural) needs, i.e., as a social relation determined by "use-value" rather than by "exchange-value."[3]

These three traits are of course by no means exhaustive. But already they enable us to understand why traditionally the three exemplary professions have been that of the physician, the lawyer, and the teacher (or professor). The physician addresses problems that seem ultimately rooted in the metasocial, "natural" condition of man: problems of life and death, sickness and health; moreover, the prevalence of curative over preventative medicine reinforces the tendency to focus primarily upon the ostensibly "natural" aspect of illness. The lawyer by contrast is concerned with the eminently social domain of legality and illegality. The lawyer satisfies the social need of upholding the legal system, but in a way that has become increasingly identified with the advancement of individual, particular interests, often at the expense of public interest. To this extent, the professional status of the lawyer has always been closer to that of the businessman than to that of the physician. One of the most visible and symptomatic changes in the culture of professionalism in recent years can be seen in the spread of malpractice suits. Traditionally, the relation of the physician to patient was considered to be based on agreement, but not of a contractual kind: since the services rendered by the physician were not considered to be a commodity, they were not

3. Burton Bledstein, *The Culture of Professionalism: The Middle-Class and the Development of Higher Education in America* (New York: Norton, 1976).

subjected to the same kind of legal and economic controls that protect "customers" or "clients" in theory, if not always in practice. The emergence of malpractice suits is a sign that medical services are becoming increasingly subject to those controls. The professional competence of the physician is, of course, by no means called into question; he must still be judged by his peers. But the necessity of such judgment can now be imposed by nonmedical professionals, i.e., by lawyers.[4]

Whereas the "disinterest" of physician and lawyer has become increasingly subject to question, thus compromising the traditional prestige of the two professions, the social status of the academic has undergone a less dramatic change in recent years, primarily because the professional standing of the professor has always been far less solidly established than that of the physician or the lawyer. The professor has never been considered a full-fledged professional, not because of an excess of (private) interest, but rather because of a lack of public interest. The utility, public or private, of the services rendered by the academic is characterized by the connotations of the word itself, for which *Webster's New Collegiate Dictionary* furnishes as synonyms: "Pedantic, bookish, scholastic," but also "theoretical, speculative"; for the word itself, it gives as one of its definitions: "Not expected to produce a practical result, as an *academic* discussion." This sense of academic attaches above all to the humanities and, to a lesser extent, the social sciences, which have made great efforts toward reducing, if not eliminating, the "speculative, theoretical" elements from their disciplines; by contrast, the natural sciences, engineering, computer sciences and, of course, business administration have developed their ties with the business community precisely in order to guarantee the practical, "non-academic" quality of their activities.

The results of such shifts are, however, contradictory: to strengthen the utility of professional training and services, their proximity to

---

4. A telling difference between the social status of professional medical practice in the United States and in France: in France, the results of medical tests (x-rays, blood tests, etc.) become the property of the patient, who is thus treated as the paying customer s/he is. In the United States, most physicians and laboratories would presumably be shocked by a "patient" who asked to be "treated" in this manner. A similar taboo exists—but this time in France no less than elsewhere—on the accessibility of information concerning the negative effects ("counter-indications") of medicines. The dissemination of the medication itself contrasts sharply with the accessibility of information concerning it.

commercial exploitation is increased; this however tends to increase doubts about the disinterested, public character associated with the profession. A related phenomenon can be seen in the increased use of advertising by the professions to attract clients (or customers). Physicians, lawyers, universities vie with other commodity-producers in efforts to increase their clientele. Similar tendencies are observable within universities themselves, state universities in particular, where the distribution of resources is often justified by the student-hours taught. In this connection, one should note not merely the growing financial dependence of universities upon private commercial enterprises, but also the increased proportion of military funding in public aid to education. Finally, within the university itself, there is an increasing tendency on the part of university researchers and research teams to treat their work as private property, to be commercially exploited by its owners in whatever way they see fit. Thus, the particularistic logic of capital has made steady inroads into the universalism that has traditionally characterized academic self-consciousness, if not always its practice.

The most obvious effect of such changes has been to undermine the deontological ideal of "disinterested service," which has traditionally allowed the professional to appear not as just a purveyor of commodities but as a representative of the common good, and hence, as a potential arbiter of social conflicts resulting from the clash of private and public interests. As a result of this shift in social standing, the need has emerged within the professions most directly affected—medicine, law, research, and teaching—to rethink the established strategies of legitimation with the aim of devising more effective ones. It is within this context that the problem of professionalism and, more specifically, that of their institutional conditions of possibility, has in recent years claimed increasing attention. At the same time, such attention has been regarded by mainstream practitioners with considerable skepticism. For they sense that the bed through which the mainstream flows is not—if I may be allowed to mix metaphors—of its own making. The very epistemological ideal of cognitive autonomy that has long informed the professionalization of the disciplines leaves these ill-equipped to undertake the urgent task of reflection that would inevitably require them to step "outside" of the discipline itself, precisely in order to reflect upon the latter *as such*. As Heidegger might have said, the "essence of the profession is not professional," no more than "the essence of technics"—with which what we call professionalism is intimately related—"is technical." The modes of thinking, the methods of investigation, the forms of analysis required for this task—none of these can be effective if they are merely extrapolations of the cognitive practices that have hitherto constituted the particular discipline at issue, no more than they can be entirely detached from those cognitive practices. In regard to this dilemma, which is determined not by individual factors but by the structure of the *episteme* that informs professionalism, the questioning of technics or *questing after* technics undertaken by Heidegger, above all in the essay, whose duplicitous title—*Die Frage nach der Technik*—I thus try to adumbrate, is of considerable interest. For the question of technics, especially as articulated by Heidegger, has much to do with that of professionalism. Both require, and promote, a certain kind of *place*, or, more precisely, a certain kind of *placement*. This is a familiar theme in recent studies of Professionalism, which presupposes established, well-defined and *stable fields*.[5] The ways in which the "technics" of Heidegger's quest(ion) entails the destabilization of such fields can be elucidated with reference to the three problems of translation posed to English readers by Heidegger's text.

The first involves the German preposition *"nach"* which Heidegger uses in his title to relate the *Frage*, the question, to its object, "technics" (which the English translation renders as "concerning" *The Question Concerning Technology.*)[6] *Nach* has both a temporal and a spatial meaning: "after," but also "toward," and that is why Heidegger's question, which comes *after* that which it interrogates, is also pointed *toward* something else; in this sense, the spatiality of "toward" is also anticipatory and hence temporal, pointing toward a future. Heidegger's "Frage nach . . . " thus designates a *questing after*, a movement and the opening of a space. In short, the reassuringly closed relationship of belonging suggested by the genitive (whether subjective or objective), as in "The Question *of* Technology," is dislocated, spaced out. And it is precisely in disrupting the clearly bounded, stable *site* that *Questing After Technics* also becomes germane for the question of professionalism.

The second point, and problem of translation, relates to the word

5. See "The Limits of Professionalism," in S. Weber, *Institution and Interpretation* (Minneapolis: University of Minnesota Press, 1987), 18–32.

6. Martin Heidegger, *The Question Concerning Technology and Other Essays*, trans. William Lovitt (New York: Harper and Row, 1977), 3–35.

used by Heidegger to continue and amplify the dislocation initiated by his title, the German word *Wesen*, rendered in English as *essence*. The problem with this rendition is that by recurring to the Latin *essentia*, it tends to arrest the very movement that Heidegger considers decisive for his argument. For this reason, I want to propose an alternative, which does not pretend to be an exact translation (whatever that might be) but which manages to preserve something of the dynamics implied by Heidegger's use of *Wesen* as a *verb*. What "*west*" or "*an-west*" in a manifestation of such as modern professional science, for instance, is simply what *goes-on* in it, or more exactly, *as* it.[7]

What goes on as technics—and this brings me to my third and last problem of translation—is what Heidegger calls the *Gestell*, which might be rendered as "stand" (in the sense of a computer stand), or as "framework," or even as "skeleton"—but which instead I will translate here as *emplacement*. The word has the following principal meanings: 1. Assignment to a definite place; localization. 2. *Fort*. a. The space in a fortification assigned to a gun or group of guns. b. The gun platform, parapet, accessories (*Webster's New Collegiate Dictionary*). The OED adds a few nuances: 1. The action of placing in a certain position; the condition of being so placed. 2. The situation, position of a building. Site. 3. Mil. A platform for guns, with epaulements for the defense of those serving them. This word seems to say much, if by no means all, of what Heidegger means by *Gestell*, namely, that the essence of technics, what goes on in it, involves the destiny of *being placed*. It is this aspect that receives a distinctive turn at the hands of modern science. In response to the destiny of being-placed, modern science according to Heidegger develops a practice aimed at *securing a place of reckoning*: a place from which to take stock and take a stand. But technics, as Heidegger insists, is ambivalent, and in this sense perhaps more complex than modern science. Its emplacement also entails a movement of what Heidegger calls *Entbergung*: usually translated as "revealing," "it connotes an opening out from protective concealing, a harboring forth," as the translators of "The Question Concerning Technology" observe.[8] I

---

7. It is, of course, evident that "going on" does not render in any direct way the two meanings Heidegger explicitly attaches to the German word, *wesen: währen*, to last or endure, and even more, *gewähren*, to grant, allow. But the colloquial expression perhaps allows the *way* that leads from "essence" to "granting" and "lasting" to be discerned.

8. Heidegger, *The Question Concerning Technology*, 11.

would therefore propose rendering this aspect of technics not as "revealing" but, wherever possible, as "unsecuring." However unusual the English, it points to the tension that informs Heidegger's conception of technics, and what distinguishes it from science: the latter is read, in a Nietzschean gesture, as a largely defensive gesture of "securing." Technics, on the other hand, even and especially as emplacement, remains a movement of *unsecuring,* "harboring forth," leaving the safety of a shelter that is already, in German, a "salvaging" [*Bergung*], and that, as such, is the response to some sort of dispersion. The danger is that, reinforced by the "securing" [*Sicherstellen*] of modern science, the emplacement of technics will attempt to eliminate the movement of "unsecuring," through which it articulates dispersion and danger, and instead will become entirely dedicated to the "placing-of-orders" (what Heidegger calls *Bestellen*). Placing everything on order also involves the organization of places to serve as secure sites for such ordering. It is here that the relation to the modern university and professionalism emerges. For if science involves the "setting after" [*Nachstellen*] and "securing" [*Sicherstellen*] of place, the professional university may be regarded both as its necessary condition and as one of its most important manifestations. For the securing of positions in this sense has long been described, by Bledstein and others, as one of the hallmarks of professionalism: the delimitation, compartmentalization, delineation of closed areas, of "fields." For Heidegger this converges with the thrust of modern science as the "theory of the real" [*des Wirklichen*]: it renders reality accountable and measurable by bringing it to a standstill in clearly defined "object fields, which it demarcates [*abgrenzen*] from one another and defines in compartmentalized subjects" [*in Fächer eingrenzen, d.h. einfächern*].[9] But on the other hand, if this process by which "object fields are demarcated and then divided into special zones" is a familiar enough fact, its basis [*Grund*] remains enigmatic to the sciences themselves, "as does their very essence." In short, what goes on as science is ultimately not accessible to scientific thinking, which cannot comprehend what it is about: "containment, objectification, and emplacement." Scientific thinking places-before-itself [*stellt vor: re-presents*], that is, *ob-jectifies*, brings to a standstill, "*em-places*," and thus, cannot think the process of emplace-

9. Martin Heidegger, "Wissenschaft und Besinnung," *Vorträge und Aufsätze*, vol. 1 (Neske: Pfullingen, 1967), 60. My translation.

ment as such. The mode of thinking that would seek to think the process of emplacement would be most "unprofessional"; Heidegger calls it *Besinnung*, another term difficult to translate (neither simply "meditation," "contemplation," nor "reflection"). Rather, it involves something like "coming to one's senses," with the connotation of a recollective movement, of remembrance:

> In "coming to our senses," we reach a place where we have long stayed without experiencing or understanding this clearly. In coming to our senses we go towards a place from which the space opens out, which our usual doings and letting-be traverse.
> [*Tun und Lassen durchmißt*, 60]

As distinct from a mode of thinking that requires predefined places in order to represent its objects, the "coming to one's senses" envisaged by Heidegger entails the "opening up of a space" which we traverse without thinking about it, insofar as the scope of our thoughts is determined by the fixity of the fields we expect to master. Thus, this movement is in a certain sense retrospective, re-memorative, although of "doings and letting-be," "goings-on" that have never been experienced or clearly recognized as such. The "opening up of a space" in this way involves the disruption of a mode of thought that is based on the expectation of stable and secure emplacements.

For some time now, different kinds of emplacements have been opening up in certain areas of university studies. These emplacements can be distinguished from the more familiar schools and disciplines by their effort to assume that "unsecuring" of knowledge that much (but not all) of modern science would like to forget. It is hardly fortuitous that such emplacements have developed from practices closely related to linguistic and literary "goings-on," in which language is approached not primarily as a medium of meaning, communication, or understanding, but as a process of signification. I will return to a few instances of these openings shortly. Should they continue to develop, it is highly likely that they will exert increasing pressure to bring about at least a partial realignment of the established academic division of labor. Such a realignment would have to entail not merely the introduction of a few new disciplines or departments, not merely the shifting of borders, but the tracing of a *different kind of borderline*, for which the term, "fault-lines" might not be entirely inappropriate. For far from defining "the

innermost motionless boundary of that which contains"—the definition of *place* [*topos*] given by Aristotle in the *Physics* (212a)—the
fault-line demarcates "an unsound or damaged place, a flaw, crack,"
to cite one of the definitions of the word to be found in the OED.
The OED also includes among its definitions a military usage that,
although obsolete, is quite pertinent in our context: "Mil. a gap in
the ranks." The result of diverging forces, fault-lines themselves always trace the contours of a dislocation. In what follows I shall discuss three instances in which such fault-lines emerge and point toward possible transformations of established cognitive paradigms
and of the professionalism with which they are complicit.

My first instance is drawn from John Searle's book, *Speech Acts*. If
Searle's book has enjoyed such a considerable vogue, both in this
country and to a certain extent in Europe as well, it is a sign that his
efforts to systematize the line of thought initiated, in a far less systematic vein by Austin, respond to a desire that is widespread among
the readers he addresses: not just professional philosophers, but also
literary critics and others working in the humanities and the social
sciences. What I want to discuss is the way Searle seeks to render
language a suitable object of a systematic and comprehensive theory.
First, he construes it as a means of understanding or communication,
and then he sets about determining the conditions under which such
communication/understanding can take place. These conditions he
conceives as constituting a fixed set of rules. Language is thus defined
by Searle as being a rule-governed activity:

> Hearers are able to understand this infinite number of possible com-
> munications simply by recognizing the intentions of the speakers in
> the performances of the speech acts. Now given that both speaker and
> hearer are finite, what is it that gives their speech acts this limitless
> capacity for communication? The answer is that the speaker and hear-
> ers are masters of the sets of rules we call the rules of language, and
> these rules are recursive. They allow for the repeated application of
> the same rule.[10]

Language is defined as the set of communications of intentions
that can be recognized for what they are by the speakers performing
speech acts. Recognition presupposes that language is constituted by

---

10. John Searle, *Speech Acts: An Essay on the Philosophy of Language* (Cambridge:
Cambridge University Press, 1970), 208. Henceforth, page numbers will be cited in the
text.

sets of rules that can be mastered by speakers and hearers by virtue of the invariance of those rules, i.e., by the fact that they remain self-identical in and through their "repeated application." Recursivity, as Searle defines it at least, presupposes that the rule remains the same throughout its repetition. Searle introduces a further distinction that is pertinent here, between "constitutive" and "regulative" rules: regulative rules he defines as those that "regulate antecedently or independently existing forms of behavior," whereas "constitutive rules do not merely regulate, they create or define new forms of behavior. The rules of football or chess, for example, do not merely regulate playing football or chess, but as it were they create the very possibility of playing such games. The activities of playing football or chess are constituted by acting in accordance with (at least a large subset of) the appropriate rules" (33–34). In this respect, language is like football or chess for Searle; it is constituted by the rules that *Speech Acts* proposes to discern and describe. Having thus introduced this distinction, Searle adds a long footnote, as if to secure it against possible objections:

> This statement has to be understood in a certain way. When I say that playing, e.g., chess, consists in acting in accordance with the rules, I intend to include far more than just those rules that state the possible moves of the pieces. One could be following those rules and still not be playing chess, if for example the moves were made as part of a religious ceremony, or if the moves of chess were incorporated into some larger, more complex game. In the notion of "acting in accordance with the rules," I intend to include the rules that make clear the "aim of the game." Furthermore, I think there are some rules crucial to competitive games which are not peculiar to this or that game. For example I think it is a matter of rules of competitive games that each side is committed to trying to win. Notice in this connection that our attitude to the team or player who deliberately throws the game is the same as that toward the team or player who cheats. Both violate rules, though the rules are of quite different sorts. [34]

The example of the competitive game is obviously no mere accident. It is of course a topos at least since Saussure's comparison of language with chess; yet what Saussure precisely ignored, the "agonistic" element of the game, Searle foregrounds, thus marking what may be a decisive shift in the professional paradigm already referred to. For Saussure the synchronic state remained the indispensable prerequisite of scientific objectification, although he fully recognized its fictional status. For Searle, by contrast, the synchronic state is, in the best American tradition, replaced by the sporting *match* divided symmetrically into winners and losers. But this in turn requires the introduction of a metarule, which determines the minimal condition of competitive sports to be "the commitment to trying to win," a commitment that must be assumed by the participants. This foot-noted afterthought, however, far from closing off the notion of con-stitutive rules and protecting it from possible equivocation, under-scores the precarity of its contours. Long before Derrida elevated it into a strategy of reading Searle against his systematic pretensions, the fault-lines of an unlimited or illimitable "incorporation" were proleptically inscribed in the margins of Searle's text, in the admis-sion that any set of moves, or "intentions" is *in principle* susceptible of being "incorporated into some larger, more complex game." And this is surely the peculiarity of language: that in it, every declaration of intention, qua declaration, is in principle capable of being "incor-porated into some larger, more complex game" than that intended by the declaring subject.

In a Heideggerian perspective, one could say that language *goes on* before and beyond the efforts of scientific theory to contain and com-prehend it as the rule-governed realization of intentionality, or, in Nietzschean terms, of the Will to Power (the subjective correlation and consummation of the technique of emplacement).

It is this Will to Power, the Will to Will, that is at work in one of Searle's most prominent critics, Stanley Fish. In "How to do Things with Austin and Searle," Fish elaborates a critique of Searle that in certain aspects resembles what I have been developing here: Searle's conceptual oppositions, such as regulative vs. constitutive rules, pre-suppose that "something is available outside of language."[11] Fish counters that such putative extralinguistic instances are themselves "interpretations," and that "Speech Act Theory" is therefore "an account of the conditions of intelligibility, of what it means to mean in a community."[12] For Fish, then, the ultimately constitutive rule is that language only makes sense, only functions as the act of a "com-munity of interpretation." The invocation of this category is designed to reestablish the borders of language, to emplace it and institu-

---

11. Stanley Fish, "How to Do Things with Austin and Searle," *Is There a Text in This Class?* (Cambridge, Massachusetts: Harvard University Press, 1980), 243.
   12. Ibid.

tionalize it. But the notion of community of interpretation is no less equivocal, no less enigmatic, no less faulted than that of constitutive rule: what it leaves unthought and indeed seeks to conjure away is quite simply that "interpretation," like "community, *goes on*, because they are steeped in language and because language, as a medium of articulation, is never entirely *unifiable* or totalizable. The interpretive community is subject to the same kinds of dislocation or incorporation as are Searle's constitutive rules. If the community of interpretation is said to be the source and addressee of "its" interpretations, it becomes itself utterly uninterpretable, indeterminate, an abstract name or claim of the Will to Interpret, the Will to Power, the Will to Will. But the notion of community is meaningless if it is not related to that which is not itself: both to other communities, and above all, to that which is not a community. To attempt to define the community strictly in terms of itself, of what its members have in common—shared sets of assumptions, etc.,—is to condemn oneself to solipsism. By taking the unifying moment of the community simply for granted, Fish's theory of the community of interpretation amounts to little more than an attempt to titillate a startled profession with a domesticated, communitarian version of the Will to Power.

By contrast, the initial elaboration of the "community of interpretation," by Josiah Royce in *The Problem of Christianity* (1913), has the virtue of clearly exposing the problem involved in any attempt to think the notion of community in immanentist terms. This crystallizes around a classical problem of modern political theory: that of reconciling individual interest with the common good, a dilemma that in Royce's text is formulated in terms of "loyalty." The dilemma of social theory and of the community itself, for Royce, is that the very idea of community presupposes a loyalty on the part of its individual members that more often than not stands in contradiction with their immediate interest. The result is a paradox that leads Royce to raise the question of the original possibility of communal loyalty. The only way Royce can conceive of such a paradoxical origin is as a mimetic circle:

> The origin of this higher form of loyalty is hard to trace, unless some leader is first there, to be the source of loyalty in other men. . . . You are first made loyal through the power of some one else who is already loyal.

> But the loyal man must also be, as we have just said, a member of a lovable community. How can such a community originate? . . .
>
> Loyalty needs for its beginnings the inspiring leader who teaches by the example of his spirit. But the leader, in order to inspire to loyalty, must himself be loyal. In order to by loyal, he must himself have found, or have founded, his lovable community. And this, in order to be lovable, and a community, must already consist of loyal and loving members. . . . One moves thus in a circle.[13]

The consequence drawn by Royce would probably shock many of those who seek to shore up the professionalist paradigm of cognitive autonomy by means of his category of the community of interpretation:

> Only some miracle of grace (as it would seem) can initiate the new life, either in the individuals who are to love communities, or in the communities that are to be worthy of their love. [130]

Royce then proceeds to describe the conditions under which such a miracle can be conceived. The only way the vicious circle can be, not so much "broken" as circumvented, is by reproducing it in a different form:

> For the new life of loyalty, if it first appears at all, will arise as a bond linking many highly self-conscious and mutually estranged social individuals into one . . . only in case some potent and loyal individual, acting as leader, first declares that for him it is real. In such a leader, and in his spirit, the community will begin its own life, if the leader has the power to create what he loves. [130]

The founding "act" of the community is thus a "speech act," a "declaration," that proclaims the reality of the community which it, literally, first "calls" into existence. Royce insists that "only the voice of a living individual leader" can call the community of interpretation into being, but also, that it can only do this insofar as it speaks in the name of another, whose absent spirit resounds in the voice of the founder. The community can thus be called into being because it has always already existed in spirit, in whose name the founder declares its reality. The founder, Paul, speaks to the community he founds in the name of the spirit, which in turn speaks in the name of the father: "Holy Father, keep them in thy name which thou hast

13. Josiah Royce, *The Problem of Christianity* (Chicago: University of Chicago Press, 1968), 129–30. Page numbers will henceforth be cited in the text.

given me, that they may be one, even as we are one" (John 17, cited
in Royce, 141).

The founding of a community—whether of interpretation or
other—can thus only be conceived in regard to a transcendence, that
is: to an *exteriority* that remains its *innermost* basis of "cohesion."
The gap between inner and outer is bridged by a *voice* speaking in
terms of a *name* that in turn is invoked to guarantee the unity of
what is separate: Father and Son. That such separateness should
nevertheless be one is what makes an appeal to the theological dimension indispensable, in hermeneutics no less than in social theory. That is why the community of interpretation, despite its ostensibly secular character, must remain an ontotheological category, even
and perhaps especially where it shows itself incapable of thinking its
origins as those of a transcendent speech act: speaking in the name
of another (one).

As the legitimation of the professionalist paradigm becomes increasingly difficult, it seems likely that the repression of its ontotheological origins will return in direct proportion to the difficulties encountered: communities defining themselves in terms of
leaders and founders who present an image or *figure:* a *Gestalt* that
in turn stabilizes the shaken *Gestell*, the established "emplacement." By transmitting a unified "image" and a consistent "voice"
of the founder and leader, *porte-parole* of the absent spirit and bearer
of the name, the media, particularly television, assume the decisive
rôle of protecting the framework of the emplacement against the
goings-on that generate its faults. Attempts to call such protective
action into question are dismissed as marginal and elitist, even (especially?) within the academy, which seeks to demonstrate its own
professional relevance and technical competence by establishing
programs of media studies which, more often than not, serve the
function of reproducing, and hence legitimating, the logic of their
subject matter.

Nevertheless, on the margins of the established emplacements,
the fault-lines of technics and of professionalism continue to be re-
traced and the fields redrawn. Nowhere, perhaps, has this been more
persistent and effective than in those rereadings generated by what
is doubtless one of the founding texts of modern aesthetics and "critical theory": Kant's *Critique of the Power to Judge*. To indicate the
kind of space that such a redrawing of boundaries might open, I
would like to discuss all too briefly, in conclusion, a passage to

which Paul de Man first called attention, one that comes toward the end of the "Analytics of the Sublime," in which Kant is reflecting upon the particular kind of suspended cognition that gives aesthetic judgment its particular and even paradoxical character:

> Therefore, when we call the sight of the starry sky *sublime,* we must not base our judgment upon any concept of worlds that are inhabited by rational beings and then [conceive of] the bright points, with which we see the space above us filled, as being these worlds' suns, moved in orbits prescribed for them with great purposiveness; but we must base our judgment regarding it merely on how we see it [*wie man ihn sieht*], as a vast all-embracing vault [*ein weites Gewölbe*], and merely under this presentation may we posit that sublimity that a pure aesthetic judgment attributes to this object. Similarly, when we judge the sight of the ocean, we must not do so on the basis of how we *think* it, enriched with all sorts of knowledge (that are not contained in immediate intuition), e.g., as a vast realm of aquatic creatures, or as the great reservoir of those vapors that impregnate the air with clouds for the benefit of the land, or again as an element that, while separating continents from one another, yet makes possible the greatest communication among them; for all such judgments will be teleological. Instead, we must be able to view the ocean as poets do [*wie die Dichter es tun*], merely in terms of what the eye reveals [*was der Augenschein zeigt*]—e.g., if it is observed while calm, as a clear mirror of water bounded only by the sky; if it is observed while turbulent, as an abyss threatening to devour [*verschlingen*] everything.[14]

In this passage Paul de Man[15] sees evidence of what he calls "a formal materialism that runs counter to all values and characteristics associated with aesthetic experience, including the aesthetic experience of the beautiful and of the sublime as described by Kant and Hegel themselves" (16). The essence of this "formal materialism," which undoes the unifying function of "aesthetic experience," whether of the beautiful or of the sublime, de Man sees in a process of "disarticulation": to take the notion of the disinterest of

14. Immanuel Kant, *Critique of Judgment*, trans. Werner S. Pluhar (Indianapolis: Hackett, 1987), 130; *Kritik der Urteilskraft* (Frankfurt: Suhrkamp, 1981), 196. English translation modified.

15. Paul de Man, "Phenomenality and Materiality in Kant," *Hermeneutics*, ed. Gary Shapiro and Alan Sica (Amherst: University of Massachusetts Press, 1984), 16. Page numbers will be cited in the text.

aesthetic judgment to its extreme is to sever "the phenomenality of the aesthetic" from the purposes or concepts that inform its representational function; this "marks the undoing of the aesthetic as a valid category" (22–23). To de Man's reading of this remarkable passage, I want to add only a few remarks. First, the "undoing of the aesthetic" as articulated in Kant's exemplary landscapes all involve the process of "framing." The starry heaven or sky must be seen without any reference to purpose, as "a vast vault" which contains everything. This vault, which Kant presents here as the perception of simple sight, is both the minimal figure of figuration itself, the container (as which Aristotle defines "place"), and also the "vault" of the eyeball, which sees merely "itself." This seeing of itself is in turn figured in the next scene: the sublime ocean, seen not as a world populated by creatures, but simply "as the poets do," by the sight of their eyes, as "a clear mirror of water bounded only by the heavens" if the ocean is at rest. This "clear mirror" contains nothing except, once again, the very condition of figuration and of perception: it is "pure boundary," "bounded only by the heavens" (or the sky: *Himmel* in German means both). The ocean, at rest, is a mirror for the eye, it is the surface of the eye, bounded by the same sky that is also the eye's socket. As de Man points out, the word that Kant uses here to designate the pure and simple sight of the eye— *Augenschein*—confounds and confuses subject and object, sight and seen, making both a function of the "eye," the *Auge*; but the status of this *Auge* is no less confused, since the *Augenschein* can be not just the "sight of the eye," but its "semblance": pure sight as the semblance of sight. But what does pure sight resemble? The final scene suggests a response: when the ocean is no longer calm, but turbulent, it becomes "an abyss (*Abgrund*), threatening to devour (*verschlingen*) everything"—everything, including above all, the very eye itself. With the site, sight itself defaults. The eye shines forth (*der Augenschein scheint*) but what its shine resembles is nothing so much as an *Abgrund*, an abyss. When the trait no longer circumscribes a *place*, the surface mirrors the boundless skies, opening to "devour" everything. The surface vaults into the vaulted sky, but as an abyss. The aesthetic bridge designed to span the gap separating phenomena from essence, nature from freedom, understanding from reason, twists and turns into a vertiginous vortex. The vault defaults.

What de Man here reads as the undoing of aesthetic experience thus comes very close to what Heidegger has described as the initial sense of "theoria" for the Greeks:

> *Thea,* (cf., Theater) is the aspect (*Anblick*), the outlook (*Aussehen*) in which something shows itself, the attitude (*Ansicht*) in which it offers itself. Plato called this outlook, in which the on-going (*Anwesendes*) shows what it is, *eidos.* To have seen this outlook (*Aussehen*), *eidénai,* is knowledge [*Wissen*]. The second root in *theorein, horao,* signifies: to look at something, take it in (the sight of the eye) [*in den Augenschein nehmen*], to regard it. What follows: *theorein* is *théan horan:* to look at the aspect wherein the on-coming appears, and through such sight to linger there while seeing."[16]

To linger in face of this faceless spectacle in which a vast, all-embracing vault frames an empty mirror that in turn opens to swallow up everything—is to open oneself to an experience of place very different from the Aristotelian *topos* that has organized the scene of Western thought and art for so long. Instead of the familiar emplacements, the possibility of another site seems gradually to be emerging, one "traversed by our usual doings," by goings-on, and which itself is not fixed, but *on-going,* albeit not going in any determinate direction. Such goings-on tend to replace the emplacements of professionalism with a different kind of platform, in which the setting and maintenance of boundaries, between spectacle and spectator, actor and acted, form part of the play. The knowledge that dwells on this *Augenschein* turns technics, and science, toward theater.[17]

16. Heidegger, *Wissenschaft und Besinnung,* 44.
17. This line of thought is explored in a forthcoming essay on "Technics and Theater: On *The Balcony.*"

KATHRYN ASCHHEIM

Belles-lettres *and the University:* *Diderot's* Plan d'une université ou d'une éducation publique dans toutes les sciences

Diderot drafted his outline for a university in response to a commission from the Russian empress, Catherine II, with a view towards a future restructuring of that country's educational system. Whether or not the plan might have been judged practicable in any sense, its foremost purpose can be understood as that of coordinating an emerging theory of knowledge, associated with the Encyclopedists, and the practical functioning of an educational institution. The construction of a university, that is, would rest on the possibility of bringing into alignment the conflicting imperatives of "universal science," pedagogy, and the state. Such a convergence could of course take different forms. Does the realm of positive knowledge contain within itself principles for regulating its own institutional transmission and diffusion, or on the contrary, is it ultimately determined by external, political forces for which it is unable to account? Can the university combine science and politics according to a formula of equal participation and cooperation? Remarkably, Diderot's answer to these questions hinges upon a problem that at first seems quite remote, that of the languages, textual corpus, aesthetic, and pedagogic tradition of belles-lettres.

By the circumstances which occasioned its writing the *Plan* was destined for a single country, but Diderot clearly believed it to be of universal application, valid for any time or place. The generality of his plan would match that of the project of public education itself, "which has nothing variable, nothing that depends essentially on circumstances," and whose goal, the making of virtuous and en-

YFS 77, *Reading the Archive: On Texts and Institutions,* ed. E. S. Burt and Janie Vanpée, © 1990 by Yale University.

lightened men, is "the same in all centuries" (756).[1] The achievement of this goal is assured by a feat of technical organization. Teaching, in Diderot's ideal university, is no longer problematic, no longer an object of philosophic reflection: it is guaranteed by a correct ordering of the institution, an optimal configuration of classes, "concours," encouragements, punishments, and so forth. But if Diderot would isolate the university as a universally valid order from the influence of historical circumstances, his text is saturated with references to a specific history of education. Composed in 1775, the *Plan* was contemporaneous with a widespread movement in France for educational reform, a movement which saw the expulsion of the Jesuits from their *collèges* in 1762, the publication of *Emile*, also in 1762, and a proliferation of reform proposals in the years following the Jesuits' departure.[2] These proposals were formally submitted by the Parliament of Paris itself as control over education shifted decidedly from the church to the state. In the *Plan*, the state will enter into the very definition of the university: "What is a university? A university is a school whose door is open *indiscriminately* to all the children of a nation, and where teachers salaried by the State initiate them in the elementary knowledge of all the sciences" (749). The effect of this definition is to situate the university within the larger operation of the state: the university becomes a function of the state, an instrument by which the state pursues its own ends. As an almost inevitable consequence, the university's purpose or goal will be explicitly linked to the reproduction of the state and of social institutions in general. That this state may be a monarchy and these institutions include the "republic" of letters underscores the considerable power of reconciliation which Diderot grants to the pedagogic project: "It is a matter of giving to the sovereign zealous and faithful subjects; to the empire, useful citizens; to society, educated, honest, and even amiable individuals; to the family, good spouses and good fathers, and

1. All page references in the text are to Denis Diderot, *Plan d'une université ou d'une éducation publique dans toutes les sciences*, in *Oeuvres complètes* (Paris: Le Club Français du Livre, 1969), vol. 11. All translations from the French are my own.

2. Cf., Jean-Marie Dollé, *Politique et pédagogie: Diderot et les problèmes de l'éducation* (Paris: Librarie Philosophique J. Vrin, 1973); Georges Snyders, *La Pédagogie en France au XVIIième et XVIIIième siècles* (Paris: Presses Universitaires de France, 1965); Gabriel Compayré, *Histoire de l'éducation en France depuis le seizième siècle* (Paris: Librarie Hachette, 1904); and Emile Durkheim, *L'Evolution pédagogique en France* (Paris: Presses Universitaires de France, 1969).

to religion, edifying, enlightened, and peaceable ministers" (747). In addition, then, to making virtuous and enlightened men, the university must also produce faithful subjects and useful citizens. This double task is assigned to the Faculty of Arts (corresponding roughly to our secondary school), while the formation of specific professional capacities is left to the higher Faculties of Law, Medecine and Theology and to extrauniversity instruction. Although the Faculty of Arts is defined precisely by its exclusive concern with general knowledge and its refusal to provide particular vocational training, this impartiality is justified less in terms of a disinterested ideal of knowledge than by the need to insure a rational distribution of professional skills within society as a whole.

In the guise of a universal plan intended for Russia, then, the *Plan* is advocating a thoroughgoing reorganization and reinstitutionalization of the existing French university. "Barbarous," "gothic," with "monstrous flaws," this university persists in an otherwise enlightened nation "despite the constant objections of all estates" (757). The failure of the university is easily identified: it lies in the overwhelming dominance of the *belles-lettres,* the massive presence within the curriculum of ancient Greek and Latin texts. At the time of Diderot's writing public instruction was still conducted for the most part in Latin, and classes devoted almost exclusively to the history and literature of the ancient world. This monopoly of the ancients can be traced in a direct line to the foundation of the university, which Diderot attributes to Charlemagne.[3] The originary scene of the university is described in these lines: "All Europe was barbarous. There were neither sciences nor arts. All those which had once existed were concealed in ancient works that were no longer understood. In these circumstances, what is to be done? The science of words, or the study of languages, became the key to these old sanctuaries closed for so many centuries" (758). This preoccupation with "the science of words" will continue uninterrupted through the Renaissance and into the seventeenth and eighteenth centuries.[4] But if

3. On the scholarship surrounding the origin of the French university, cf., Durkheim, op. cit., 90 ff.

4. The education statutes of 1600, for example, contain an absolute interdiction of the vulgar tongue; a parliamentary edict of 1624 prohibits the teaching of Descartes and forbids "à toute personne, à peine de vie, de tenir ni enseigner aucune maxime contre les anciens auteurs et approuvés" (Snyders, op. cit., 32); the teaching of Descartes is not authorized until 1721.

study of the ancients was strictly unavoidable during the early period of the university, Diderot argues, their subsequent translation into French, the development of a national culture, the progress of science, which "began to speak in the vulgar tongue," and the declining usefulness of Greek and Latin, all require that the traditional privilege of these languages be reexamined.

What are the consequences of this displacement of the ancient languages for the organization of the university? What is the place of the ancient languages, if any, in the modern curriculum? According to Diderot, none of the many reform proposals of the period has found a satisfactory answer to these questions. The solution, as outlined in the *Plan*, entails a major restructuring of the traditional curriculum in which new subjects are introduced (eg., natural sciences, modern languages), old ones reconceived (eg., logic, grammar), and belles-lettres limited to a single class—the last and least useful one in the curriculum.[5] Thus the problem of belles-lettres is solved by an act of reordering: the dominant subject in the old university is moved to the least dominant position in the *Plan*. But in what sense is this a solution? If belles-lettres are the embodiment of the gothic and the barbarous, why are they not simply excluded altogether? What is the status of belles-lettres in the new curriculum? To begin to answer these questions we must look at the university which Diderot puts in their place.

We have said that Diderot's central task in the *Plan* is to reconcile the teaching of science and the needs of the state. Thus the university is founded upon two principles—an epistemological principle according to which the sequential order of the curriculum must correspond to the "liaison essentielle des sciences" [the essential linking of the sciences] and a political principle requiring that the university teach what is most "useful" to the greatest number of people. That these two principles are in fact compatible, that each would generate precisely the same curriculum, can hardly be assumed, yet no attempt is made to account for their intersection beyond the statement that they are both equally "inaltérable" [unchangeable]. Or, more precisely, the question of utility is raised to the level of necessity already associated with the "liaison essentielle," "lien," or "en-

5. Although Diderot stresses the radical nature of this solution ("Je m'élève contre un ordre d'enseignement consacré par l'usage de tous les siècles et de toutes les nations" [788]), its essential features were proposed by Locke almost a century earlier, cf., *Some Thoughts Concerning Education* (1693).

chaînement naturel" of the sciences: "The order of exercises and of instruction is as inalterable as the "lien" [link] between the sciences. Proceed from the easy thing to the difficult thing; go, from the first step to the last, from what is most "utile" [useful] to what is less so; from what is necessary to all to what is necessary only to a few; spare time and fatigue; or accommodate teaching to age, and lessons to the average aptitude of students" (756). These diverse rules for the ordering of the curriculum have two distinct spheres of operation. Some attempt to define a temporal pedagogic strategy, an efficient, timesaving method for conveying a given body of knowledge. Others refer to the practical utility or "public interest" of knowledge, its usefulness to the greatest number of people insofar as they belong not to particular corporations but to the general body of the nation. This second consideration—the principle of utility—is later designated the cornerstone, the "pierre angulaire" of the university edifice.[6] Since not all students will complete the full course of studies, the principle of utility requires that the sciences be classified and taught according to an order of decreasing usefulness. This descending scale is then framed by a division into two blocks: "essential" knowledge, which is useful to everyone, and "accessory" knowledge, useful only in the practice of a particular profession. The concept of essential knowledge defines the limits and purpose of the Faculty of Arts. Although it accumulates meaning that has to do more often with utility (eg., the university must teach general knowledge "the ignorance of which . . . would be harmful in all stations of life, and more or less shameful in a few" [763] and less often with epistemology (it teaches the "fundamental principles" [763] of the sciences, the order of the curriculum is clearly meant to respect both of these conditions simultaneously. Hence the conclusion of the first, "theoretical" part of the *Plan*, which claims that except in a single instance (the placement of astronomy) the curriculum represents a perfect synthesis of the principle of utility and the "enchaînement naturel" of the sciences. The second part of the *Plan*—the "execution"—touches on questions of discipline, administration, examinations, architecture and the like, but its primary concern is with the curriculum: what classes

6. Diderot's stated emphasis on utility clearly distinguishes his university from the German plans of the following decades. Cf., Jacques Derrida, "Mochlos ou le conflit des facultés," *Philosophie* 2 (1984); and Luc Ferry, Jean-Pierre Pesron and Alain Renaut, *Philosophies de l'université: l'Idéalisme allemand et la question de l'université* (Paris: Payot, 1979).

should be taught, how they should be ordered, the classical texts they might require.

In broad outline, the order of the curriculum proceeds from mathematics and the natural sciences to the sciences of thought and language to the belles-lettres. The first class is mathematics: "I begin with arithmetic, algebra, and geometry; because in all stations of life, from the highest to the least of the mechanical arts, these sciences are needed. Everything can be counted, everything can be measured. The exercise of our reason often comes down to a rule of three. There are no objects more general than number and space" (771). The movement of this opening paragraph—from the usefulness of mathematics in all occupations to the generality of number and space—already suggests what the rest of the section will confirm: that the priority of mathematics has less to do with its utility than with its privileged relation to truth, or, in other words, that the utility of mathematics flows from its authority within an epistemological discourse of truth and error. Mathematics offers "models of reasoning of the first evidence and of the most rigorous truth" (773); geometry is the "best" and the "simplest" of logics. Indeed geometry is said to provide models against which to compare and measure *all* other sciences, not excluding the sciences of language. If languages are too "imperfect," the meanings of words too "indeterminate" to lend themselves easily to geometric method, the "perfection" of geometric definition remains the distant goal of any science of language: "If our dictionaries were well made; or what amounts to the same thing, if ordinary words were as well defined as the words "angles" and "squares," there would remain few errors and disputes among men. It is toward this point of perfection that all work on language must tend" (774). These quotations taken together describe a distinct taxonomy of knowledge: a hierarchization of the sciences based on concepts of "truth" and "perfection" which descends from mathematics to logic to language.[7] Mathematical language is the locus of truth, natural language the source of errors and disputes. This model is in fact faithfully reproduced in the order of the curriculum (preempting the cornerstone principle of utility and giving content to the idea of the "liaison essentielle des sciences")

7. For a discussion of the interrelation of these sciences in terms of the classical theory of the *trivium* and *quadrivium*, cf., Paul de Man, "The Resistance to Theory" in *The Resistance to Theory* (Minneapolis: University of Minnesota Press, 1986).

and goes a long way toward explaining why the imperfect and dangerous science of the belles-lettres is placed last. Mathematics not only precedes the sciences of language, it would eventually orient and control them, a possibility that evokes the extravagant image of a universal, nonmathematical language by which all error and social conflict are eliminated. We are reminded here of another text written some twenty years before the *Plan*, the Encyclopedia article "Encyclopédie," in which it is precisely Greek and Latin that are suggested as possible candidates for such a language. There, Diderot has recourse to the ancient languages when his proposal for an encyclopedic dictionary in which language would be "fixed and transmitted to posterity in its full perfection"[8] by means of an exhaustive definition of vocabulary runs up against its inevitable limit. In an effort to break the "vicious circle" of definition—that words are defined by other words which themselves have to be defined—Diderot turns to the "dead" languages of Greek and Latin for "an exact, invariable and common measure."[9] By the time we arrive at the *Plan*, however, the ancient languages are described on the contrary as the most difficult, most inaccessible and least useful of languages.

Mathematics is followed by four classes on the natural sciences, all of which share an emphasis on utility, experimentation, observation, the education of the senses. The primacy given to the natural over the human sciences, to things over words, marks a profound break in the history of French education. Similarly, Diderot's approach to the sciences of man produces an inversion of the traditional pattern. The old university taught rhetoric before logic, "the art of speech, before the art of thought, and that of speaking well, before having ideas" (752). For Diderot, on the other hand, logic is the first of the human sciences and rhetoric the last. The sixth class, directly following the natural sciences, is composed of "logic, criticism, and general reasoned grammar" in that order.

Logic teaches the art of thought, the proper use of reason and method in the search for truth. As the "instrument" of all learning,

8. Article "Encyclopédie," in *Oeuvres complètes*, vol. 2, 381.
9. How can we fix the meaning of radicals once and for all? "[I]l n'y a, ce me semble, qu'un seul moyen . . . Ce moyen est de rapporter la langue vivante à une langue morte: il n'y a qu'une langue morte qui puisse être une mesure exacte, invariable et commune pour tous les hommes qui sont et qui seront, entre les langues qu'ils parlent et qu'ils parleront. Comme cet idiome n'existe que dans les auteurs, il ne change plus; et l'effet de ce caractère, c'est que l'application en est toujours la même, et toujours également connue." (Article "Encyclopédie," op. cit., 388).

the study of logic ought to precede that of all other sciences: "It is assuredly with logic that one ought to begin, that is with the perfecting of the instrument that one must use, if this abstract subject were accessible to children. But having arrived at this point, they will have been prepared for it by a sufficient exercise of their reason" (783). The introduction of logic provokes a conflict between two ordering principles which were meant to act in harmony. From the perspective of pedagogic efficacy, logic is too "abstract" to be taught first, whereas from a purely cognitive standpoint, presumably for the same reason, it is the necessary preparation for any study whatsoever. Diderot gives precedence to pedagogy while at the same time trying to diminish the conflict: logic is placed after the sciences and the transition from one to the other represented as a movement from the "exercise" of reason to the study of its formal principles. Logic will bring to light and formalize the operations of reason that were always implicit in the study of the sciences. By turning reason upon itself, the principles of reason common to the plurality of scientific practices will be set out within the confines of a single discipline.

Despite his frequent references to the "liaison essentielle des sciences," Diderot has little to say in the *Plan* about the links or transitions between classes. That the transition from science to logic, experience to reason, exercise to principles may be more problematic than it at first appears is suggested only by a minor effect of juxtaposition. After logic Diderot places "criticism"—at the time a novel, untaught subject. Criticism is defined as "the art of evaluating the different, quite often contradictory, authorities, on which our knowledges rest" (783). These different and often contradictory authorities form a long and heterogeneous catalogue: "There is the authority of the senses" it begins, "and that of reason. The authority of experience and that of observation" (783). Criticism, in other words, takes as an object of investigation the very disjunction between experience and reason that structures the relation of the natural sciences and logic. The list of authorities continues with: the danger of analogy; witnesses (historians, writers of all kinds, philosophers, orators, poets, nations, tradition); natural and supernatural facts; possibility, existence, evidence, verisimilitude, certitude, persuasion, conviction, doubt; opinions and systems. The function of criticism is thus to cope with the multiplicity of our sources of knowledge, to construct a common conceptual space in which differences can be registered and disputes adjudicated. But the summary that concludes the list of authorities locates this meta-philosophical discourse strictly in the future: Someone needs to write "the treatise of philosophical places [*loci philosophici*] as the theologian Melchior Canus has written the treatise of theological places. A work of the greatest importance of which the first page is not yet written" (784).

We have seen that Diderot's general strategy for ordering the curriculum is to privilege mathematical over discursive knowledge. But this strategy is of little use when it comes to ordering the linguistic sciences among themselves: general reasoned grammar, the grammar of the national language (in this case Russian and Slavic), and belles-lettres ("Greek and Latin, eloquence and poetry"). How is this order justified? General reasoned grammar is defined as the study of the "general rules," the "single machine" governing all particular languages. Which should be studied first: a foreign, natural language, whether ancient or modern, or the rules common to all languages? Diderot hesitates before choosing general grammar, and this hesitation seems visible in what appears to us as a surprising explanation: general grammar is apparently *less* general than a foreign language, less like general rules and more like the practice of a natural language. "But when I consider that it is not a matter of an entirely new object; that we all possess a mother tongue; that the long exercise of speech disposes us from our childhood to the study of its principles; or to their application to the idiom which is familiar to us and whose elements we learned from our parents, when they surrounded our cradle or carried us in their arms; when I see the "liaison étroite" [close link] of this science to logic, I leave it where I placed it" (786). Unlike any other science, general grammar does not confront us as an entirely new object; it is contained implicitly in the elementary knowledge which we all "possess," which we learned in the cradle: our mother tongue. The "method" by which we learn to speak is both the least methodical of pedagogies—it works "by use, by daily exercise"—and the most successful. Diderot even imagines transporting it inside the university, namely, to the teaching of Greek and Latin, though he immediately deems it "impracticable" in the environment of the public school.

It appears, then, that the position of general grammar in the curriculum follows from its unique proximity to natural language, that the study of language calls for an inductive method which moves from "particular facts" to "first principles." But this would not explain why the "reasoned" study of the mother tongue, the grammar of the national language, is placed *after* general grammar. According to the passage quoted above, general grammar is not only closely related to natural language, it also has a "close link" with logic—perhaps the least natural, most abstract of languages. Just as criticism was intended in part to control the transition from the natural sciences to logic, so general grammar forms a bridge between logic and natural language: "General reasoned grammar is only a very subtle application of logic or the art of thought, to grammar or the art of speech" (784). Thus the ordering of the sciences of language is justified not by reference to their utility but to the "liaisons" [the links] between them. General grammar may consist "only" in a subtle application of logic to speech, yet it shares the same problem that we found in the case of criticism. The review of classical texts for general grammar notes simply: "It is a work to be written" (785). The *Grammar* of Port-Royal, for example, is only "a superficial attempt" (785); Dumarsais's *Tropes* is limited to a single language. In the chain of knowledge that moves from mathematics and the natural sciences to logic to language, the two connecting links—criticism and general grammar— are yet to be written.

But the breakdown of the curricular chain is not limited to the blank spaces indicated by the terms "criticism" and "general grammar." In a short section on "classical books"—books for the classroom—Diderot remarks that a classical text is simply a summary, an abbreviated presentation ("abrégé") of the great treatises of a field; nevertheless, "Almost all classical books are still to be written. . . . They are needed for all ages and for all the sciences" (856). What explains this lack? Only a few people are capable of writing such books, of "ordering the truths, defining the terms, distinguishing what is elementary and essential from what is not" (856). And those who can, it seems, have chosen to advance the progress of science rather than to document its history. To write a classical text is to delimit the essential knowledge of a science. It is a labor of abbreviation and systematization by which a diverse group of treatises is inscribed within the homogeneous space of a single book; thus it figures the very constitution of the science as an autonomous, self-consistent discipline. The generalized lack of classical texts is complicated by the fact that the qualities needed in their authors cannot be taught. ("But can one teach genius? It is enough that a public education does not smother it" [751]. "The object of a public school is not to make a profound man, in any genre whatsoever . . . " [763]). Profundity and genius are not the product of public education, though a firm grasp of essential knowledge is said to be the best preparation for them. But the difference between essential and accessory knowledge, the difference on which the university is founded, is not within its power to teach. To the extent that there *are* classical texts it can presumably teach examples of this difference, pieces of essential knowledge, but the principle of the difference is located outside of it.

At the end of the curriculum Diderot appends a class in *belles-lettres*, thereby reinscribing within his university the long pedagogic tradition that it is intended to supplant. Why, indeed, given the basic antagonism between the two universities, is ancient literature included at all? The last class, we will see, is a response to the classes that precede it, to the inability of the curriculum to define its boundaries or to delimit the field of essential knowledge. The anachronistic presence of belles-lettres is not simply a form of nostalgia,[10] then, but a reflection of fundamental tensions within the university as a whole. Belles-lettres, in other words, must be both excluded and included: excluded, in order to construct the university, and included, not as one class among others, but as a possible solution to the failure of this effort at self-construction.

Diderot's case for exclusion is roughly consistent with the university's framing principles, the principle of utility and the "liaison essentielle des sciences." First, literature is characterized repeatedly as a force of moral and social corruption, a danger that calls for vigilant censorship and a constant level of moralizing commentary on the part of the teacher.[11] A further argument is made for the extreme difficulty of the ancient texts in both their grammar and content; contrary to what is commonly believed, the study of these texts far exceeds the abilities not only of children but of most adults. Finally,

10. Cf., Peter Gay, *The Enlightenment: An Interpretation* (New York: Knopf, 1969), vol. 2, 497–511.

11. This is one of several respects in which Diderot seems merely to mimic the practices of the existing ecclesiastical *collèges*. In order to counteract the continual threat arising from its reliance on pagan literature the church came to develop ingenious strategies of interpretive censorship. The burden fell in particular on oral commentary: it became the responsibility of the teacher to "rendre Chrétien [les livres païens] par la manière dont il les explique." (Nicole, *Traité de l'éducation d'un prince*, lettre 17 (1670), cited in Snyders, op. cit., 62).

ancient literature is said to be the least useful of subjects—essential, that is, only to the "least necessary" class in society: poets, orators and other "littérateurs de profession" ["professional men of letters"]. Familiarity with Greek and Latin is no longer needed for the practice of medicine, law, theology, and the other professions because scientific knowledge can now be acquired directly in French ("The teaching of a science, any science, can be taught in the language of the nation . . . " [791]).

What is the relation of science and its teaching to national, natural language? The question lies at the center of the controversy over ancient literature, and the deep puzzle that it held for Diderot can be seen in his belated retreat from his strong claim that the sciences can be taught in French, that Greek and Latin are no longer essential. This retreat occurs by way of a single sentence in which for the first time the claim is made to depend on the possibility of translation. Ignorance of Greek and Latin has not prevented great jurisconsults, theologians and physicians from acquiring the essential knowledges of their professions because the relevant texts have all been translated: "Haven't their ancient authors been translated and retranslated a hundred times?" (792). From this it follows that Diderot's "translation" of the university will have to include translations of the ancient authors as an important, even indispensable feature. But the sentence suggests something further: through a process of multiplication ("translated and retranslated a hundred times"), translation would cancel itself out, render itself transparent, permitting a fully adequate transmission of the ancient storehouse. The condition of abandoning the ancient texts seems to be nothing less than a perfect mastery of them. After this sentence the claim on which Diderot's entire project can be said to rest—the nonessentiality of the ancient languages—is turned into an open question: "Among sciences, in what should they be placed: essential or accessory?" (792). If we also recall here a number of other passages in which Diderot insists on the nearly insurmountable difficulties of translation,[12] we are brought to the following conclusion: that Diderot's attempt to do away with the ancient texts relies implicitly on a dream of perfect translation, and that the failure of this attempt is at bottom a failure of translation. The question remains: in what category are ancient languages to be

12. Cf., 787 ff. "Je ne connais pas de science plus épineuse . . . " The point is also made in *La Lettre sur les sourds et muets.*

placed? To classify them as essential is to acknowledge the irreducibility of the linguistic, textual dimension of these sciences; to classify them as accessory is to affirm that essential knowledge can be learned entirely in French. Diderot leaves the question unanswered, and indeed it is not in terms of utility that the placement of *belles-lettres* is ultimately justified. Rather, they are deferred until "the time when it is appropriate to learn them," though in what sense such a time can actually be said to exist is left unclear: "But were I to admit the full advantage of these languages, for certain occupations, the question would remain no less undecided, for it is not a matter here of their utility, but rather of the time when it is appropriate to learn them. . . . One would study at five or six what could never be learned well and could never be useful before twenty-five or thirty, perhaps later; for at what age is a doctor able to perceive the truth or falsity of an aphorism of Hippocrates?" [792]. The ancient text is the site of a particular opacity or resistance which is indifferent to age and which prevents it from being appropriated as teachable, useful knowledge. At the same time, however, the place of ancient literature in the university proves to be absolutely necessary.

Although the question of the utility of ancient languages for the majority of professions is left undecided, Diderot insists that in the case of the marginal profession of *littérateur* they are strictly essential. Ancient literature is the repository of the highest models of "goût" [taste], and the achievement of the *littérateur* combines the greatest "originality" with the most successful "imitation" of the ancient models. The figure of imitation, which is simultaneously a figure of translation, inscribes in the modern text a legible trace of the ancient language: "He who has a little tact will soon discern the modern writer who has familiarized himself with the Ancients from the writer who has had no commerce with them" (797). We can appreciate the level of "tact" that is involved here when we note that the important distinction is not between reading the ancients or not reading them, but between reading them in the original or reading them in translation. With a little tact, that is, one can discern whether a modern French writer has imitated an original ancient text or a translation. Unlike the other sciences, then, literature clearly cannot be acquired in translation. And as belles-lettres are essential to the *littérateur*, so the *littérateur* is necessary for the definition of essential knowledge itself. This would mean that belles-lettres are necessary not only for the elaboration of the curriculum as a whole, but also in order to resolve the question of their own status—essential or accessory—in the curriculum.

In the class in belles-lettres previously acquired knowledges are put to use, ideas rendered, ancient models imitated, and genius, if not imparted, at least encouraged and promoted. Genius, indeed, becomes a characteristic, even indispensable attribute of the literary professions as such, "which do not suffer mediocrity, and in which education "ne sert de rien" [is useless] without genius" (762). But to say that the relation of the *littérateur* to the problem of essential knowledge is that of the genius is to describe it by an empty figure, for genius is by definition undecipherable and uncodifiable. Still, we can define it somewhat further through the related notions of generality and history.

Essential knowledge, whether understood as the fundamental principles of the sciences or as knowledge that is useful in all professions, is consistently linked to the idea of generality. The university is ruled by "la généralité des esprits" [the generality of minds], "la portée commune de l'esprit humain" [the common capacity of the human mind] (751); it represents the "public interest" against the private, "la lumière générale" ["the general light"] (758) against that of particular corporations. This general perspective is attained only by the *littérateur*. "Let us take another example, less important; the poet. What object in art or nature is not within his scope?" (761). The profession of *littérateur* is the only profession that comprehends the totality of the sciences, standing outside the other professions as their common ground. In this way the *littérateur* resembles the author of the *Plan d'une université* himself, who claims his most important and unique merit to be that of impartiality.

Another aspect of essential knowledge can be seen in the requirement that of the three parts of every science—history ("erudition, or the exposition of its development"), theory ("the speculative principles with the long chain of consequences that has been deduced from them"), and practice ("the application of the science" [764])—only history is to be taught in the university. Essential knowledge takes the form of a history of its progress—a teleological structure which accounts for the remarkable statement that the writing of a classical text must await the "perfection" of the sciences ("A good classical book presupposes that the art or science is reaching its perfection" [856]). In the first lines of the section on *belles-lettres*, the work of the *littérateur* is identified with the possibility of historical representation as such: "Great actions fall out of memory or degenerate into extravagant fables without a faithful historian who recounts them, a great orator who recommends them, a sacred poet who sings them, or plastic arts which represent them to our eyes. No one is thus more interested in the birth, the progress and the duration of the *beaux-arts* than good sovereigns. When powerful men have not been able to merit the homage of the arts through virtuous behavior, they have corrupted them through generosity" (787). It is by "letters" and "monuments" that the centuries are distinguished and the past constructed. "The past" Diderot writes, "exists only through them" (787). No sooner, however, does he affirm the *beaux-arts'* power of representation than he invokes the possibility of corruption; indeed it is precisely because of this power that they are immediately subject to appropriation for political ends. Whatever bad faith may be involved in the recommendation that Catherine support the *beaux-arts* out of political self-interest is offset by the complementary recognition that the *beaux-arts* are in fact corruptible. If they make history possible, if they protect it from falling into extravagant fables, they are also a primary means for the legitimation of sovereign power. Thus the last class in the curriculum forms a bridge between the university and the state, uniting them in a relation of mutual dependence.

If we recall here Diderot's repeated warnings about the threat that literature poses to the social order, we can begin to measure the radically equivocal position that belles-lettres hold in the *Plan*. The least essential subject is also the most essential; the subject that is marginalized in the effort to link knowledge and utility is also indispensable to that very effort. Neither essential nor accessory, belles-lettres are essential to the ever-renewed attempt to determine the difference between essential and accessory. In Diderot's terms, this is to say that the *littérateur* is needed less for the production of knowledge than for its transmission, for the process that enables knowledge to become useful, just as the authors of an encyclopedia organize and disseminate masses of information which, previously scattered through a multitude of texts, "restent sans produire aucune sensation utile, comme des charbons épars qui ne formeront jamais un brasier" [remain without producing any useful sensation, like dispersed coals that will never form a blaze].[13] How far this strategy can be said to work, how far the plan can be said to have succeeded, remains an open question.

13. Article "Encyclopédie," op. cit., 371.

RICHARD KLEIN

The Future of Nuclear Criticism

If the institution of Nuclear Criticism has a future, which is by no means certain, for the moment only a hypothesis, it would depend on its capacity to give us to think the future differently. The future of Nuclear Criticism, objective genitive, depends on the future of Nuclear Criticism, subjective genitive, its ability to produce a new concept, hence an altered model of anticipation, perhaps a new, nonnarrative future tense. Nuclear Criticism seeks to differentiate itself from abundant past efforts to imagine narrative scenarios, fictional or pseudo-documentary, that aim to represent or pretend to document a war without precedent, perhaps without model. That sort of mimetic imagining and its criticism, in the genres of fiction, of history, of political science, of journalism, has been productively going on for decades without need of a new concept of the future, without benefit of Nuclear Criticism—if there is such a thing and if it has a future. Indeed, the bibliography of those narrative representations is now enormous, in itself a vast archive remembering what until now has never occurred. From the englobing perspective of the archive, what is called Nuclear Criticism, despite its overweening ambition to think a new new, or new anew, is no news. Despite its ambition to institute a new concept of the future, another model of anticipation, Nuclear Criticism can only with difficulty avoid the claims of narrative—above all, the assumption that the future has a future, that there is, potentially, a story in the future of everything that has a future. Nevertheless, it aims to generate a concept, and institute a discourse that does not lend itself readily to narrative configurations—a discourse whose possibility has been created by the

YFS 77, *Reading the Archive: On Texts and Institutions,* ed. E. S. Burt and Janie Vanpée, © 1990 by Yale University.

paradoxes of the nuclear condition, with consequences for the production of culture that have only begun to be drawn.

It must not be assumed that thinking the future differently means
anticipating anew the unthinkable prospect of total nuclear war; it
has already been amply demonstrated that that task, thinking the
unthinkable, is probably unavoidable, since it is not only the explicit
aim of the project associated with eighteenth-century reflection on
the sublime*, but, more permanently perhaps, the ambition of philosophical interpretation of future time since Plato. The nuclear sublime is that all too familiar aesthetic position from which one antic-
ipatorily contemplates the end, utter nuclear devastation, from a
standpoint beyond the end, from a posthumous, apocalyptic perspective of future mourning, which, however appalling, adorably presupposes some ghostly survival, and some retrospective illumination
[apo-calypto: the emergence of what is hidden (in the secret cave of
Calypso) out of the darkness into the light—the end as revelation of
some essential truth: "Tel qu'en lui-même l'éternité le change."
(Mallarmé)]. From a godlike perspective, beyond time and finitude, in
the infinity of a pious fiction, future total nuclear war is contem-
plated; the paradigm of that perspective is Carl Sagan beyond the
Earth, alight in his spaceship, intoning the end while the planet
darkens under the inexorable progression of a cruel nuclear winter.
The time or tense of the nuclear sublime is the already of a not yet,
the mimetic reassurance of a future anterior: as when Plato, in the
Philebus,[1] solves the problem of thought representing the future
(since imitation, mimesthai, in a second time always follows what it
re-presents, doubles the first) by treating the future as having past.
Seen from the perspective of the present, in the precipitation of anticipation, headlong, ahead of its head, the future is envisaged as if it
were the past. Nuclear Criticism denies itself that posthumous, apocalyptic perspective, with its pathos, its revelations, and its implicit
reassurances; it supposes that the only future may be the one we
project forward from the time when total nuclear war, for the time

* See Frances Ferguson, "The Nuclear Sublime," Diacritics 14, no. 2 (Summer
1984): 4–10.

1. Cf., Plato's Philebus (38e–39e), and Derrida's discussion in "The Double Session": "Socrates: We said previously, did we not, that pleasures and pains felt in the soul
alone might precede those that come through the body? That must mean that we have
anticipatory pleasures and anticipatory pains in regard to the future." In Dissemination, Trans., Barbara Johnson. (Chicago: Chicago University Press, 1981), 175. Page
numbers will henceforth be cited in the text.

being, has not taken place. Nuclear Criticism may even risk a jocular tone in order to signal its resistance to assuming the implications of the doleful language of anticipatory mourning, whose account of some total, unthinkable future loss inevitably presupposes that it is less than total, that the narrator, if only in imagination, survives. The lugubrious tone of the nuclear sublime conceals the interest that may be derived from evoking, in the present, the future possibility of total nuclear war; beneath its grim prospect, it masks some pleasure being taken or some profit being made—here and now.

Of course, historians may justifiably suspect the precipitation with which we leap to assume that the nuclear age is without precedent, that there is something new in the nuclear predicate. Is the magnitude or the nature of the horror, after all, incomparable? "What might prove," asks Derrida in "No Apocalypse, Not Now,"

> that a European in the period following the war of 1870 might not have been more terrified by the "technological" image of the bombings and exterminations of the Second World War (even supposing he had been able to form such an image) than we are by the image we can construct for ourselves of a nuclear war? [23]

The question forces us to wonder whether the haste with which we anticipate unprecedented destruction may be only the sign of an ideologically motivated ego's wish to be historically undetermined, narcissistically unique in history, and thus relieved of its burdens. For neither should we forget that there are those who never forget the holocaust and without hesitation assimilate its horror to the prospect of total nuclear war. For them, the first holocaust is a model, we might better say, a referential analogue for what then would be a second nuclear one. But Nuclear Criticism determines the specificity of what it calls total nuclear war in so far as it is, potentially, a burning of practically everything, including memory. The difference is one between destruction on a vast scale that is collectively survived, archivally remembered, and politically mourned, and a total burning—a true *holos-kaustos*—in which no public survival, no collective recollection, no institutional mourning, remains.

Against the risk that the notion may acquire merely metaphorical significance, we will consider to be total any nuclear war which results in the exchange of at least one half of the strategic arsenal of both superpowers. It represents the exchange of not more than 5000 of the more than 12,000 strategic weapons each side possesses—that number only a fraction of the 50,000 weapons in toto, of which the majority are designed for so-called tactical deployment (the distinction at those levels of magnitude may in reality be difficult to maintain). Imagine the effect on our society if one bomb, at very least twenty to forty times the power of the one that fell on Hiroshima, were to strike each one of the 197 cities in the United States with populations above 120,000. But then, instead of 197 bombs, imagine that 5000 fell, twenty-five for each such city—less than one half, I repeat, of the Soviet strategic weapons armed and pointed at this moment in our direction. Let that far from total engagement of the strategic nuclear arsenal, less than one-fifth of the total number of weapons, constitute what we are calling total nuclear war.

Total nuclear war does not refer to anything that is or ever has been, so far; its real referent is in some still hypothetical future. Until the mirror is broken, we are suspended in this hypothetical phantasm, what Derrida with some qualification, has called "a fable—a pure invention: in the sense in which it is said that a myth, an image, a fiction, a utopia, a rhetorical figure, a fantasy, a phantasm, are inventions" (22). "We are suspended in this fabulous condition in which all our plans, and all our strategies, personal and public, are conditioned by a non-real referent, one which until today exists only as a thing without a model, about which we can only talk, and opine, and hope. If the mirror breaks into total nuclear war, if we were to escape the condition of the phantasm or fable, and enter the so-called real, the entry of the real of total nuclear war is expected to coincide, according to the fable, with the exit from all textuality, fabulous or otherwise. On that day, the fable has it, there may be no discourse left, no memory and no work of mourning capable of registering the then real referent; there will have been no more letters to take the news that there were no more letters. The conditions for any cultural record of the mirror having been broken will by virtue of its shattering cease to exist; the escape out of this imaginary relation to the nuclear phenomenon will have coincided with the end of the archive."[2]

Of course to call total nuclear war a kind of fable does not mean it could not occur; we are constantly preparing for it or against it, and it is already producing massive effects in the present, here and now,

2. Richard Klein and William Warner, "Nuclear Coincidence and the Korean Airline Disaster," Diacritics 16, no. 1 (Spring 1986): 2–21, 3. Page numbers will be cited in the text.

insofar as the arms race, its corollary, may indeed have become the dominant mechanism of capitalization in the world, the motive and motor of capital formation itself. Nuclear Criticism is interested not only in the fable of total nuclear war, but in the difference between the fable of total nuclear war in the future and the reality, here and now, of the arms race. It is the relation between that fable and that reality that already constitutes what we might venture to call, at the risk of not being seriously understood, a literary problem for Nuclear Criticism.

But what we call literature may be precisely what is most at stake in the fable of total nuclear war. Being most at stake does not mean that we are more concerned with the survival of literature than with the loss of lives or the destruction of the ecological system. For indeed, it is not impossible to imagine, it is even likely perhaps, that human beings will survive, that the human habitat could regenerate, that even literature, epic poetry for example or lyric song, might revive in some form. But if total nuclear war meant the end of the archive, the destruction without a trace of the institutions of collective memory, then what is most absolutely vulnerable in the nuclear age is the institution of literature, and everything like literature which, at least since the eighteenth century, utterly depends on the archive's existence. Nuclear Criticism is an attempt to reflect on the peculiar vulnerability of literature in light of the prospect of total nuclear war. The repository of the archive, the institutions of public memory, not only insure the literal preservation of this text and that, fragments of which could of course survive total war. The institution of the archive not only makes possible positive remembering; it also permits systematic forgetting—all the possibilities for wandering, for error and discovery, for allusion and influence, for censorship and its undoing, that arise from the intertextual organization of the archive. That organization of course includes as well all the rhetorical and generic conventions, the protocols of commentary and criticism, canons and resistance to the canon, all the laws of copyright, and principles of authorship, all the technologies of publication and dissemination, all the systems of retrieval, cataloguing, bibliography, which have made access to the archive possible, at least since the eighteenth century. It is that institutional organization and that access, which is most utterly vulnerable in the prospect of total nuclear war; that, at least, is the hypothesis of Nuclear Criticism. If it were the case that what is for the moment a fable were to acquire a real referent, what conclusions then could one draw now, in advance, about the nature and the conditions of our contemporary cultural production? What effect does that fabulous possibility exercise here and now on the forms and themes, the substance and the shadows of our cultural products? Nuclear Criticism seeks to discover signs of that fabled future at work in the present and to determine how they may be read, with implications not only for the cultural critic, but perhaps as well for the historian, the political scientist, the nuclear strategist.

What may be most vulnerable is the collective memory of our culture, not merely its existence but the persistence of the memory of its loss. Its loss may be lost, with no trace of survival—a possibility that literary fiction has always claimed the prerogative of proposing: the fiction or fable of the loss of the trace of the loss of the trace. If the memory of the destruction of collective memory is lost there will be no one to mourn, no mourning that will internalize and preserve the memory of what will have vanished—destruction on a scale incomparable with the burning of the library at Alexandria. Our culture, such is the hypothesis, is facing the possibility of a futureless future, a time in which it may no longer be possible collectively to mourn the past, a future in which there will not have been a posthumous perspective. It is this altered relation to mourning in a future without future, this negative future anterior, that differentiates what the nuclear fable allows us to imagine from the Nazi holocaust in Europe, whatever its hideous magnitude, which will still have permitted the consolation, the interiorization, the working through of memory, in order to preserve the future from repetition.

"The practical or pragmatic implications of this nuclear perspective, the standpoint of temporal narrativity which it imposes, have already begun to affect our culture, massively, and to determine our cultural productions in ways we are only beginning to discover. The dilemma is that we are obliged to become the cultural historians of a time without a model, anticipating in the tense of the future anterior a decisive historical possibility which, if it occurs, our culture might never view historically. We are left to become the historians of the future, to invent its history before it happens, because if it happens, it may never have a history—if the fable means the end of discipline, organized memory. If it will have been the case that there was no future, then the only existence the future may have for us is behind us, in the present imagined from the anticipatory standpoint of its having already occurred" (Klein, 3).

The nuclear age under the shadow of the nuclear fable implies a different relation to the future of mourning; it obliges us to think the possibility of another concept of the future, which the nuclear condition has fabulously erected alongside and in the interstices of the Platonic one with which we are accustomed, in our culture, to think. If it could grasp the structure and the implications of this new future, Nuclear Criticism might perhaps begin to operate, not only rhetorically with a new style of argument, but grammatically in a new future tense, perhaps under a new logical model of a hypothetical future, one whose concept may be readable in certain paradoxical logical formulations concerning the way we can anticipate future certainty from within the horizon of the nuclear condition. If the institution of Nuclear Criticism has a future, which is by no means certain, for the moment only a hypothesis, it would depend on its capacity to determine the existence of an alternate concept of the future whose logical consequences for the possibility of anticipated certainty might, in certain crucial circumstances, alter the calculations of our strategies, and effect the very conditions of strategic thinking itself. Its effects might erupt in discrete and punctual forms at certain moments of strategic consideration, not only with fearful implications for our military and diplomatic calculations but with intimate consequences for the conditions of our experience. It would be the future task of Nuclear Criticism, if it has a future, to uncover the work and display the effects of this revised concept or altered tense, in places where, unobserved, that concept is already decisively affecting our cultural productions.

As a contribution to formulating the concept and extending the implications of the nuclear future, I would like to turn your attention to a well-known paradox which broke into print for the first time in 1948 in *Mind*, the British philosophical journal, in the course of an article by the famous Scottish logician, Donald John O'Connor.[3] Known in its first incarnation as the Class-A Blackout paradox, it has had a remarkable history. For, despite having been considered by O'Connor himself to be "a frivolous example" of those his article

3. Donald J. O'Connor, "Pragmatic Paradoxes," *Mind* 57 (July 1948): 358–59.

entitled "Pragmatic Paradoxes," it prompted more than thirty responses over the next twenty years. Quine's decisive intervention in the debate is republished from *Mind* as the first article in a book entitled *The Ways of Paradox*.[4] His brief piece, only two pages long, is called "On a So-called Antinomy," because it seeks to demonstrate the fallacy in the Class-A Blackout paradox that disqualifies it as an authentic antinomy—one which might bring on a genuine crisis in thought by producing a self-contradiction arrived at by accepted ways of reasoning. As Quine writes: "[An antinomy] establishes that some tacit and trusted pattern of reasoning must be made explicit and henceforward be avoided or revised" (Quine, 5). Authentic antinomies have been the basis for important technical progress in the history of logic, and have produced earthquakes in the discipline, as when Bertrand Russell sent a letter to Frege containing his discoveries on the self-membership of classes whose self-referential logic derived from his meditation on the presocratic paradox of Epimenides the Cretan, commonly known as the *pseudomenon*, or liar paradox. It was the ground-shaking discovery contained in that letter that caused Gottlob Frege, in shock, to write, in 1902, an appendix to his just-finished *Grundegesetze des Arithmetik*, which began: "Arithmetic totters. . . . A scientist can hardly encounter anything more undesirable than to have the foundation collapse just as the work is finished. I was put in that position by a letter from Bertrand Russell."[5]

Quine's article seeks to demonstrate that the Class-A Blackout is merely a puzzle, a so-called antinomy, whose appearance of paradox, depending on a fallacious assumption at a decisive moment in its argument, may hence be dismissed as an illusory threat to the integrity of logical procedures, with no power to deconstruct the unshaken foundations of logic. But I particularly wish to draw your attention to the title of another paper, by Richard Montague, "A Paradox Regained."[6] Montague counters what he considers to be Quine's evasion of the paradox by proposing a logical formulation that reinstates the antinomy. The Miltonic allusion in Montague's title suggests that for

4. W. V. Quine, "On a Supposed Antinomy," *The Ways of Paradox, and Other Essays* (Cambridge, Massachusetts: Harvard University Press, 1979), 19–21. Page numbers will be cited in the text.

5. Quoted by Quine, 11.

6. Richard Montague and David Kaplan, "A Paradox Regained," *Notre Dame Journal of Formal Logic* 1 (1960): 79–90. Page numbers will be cited in the text.

a logician, paradise is an authentic antinomy, and to regain one that had been considered lost is the most blessed culmination of a logician's thorny path.

The following abbreviated history of the Class-A Blackout paradox aims to demonstrate the way its capacity to be a true antinomy has been repeatedly lost and regained. There are those in the tradition whose whole aim is critical, and consists in discrediting the paradox, revealing the fallacies in the presentation of its premises and arguments that disqualify it, and reducing it to a "frivolous example." Others like Michael Scriven[7] and Richard Montague have worked, as the latter writes, "to discover an exact formulation of the puzzle which is genuinely paradoxical" (79). There are those who seek to interpret the paradox with the view of mitigating the disruptive negativity it seems to propose; others have sought to exacerbate its negativity by discovering an authentically paradoxical formulation. For the latter, the paradox is not a menace to be overcome but an invitation to be taken up, one that solicits them to think anew about possibilities of anticipated certainty.

The alternating history of paradox lost, paradox regained signals the difficulty, in certain instances, of deciding whether we are speaking rhetorically or analytically, poetically or logically, about future possibilities of knowing the future. This narrative aims not only to repeat the logical arguments which have been advanced, but to analyze the rhetorical terms and the narrative frame, what Quine calls "the embodiments of its plot" (20), into which the logical argument has been cast—in order to justify the perhaps abusive extension of its implications for the possibility of Nuclear Criticism. But this history of the paradox wishes also to point to the punctual nature of its appearance, as if its emergence in the philosophical literature after the war signaled some deeper crisis in logical thought of which the debate surrounding this paradox may be a historically determined index—or perhaps only a rhetorical phantasm, whose philosophical seduction an analyst might wish to explore, but whose logical terms remain entirely within the capacious confines of millennial Western conceptions. If the paradox proves to be only a puzzle, the fiction of a true antinomy, it may nevertheless betray, beneath its apparent frivolity, a heightened anxiety of anticipation prompted by the nuclear condition; if no puzzle, but an authentic paradox, its punctual erup-

---

7. Michael Scriven, "Paradoxical Announcements," *Mind* 60 (July 1951): 403–07.

tion after the war may signal a crisis in the logic of the future inaugurated by the prospect of total nuclear war.

In *The Unexpected Hanging and Other Mathematical Diversions*, Martin Gardner reports that Lennart Ekbom, who taught mathematics at Ostermalms College, in Stockholm, may have pinned down the apocryphal origin of the paradox that first appeared in print in O'Connor's published version. Gardner writes:

> In 1943 or 1944, the Swedish Broadcasting company announced that a civil-defense exercise would be held the following week, and to test the efficiency of civil-defense units, no one would be able to predict, even on the morning of the day of the exercise, when it would take place. Ekbom realized that this involved a logical paradox, which he discussed with some students of mathematics and philosophy at Stockholm University. In 1947 one of those students visited Princeton, where he heard Kurt Gödel, the famous mathematician, mention a variation of the paradox. [21][8]

It does seem plausible to imagine that the origin would lie with Swedish philosophers, suspended in precarious neutrality, anxiously anticipating a blackout, while all around Europe was in flames; in the pleasant groves of their academy they had ample incentive to demonstrate with anticipated certainty that the worst is never sure—a conclusion at which the sage of Princeton had presumably, in other terms, arrived. It is not, however, until 1948 that O'Connor gives the world this inaugural formulation of the problem:

> Consider the following case: The military commander of a certain camp announces on a Saturday evening that during the following week there will be a "Class A blackout." The date and the time of the exercise are not prescribed because a "Class A blackout" is defined in the announcement as an exercise which the participants cannot know is going to take place prior to 6:00 p.m. on the evening in which it occurs. It is easy to see that it follows from the announcement of this definition that the exercise cannot take place at all. It cannot take place on Saturday because if it has not occurred on one of the first six days of the week it must occur on the last. And the fact that the participants can know this violates the condition which defines it. Similarly, because it cannot take place on Saturday, it cannot take

8. Martin Gardner, "The Paradox of the Unexpected Hanging," *The Unexpected Hanging, and Other Mathematical Diversions* (New York: Simon and Schuster, 1969), 11–23, 21.

place on Friday either, because when Saturday is eliminated Friday is the last available day and is, therefore, invalidated for the same reason as Saturday. And by similar arguments, Thursday, Wednesday, etc., back to Sunday are eliminated in turn, so that the exercise cannot take place at all. [358]

Before considering the history of the interpretation of this puzzle, I wish to make two parenthetical remarks. The expression, "anticipated certainty," with which this history characterizes the object of the dilemma, does not belong in the first place to the Anglo--American tradition, but comes from the treatment of its logic in another puzzle, the "Three prisoner problem," a version of which Jacques Lacan discusses in a brief, but crucial article entitled "Le Temps logique et l'assertion de certitude anticipée."[9] Lacan's treatment of that puzzle, or sophism, as he called it, appeared only a few years before O'Connor's Class-A blackout paradox, at the end of the Second World War. It would require another essay to demonstrate the remarkable similarities between these two puzzles, whose almost simultaneous appearance in two independent traditions, at the dawn of the Nuclear Era, could be taken to constitute the emergence of something like a new episteme—an index of a crisis in our conception of the future whose implications we are only beginning to gauge.

The second parenthesis concerns the anecdote. The puzzle over the years has been variously known as the Hangman, the Unexpected Egg, the Surprise Quiz, the Senior Sneak Week, the Prediction Paradox, and the Unexpected Examination. In principle, of course, the anecdotal form has no bearing on the logical dilemma that the puzzle advances. Still, it cannot be uninteresting to a literary mind, to one that wishes to discover here a decisive adumbration of a new nuclear temporality, that in the earliest and most common forms of the puzzle, the theme of a fateful blackout at the end persists, even in its domesticated version of a surprise examination—which for students, and the academic philosophers who invented that anecdotal variant, is the functional equivalent in terms of absolute anxiety to programmed certain death. What one hears in the anecdote, mostly repressed in the logical discussions, is the anxiety of anticipation, what the paradox engenders and risks exacerbating by converting it into a

9. Jacques Lacan, "Le Temps logique et l'assertion de certitude anticipée," *Ecrits* (Paris: Seuil, 1966), 197–213. This article was not included in the two volume Livres de Poche, nor to my knowledge was it ever translated.

permanent, unavoidable antinomy, the anxiety of anxiety. It risks, for example, deconstructing the distinction, which Freud requires as a condition for therapy (in *The Problem of Anxiety*) between normal anxiety that inoculates us against real potential threats and neurotic anxiety that endlessly reproduces itself.

Before we begin to examine the earliest treatments of the paradox, which dismissed it, let us dispense with one of the most general, metaphysical objections to it, advanced by Paul Weiss in a subsequent discussion, in a famous article entitled, "The Prediction Paradox."[10] Put simply it is this. The Class-A Blackout is no paradox because it illegitimately presumes a predictive, logical certainty (as distinct from probabilistic or empirical certainty) that one of a collection of future possibilities will actually occur. Operating with distinctions he borrows from Aristotle's *De Interpretatione*,[11] Weiss discovers an ontological gap between knowing a range or tissue of possibilities and knowing in advance that one or the other of those possibilities will actually fall out. In metaphysical terms, one must distinguish between "the realm of possibility" and "the realm of time, history, becoming" (267). Weiss disputes the premise of the paradox that on the first day of the week, faced with a range of possible days, one may be permitted to leap ahead in thought to the penultimate sixth day, Friday, and know for certain that on that day one will know for certain when the blackout must occur. Leaping ahead in imagination, says Weiss, presupposes that we have left the realm of possibility for the realm of time, history, becoming. The power of imagination introduces the factor of history; its anticipatory leap is logically equivalent to time having already eliminated the alternative possibilities which the commander had announced. What allows us in leaping ahead to be certain, on the basis of the decree that the event will occur on Saturday, the last day, is that we have already eliminated in imagination all the other days of the week, all the other possibilities which on the first day remained open. Eliminating them, "there will be no uncertainty regarding the remaining alternatives" (269); after Friday, faced with no other possibilities, only a necessity, Saturday, remains open. But that condition cannot be predicted with logical certainty from the perspective of the beginning of the week when all the pos-

10. Paul Weiss, "The Prediction Paradox," *Mind* 61 (April 1952): 265–69. Page references will be made in the text.

11. Aristotle, "De Interpretatione," *The Complete Works of Aristotle*, ed., Jonathan Barnes (Princeton: Princeton University Press, 1948), 30; 18b ff.

sibilities still obtain. On Friday, we are treating the last day as "distinct from all the rest": at that time there is no longer a collection of alternatives, only a single distributive one. Weiss writes:

> I can say that I will positively do 'something or other' tomorrow and yet not know positively what it will be. I can be positive that 'this or that will be,' i.e., of a range of possible occurrences connected by a collective 'or,' which allows no one of these occurrences to stand apart or be distinct from the others. This does not make it possible for me to know that just this will be done, or that something other than this will be done. There is a great difference between 'It is true that either x or non-x is the case' and 'it is true that x is the case or it is true that non-x is the case,' between $f(x \vee non\text{-}x)$ and $f(x) \vee f(non\text{-}x)$. The former is a necessary truth, the latter is true only when one has isolated the x and the non-x, an act which requires that one leave the realm of possibility for the realm of time, history, becoming. To become is to convert the collective into the distributive 'or.' [267]

For Weiss, the conversion of a range of collective possibilities into a single distributive alternative formally marks the passage, in the metaphysics of Aristotle, between *dunamis* and *energeia*, between what is only a possible world and what becomes effectively real. The Class-A blackout results from the confusion of those two realms; it depends on the power of imagination to substitute surreptitiously for the calculations of logical time, the stark necessity of history. Given a range of possibilities, one can never predict, with logical certainty, that this or that will really occur; not even the commander, when he makes his decree, can know for sure what will actually happen to his decree until the day he proceeds to fulfill it. For Weiss, it is only an illusion to think that the Black-out, whenever it occurs, even on the last day, will not be Class-A, one whose precise occurrence cannot be predicted at the beginning of the week.

W. V. Quine locates an even more fundamental error in Weiss's willingness to credit "a false notion abroad that actual paradox is involved" (19). For indeed Weiss does argue as if the paradox might be logically sustained, if only one overlooked the confusion it promotes between possible being and actual becoming. But it is that initially false notion, says Quine (with a logician's ill-disguised contempt for metaphysics), that "has even brought Professor Weiss to the desperate extremity of entertaining Aristotle's fantasy that 'It is true that p or q' is an insufficient condition for 'It is true that p or it is true that q' "

(19).[12] Quine, himself disputing the paradox, will have no recourse to that fantasy; he argues, as most logicians have, that it is plausible to assume, under some circumstances, that certain propositions about the future can be known analytically, and that it would be absurd and dangerous to assume that the time series, Sunday to Saturday, cannot be treated like a logical sequence of distributive alternatives. Without benefit of metaphysics, Quine's argument, we will see, claims to locate the strictly logical fallacy the paradox conceals.

D. J. O'Connor, L. Jonathan Cohen, and Peter Alexander, the first logicians who treated the paradox, dismissed it, not because of its faulty metaphysical assumptions, nor on strictly logical grounds, but because they considered its argument to be pragmatically, not formally, contradictory. Since a Class-A blackout is defined as one whose occurrence cannot be known in advance of the evening on which it is ordained, the order both decrees its occurrence within a specific time period and decrees that it will be a surprise. Such an announcement, writes O'Connor, "is merely pragmatically self-refuting. The condition of the actions are defined in such a way that their publication entails that the action can never be carried out" (358). The performance of the constative announcement, "There will be a Class-A blackout during the following week," itself precludes the possibility of ever verifying the truth of its performative accomplishment. The public enunciation of the decree disrupts the contextual condition for enacting its fulfillment: if the commander had merely whispered to himself that the Class-A blackout will take place during the week, there would have been no contradiction involved in its occurring and in its being a surprise. According to L. Jonathan Cohen, the decree, although not a statement involving self-referential, ego-centric particulars (of the sort, "I am speaking French now") resembles them insofar as its truth "can be falsified by its own utterance."[13] Peter Alexander went even further in contemptuously dismissing the decree, "There will be a Class-A blackout during the

12. "And the same account holds for contradictories: everything necessarily is or is not, and will be or will not be; but one cannot divide and say that one or the other is necessary. I mean, for example: it is necessary for there to be or not to be a sea-battle tomorrow; but it is not necessary for a sea-battle to take place tomorrow, nor for one not to take place—though it is necessary for one to take place or not to take place," (Aristotle, 30; 19a).

13. Jonathan L. Cohen, "Mr. O'Connor's 'Pragmatic Paradoxes'," *Mind* 59 (January 1950), 85–87.

following week," by comparing it to a conditional statement whose condition is empirically, not even pragmatically unrealizable—of the species, "If I can be without air, I will not breathe all day tomorrow."[14] "Of course," he says, "I might be able to live without air tomorrow but, similarly, men might cease next week to be able to realize that if the blackout had not occurred by Friday it must occur on Saturday and then the condition would be realizable" (539). For Alexander, the decree amounts to saying, "There will be a surprise blackout next week" if a surprise blackout next week were possible, which it is not, if the surprise is announced in advance. For these first analysts, there is no authentic paradox, no true antinomy; the decree itself conceals a contradiction that the argument, leaping forward and devolving backward, serves only to display.

Consider the fate of K, as he is called by Quine and others, in the Hangman anecdote, who sits in his cell on Sunday with his lawyer reflecting on the judge's decree that some day during the following week he will be hung at noon and will not know until a few minutes before noon, what day that will be. Having arrived at the conclusion of O'Connor, Cohen, and Alexander, he begins to smile, because he realizes that the judge's decree is contradictory and therefore he cannot be hung as promised. Anxiously anticipating the end of the week, in an imaginative gesture of anticipated certainty, he logically determines what conditions will prevail, on the basis of the decree, on the penultimate day before the last day of the week, and knows that if he survives until then, he will know when he must be hanged. But knowing that he must be hanged on Saturday contradicts the definition of a Class-A blackout, so on that day, the last possible day, there can be no blackout for K. Having eliminated the last day, by the same argument he retrospectively eliminates the rest of the days of the week. Concluding that there is no day of the week on which the hanging can be performed by surprise, K concludes that the decree cannot be fulfilled, and he has every reason to smile.

K would take less consolation if he knew the argument of Judith Schoenberg who asserts, also in *Mind*, that K's initial hypothesis that he survives until Friday contradicts the judge's decree. It is not, as Weiss has claimed, that leaping ahead in imagination puts history in the place of possibility. The assumption of K's being unhanged on Friday requires the conclusion, based on the judge's specifications,

14. Peter Alexander, "Pragmatic Paradoxes," *Mind* 58 (October 1950): 536–38.

that he cannot be hanged on Saturday and thus cannot be hanged at all under the prescribed conditions, which include a specified time interval. "But this conclusion is in plain contradiction with the [judge's] order, which states that the [hanging] is going to occur during the specified interval. Therefore, the proposition cannot be considered to be an inference from the defined conditions. On the contrary, its conclusion contradicts the [judge's] order, and it follows that the assumption of [K being unhanged] on Friday is incompatible with the order."[15] Skipping over the week, the argument thus *begins* with the premise that the hanging has not occurred under the prescribed conditions. "It is not so much that the argument reverses the temporal order as that its premise skips over the week, while the argument itself is a kind of smokescreen that conceals the implications of the premise" (126).

K, continuing to hope, might have countered the charge (that his premise, the assumption that he is unhanged on Friday contradicts the judge's specifications) by appealing to the judgment of Quine, who defends his argument on this point—and whose objections to it lie elsewhere. Quine finds nothing wrong in K's assuming, for the space of a recursive argument, that he is unhanged on Friday, in order to prove that the decree will not be fulfilled: "This," he says, "would be good *reductio ad absurdum*" (20):

> Suppose that a mathematician at work on the Fermat problem assumes temporarily, for the sake of exploring the consequences, that Fermat's proposition is true. He is not thereby assuming, even as a hypothesis for the sake of argument, that he knows Fermat's proposition to be true. The difference can be sensed by reflecting that the latter would actually be a contrary-to-fact hypothesis, whereas the former may or may not be." [21]

By leaping ahead to Friday, K assumes he is unhanged, for the sake of the argument, whereas in fact he may or may not be. He does not assume, even as a hypothesis for the sake of argument, that he *knows* he will be unhanged, which would contradict the specification of the judge's decree.

But the happiness of K turns to despair when, having decided on Sunday that he cannot be hanged at all because the decree is contra-

---

15. Judith Schoenberg, "A Note on the Logical Fallacy in the Paradox of the Unexpected Examination," *Mind* 75 (January 1966): 125–27. Page numbers will be cited in the text.

dictory, the hangman walks in at 11:55 A.M. on Thursday and the hanging occurs at noon exactly as the Judge has specified, i.e., during the week and by surprise.

Michael Scriven, who was the first to regain the paradox, writes as follows:

> I think this flavour of logic refuted by the world makes the paradox rather fascinating. The logician (namely K) goes pathetically through the motions that have always worked the spell before [i.e., the spell of contradicting the judge's decree], but somehow the monster, Reality, has missed the point and advances still. [403]

K is hanged on Thursday and it is a surprise, just as the judge decreed.

Scriven regains the paradox, if not K, by adopting K's assumption that he survives until Friday, embracing his perspective on the penultimate day, and concluding as follows. Either K will be hanged on Saturday, and it will not be a surprise—which would falsify the judge's decree; or he will not be hanged on that day, which would also falsify the decree. Either way, hanged or unhanged, K knows on Friday that the decree will be self-refuting. Arguing in the same way, K regressively eliminates the other days. Thus, he realizes in advance that, since he cannot draw any proper conclusion concerning the occurrence of the blackout relative to the governing announcement, if the hanging does occur on any day of the week, if the monster reality enters the cell on Thursday just before noon, it will be a surprise; and since the definition of a Class-A blackout is framed in such a way that the precise date of its occurrence cannot be deducible from the announcement made, the decree will have been fulfilled: "Now if the governing announcement . . . is self-refuting and a blackout occurs on any night of the week, the statement, 'There will be a Class-A blackout next week' will be verified. And if it was publicly stated, it would still be correct" (Scriven, 407). Exit K; the logician goes refuted to the gallows. For Michael Scriven, the paradox regained consists in this: since all the days have been negated as possible days, any day is possible; since the decree is self-refuting, cannot be logically fulfilled, it will in all instances, pragmatically, be fulfilled. Its "suicide," he says, "is accompanied by its salvation" (407). Of course, for K, sitting in his cell, the death and life of the paradox is a matter of life and death. What must be his state of mind when at the beginning of the week he concludes, on the basis of the decree, that his hanging is impossible, and because it is impossible, that the hangman may appear on any morning before noon? It must seem to him as if the anticipated certainty with which he concluded his calculations was itself responsible for confounding the possibility that his calculations might prove to be true.[16]

At the very moment in the history of the paradox when it was thought to have been regained, W. V. Quine, the astringent Boston logician, shattered its pretensions to be an authentic antinomy, by proposing an interpretation of the paradox that seemed definitively to reveal its fallacy.[17] He attacks it at the point where K, leaping ahead to Friday, concludes, on the basis of the governing decree, that a Class-A blackout, an unexpected hanging, cannot occur on Saturday, the last possible day of the week. K at that moment seems to be making what all previous commentators had taken to be an unimpeachable valid inference from the defined conditions of the event, "and as such [it] was accepted as the original premise upon which the whole argument rests" (Schoenberg, 127). Even Scriven and Nerlich, whose hyper-paradox requires the elimination of Saturday as a possible day, make an argument that begins by first assuming the validity of the premise: on Friday K knows that he must be hanged on Saturday. According to Quine, the fallacy arises at the moment K leaps to the penultimate moment and concludes either (a) the event will have occurred at or before that time; or (b) the event will (in keeping with the decree) occur on the last day and K will (in violation of the decree) be aware

16. Judith Schoenberg, following G. C. Nerlich's treatment of the paradox in 1961 (which cites Scriven), locates the turning point which "transforms" the paradox and negates its initial negation. She then regains it at another level, when a valid inference from its defined conditions allows her to conclude that what at first was paradoxically impossible proves by that very result to be both impossible and possible. "He points out that if all the days are negated as possible days for the event, then there are no grounds for assuming that it will occur, so that whenever it does occur it comes as a complete surprise. It might also be argued, perhaps, that if all the days are negated, then all the days are the same insofar as their probability of being the day of the (hanging). But a difficulty appears here, for this turning of the argument makes the possibility of the event follow from the previously established negation. The result is that Saturday becomes a possible day, and this would seem to be a fatal result. Because the impossibility of Saturday was accepted at the beginning as being a valid inference from the defined conditions of the event, and as such was accepted as the original premise upon which the whole argument rests. To negate it, is to negate the point of departure of the argument. So that this constitutes a *reductio ad absurdum,* and if the reasoning leading to it were valid, this could only prove that the defined conditions lead to a contradiction. That is, Saturday would both be impossible and possible. Thus the original paradox is transformed, but not resolved" (127).

17. W. V. Quine, "On a So-called Paradox," *Mind* 54 (July 1953): 65–67.

promptly after noon on Friday that the event will occur on Saturday. Rejecting (b) because it violates the decree, K elects (a) and turns to considering earlier days. Actually, says Quine, K should have envisaged four possibilities instead of merely two. On Friday, he should consider the possibility that (c) the event will not occur on Saturday, in violation of the decree, or (d) the event will (in keeping with the decree) occur on Saturday and K will (in keeping with the decree) remain ignorant meanwhile of that eventuality (not knowing whether the decree will be fulfilled or not). "He erred in not recognizing that either (a) or (d) could be true even compatibly with the decree. The same fault recurred in each of his succeeding steps" (20). K cannot assume at the beginning of the week, even as a hypothesis for the sake of argument, that on Friday he will know that he must be hanged on Saturday; he might legitimately suppose that he will be hanged, but not that he will know it, with anticipated certainty, even a day in advance. "It is notable," Quine adds,

> that K acquiesces in the conclusion (wrongly according to the fable of the Thursday hanging) that the decree will not be fulfilled. If this is a conclusion which he is prepared to accept (though wrongly) in the end as a certainty, it is an alternative which he should have been prepared to take into consideration from the beginning as a possibility. [20]

That K accepts the (erroneous) conclusion that he will not be hanged points up the fallacy of his embracing the premise that on Friday he will know that he must be hanged. His conclusion should have led him to realize from the first that one can never know analytically what will happen on the morrow. With the pious realism of a Boston Puritan submitting to the uncertainty attending predestined grace, Quine admonishes the victim: "If K had reasoned correctly, Sunday afternoon, he would have reasoned as follows: 'Rather than charging the judge with self-contradiction, therefore, let me suspend judgment and hope for the best'" (20).

In a final turn, in an article to which we have already alluded, Richard Montague disputes Quine's judgment that the unexpected Class-A hanging is merely a "so-called paradox," "a supposed antinomy." Montague's solution not only achieves the salvation of K but brings us the blessing of a "A Paradox Regained." I may perhaps be allowed merely to indicate the direction of the solution he proposes, for to follow the steps of the demonstration in all its complexity would require having recourse to the symbolic language with which he formally represents both the logic of elementary syntax and intuitive epistemological principles.

"Treatments of the paradox," writes Montague,

> have for the most part proceeded by explaining it away, that is, by offering formulations which can be shown not to be paradoxical. We feel, with Shaw, the interesting problem in this domain is of a quite different character; it is to discover an exact formulation of the puzzle which is genuinely paradoxical. The Hangman might then take a place beside the Liar and the Richard paradox, and, not unthinkably, lead like them to important technical progress. [79]

For Montague as well as for Shaw, Quine is guilty of evading the paradox rather than resolving it: "To see that this is the case, it is only necessary to state explicitly and unambiguously what is meant by 'knowing' that the examination will take place on the morrow."[18] Neither Quine nor Montague dispute Quine's diagnosis of the fallacy in K's argument; he is right to say that K cannot know, simply on the basis of his not having been hanged before Friday, that he will be hanged on Saturday; to the extent such knowledge cannot be logically deduced from the conditions of the decree, it is not analytical knowledge, and as Montague says, "one cannot know a non-analytic sentence about the future."[19] Knowing nothing for certain, K can only hope for the best. It might seem plausible to suppose that K draws the conclusion that he must be hanged from the assumption that the decree will be fulfilled; for on that assumption K could indeed deduce on Friday that he must be hanged. "But it is unreasonable to suppose that K knows the decree will be fulfilled, especially in view of his attempt to prove the contrary" (Montague, 82).

But whereas Quine adopts a vague common sense notion of knowing, Montague proposes to make the meaning of the decree depend explicitly, unambiguously, on K's "knowing" in the sense of being able to predict *on the basis of the decree*" (80). "As Shaw has remarked, the paradoxical flavor of the hangman decree derives from a self-referential element in the decree which was not incorporated in

18. R. Shaw, "The Paradox of the Unexpected Examination," *Mind* 67 (July 1958): 382–84. Page numbers will be cited in the text.

19. Knowing here is used in the sense of being able logically to be deduced from pre-existing conditions assumed to maintain. That is not at all to deny that we can have nonanalytic, empirical certainty concerning possible future events: we know the sun will rise. By inference it does however reject Weiss's claim, following Aristotle, that no statements concerning future possibilities can ever be known analytically in advance.

Quine's formulation" (80). Montague permits K to propose a version of the decree which warrants his arriving at the conclusion that he will not be hanged; he is allowed to assume that the judge's decree may be expressed as follows: K will be hanged at noon on one of the days of the following week, and he will not be able to know, on the basis of the present decree, what day it will be. What distinguishes this formulation of the decree from the one that Quine proposes is that it restores a self-referential element to the decree. Leaping ahead to Friday, K is not now obliged to assume, as Quine has him doing, that the decree must be fulfilled on Saturday (a hypothesis contrary to the fact he wishes to prove), or that having eliminated the other alternatives, on the last day he will know he must be hanged (a non-analytic statement about the future). In the self-referential version of the decree that K advances, he needs only to be able to claim that on Friday he will know, *on the basis of the decree,* that the decree itself logically implies that he will be hanged on Saturday. But since knowing that, and knowing that he will know it, contradicts the ordained surprise, the decree will be seen to be contradictory and K has nothing to fear. His argument is closely analogous to the earlier fallacious argument with which he had illegitimately concluded his salvation, but whereas in Quine's version he is obliged to assume, as a condition of his argument, that the decree will be fulfilled, in the self-reflexive version he concludes only that the decree itself logically implies that on Saturday he must be hanged, if the alternatives are eliminated. Arguing *on the basis of the decree* means that he takes its requirements not as conditions which must be fulfilled but as rules acting like axioms that lead to a logically contradictory conclusion.

Montague, following Shaw, has produced a plausible version of the decree that proves to be self-contradictory; K may be spared, but the logician has not yet regained the paradox, an authentic antinomy— one that would allow K to conclude analytically that he cannot be hanged while at the same time permitting the judge to prove that the conclusion is a nonanalytic statement about the future. To do that requires a final step, a last desperate attempt on the part of the judge to "avoid official embarrassment by reformulating his decree with an added stipulation" (84). The judge stipulates that K will be hanged unexpectedly during the following week, *unless he knows at the beginning of the week that the present decree is false.* Deviously, the judge seems to have confounded K's triumphant demonstration by making its conclusion an integral part of the decree: if K wins, he loses. If he proves that the unexpected hanging entails a contradiction, he knows that he knows that the decree cannot be fulfilled which fulfills the decree. "But in avoiding official embarrassment the judge has plunged himself into contradiction. Now we have a genuinely paradoxical decree" (84–85). Reduced to its simplest form, the stipulation comes down to the judge ordaining that the following condition will be fulfilled: K knows at the beginning of the week that the present decree is false. It is short work to demonstrate that if the judge's decree is false and if K knows it at the beginning of the week, then he has fulfilled the condition of the judge's decree which ordained that K would know that the present decree is false, with the result that the decree is fulfilled. Montague writes: "In view of certain obvious analogies with the well-known paradox of the Liar, we call the paradox connected with [the judge's decree] the Knower" (88). Its assumptions lead to the genuinely paradoxical consequences that the decree cannot be fulfilled and that the decree necessarily will be fulfilled. Thus if the judge's formulation of the decree is adopted, Montague exclaims "Both K and the hangman are correct!" (87). K knows, with analytical anticipated certainty that the trap must fall and cannot fall on the appointed future date. Neither hopeful nor anxious, free of any uncertainty, he faces the future prospect of this decreed blackout with absolute terror as to its necessity and absolute confidence in its impossibility.

I fear I may have strayed so far into the history of the institution of this paradox, within the institution of logic, that I have long ago lost your willingness to hear this story in light of the question of the nuclear fable. And I fear even more that I will not be able to persuade you that the exacerbation of the negativity of the Class-A Blackout paradox points to logical problems concerning the anticipation of the future in a nuclear condition. Let me invite you to reflect, briefly, on the implications of the Class-A blackout for the condition of launch on warning strategies that could be devised by our leaders. Consider the consequences of one of the prominent features of the Class-A blackout paradox, the way it seems to be pragmatically self-refuting-—the way the publication of an order appears to make the order self-refuting. And yet, as we have seen, that appearance is itself the result of a perhaps fallacious interpretation of the decree that overlooks the way the order can seem, at another level of interpretation, to be perfectly capable of being fulfilled. Consider generally how this paradox reveals, in certain circumstances, that timing is decisive not merely for survival, but for the production of logical truth. If K waits too long before leaping ahead in thought to formulate the argument which saves him from the hangman, even though he might have proved that the decree was logically contradictory, having procrastinated, the decree is pragmatically fulfilled and he is hanged during the week and by surprise. Although the time of a logical syllogism is said to be the time of eternal truth, we seem to have here an instance in which the timing of the enunciation of a proposition determines its truth. Speed of utterance has become a crucial issue in the moment of firing, when one has to decide to make a response, before the enemy missiles have detonated, to what has not yet occurred. And this response may then in turn become an inaugurating moment in the production of the anticipated event—a future that has become the determining past of an event, total nuclear war, that if it occurs will never have a future, will never be said to have occurred. At that moment there is something like the reversibility of the times series; at that moment one may simultaneously know, as K knows with anticipated certainty, that a Class-A blackout, which must occur, can never occur, if leaping ahead in anxious anticipation produces the very consequences it forestalls. In those scenarios of total nuclear war, in the systems of what is called deterrence, lie possibilities for hallucinatory coincidence to arise of the sort William Warner and I undertook to analyze in our "Nuclear Coincidence and the Korean Airline Disaster."

All strategy depends on anticipated certainty, the confidence that, under certain conditions, a statement concerning the future may be performatively enacted, that an announcement projected in the future (say, knight takes rook) will be capable, under the right circumstances, of ordaining an anticipated result. It requires being able, on the basis of plausible assumptions, to draw logically impeccable conclusions concerning the possibility of future enactments. The gravest consequences may follow from the failure to understand in what way statements about the future can be analytic or nonanalytic, entailing contradictions, with the result that what is ordained may not be fulfilled as anticipated—or fulfilled for the wrong reason, or, paradoxically, despite reason. These possibilities for error are not of a statistical variety, inevitable margins of error that attend most announcements about the future, which disrupt the context a command may require in order to be carried out; rather they reside in the very logic of anticipated certainty whose paradoxical implications have been aggravated by the nuclear condition, perhaps even engendered by it.

Whether the nuclear condition may be thought to have given rise to a new concept, or to have exacerbated logical implications of the future hitherto unobserved, strategic calculations are menaced by the existence of paradoxes of command lurking in the logic of our strategic calculations. All our strategies, private as well as public, are effected by the existence of a nuclear future, alongside or within the Platonic one, with which our thinking traditionally negotiates. Not a critique or a deconstruction, but a new version of the future, having become literalized in the nuclear fable, it risks giving rise to unexpected effects, strange encounters, phantasms, hallucinations, significant coincidences. Nuclear Criticism aims to uncover the ways in which the nuclear future may already be effecting our strategic decisions by observing its obscure influence, not only in the realm of military, diplomatic strategy, but in the production of cultural artifacts. Where its effects are produced cannot be determined in advance; Nuclear Criticism cannot be supposed even to know where to look for the intrusion of its uncanny power to disrupt our strategic considerations. Evidence of nuclear thinking may emerge, will emerge in the most unexpected and provocative ways; it carries risks which we cannot afford to ignore.

But let me insist, Nuclear Criticism is not an answer, it is a question—a way of asking how to ask the question of whether the production of culture in our society is being shaped and determined, mediated down to the smallest details, by the implications engendered by the nuclear fable for the way we think about the future. Not only for our thoughts, I would add, but also for our dreams.

Nuclear Criticism considers it essential to our understanding of the current cultural moment to explore literature insofar as it can be seen anachronistically to have always enacted in the mode of fiction what the Nuclear era has made terrifyingly literal—the perspective future of memory disappearing without a trace, without leaving a trace. Its capacity to represent that possibility in fiction is linked to what makes it, in the Nuclear age, the most fragile of all institutions, since, being without a real referent, its survival absolutely depends on the survival of the organized archive, on institutions of collective memory. Its acute vulnerability allows us to measure the vulnerability of all other institutions which, like it, depend on the archive for their perdurance. Its existence has become synonymous with the existence of our culture itself at the historical time of the nuclear condition; it is to it that we must turn to find anticipated figures of an altered future, representations of anticipation that the nuclear era allows us retrospectively to uncover.

Consider, for example, more or less than an example, the possibility of the future summoned by these lines from Mallarmé's sonnet: "Ses purs ongles." They invite you to observe, there on sideboards or altars, the manifestation of the absence of anything where a ptyxis [Ptyxis, from the Greek, *folding* is used as a general term for the folding of a single part, of an individual leaf, or page] had been, after the Master, at his death, had taken it with him, this voluminous, bookish shell,[20] in order to dip for the water of forgetfulness in the river Styx. And I ask that you consider, narratologically as it were, the posthumous perspective of a narrator of this poem speaking about the loss of loss in a future, in the tense, in the time of a negative future anterior, from which all mourning is absent.

> Sur les crédences, au salon vide: nul ptyx
> Aboli bibelot d'inanité sonore
> (Car le Maître est allé puiser des pleurs au Styx
> Avec ce seul objet dont le Néant s'honore).

> On the credenzas, in the empty salon: no ptyxis
> Abolished bibelot of sonorous inanity
> (For the Master has gone dipping in the Styx
> With only this object with which Nothingness is honored).

20. Cf., E. S. Burt, "Mallarmé's 'Sonnet en yx': The Ambiguities of Speculation," *Yale French Studies* 54 (1977).

II. Contesting Limits

ALICE YAEGER KAPLAN

Working in the Archives

I.

The archive owes its existence to the archivist's passion. An archive can be anyplace, but for the archive to be, there should be too much of it, too many papers to sift through. And there must also be pieces missing, something left to find. The best finds in the archives are the result of association and accident: chance in the archives favors the prepared mind.

Etymology doesn't appear to be of much help in getting at the special quality of an archival search. Arche—from Greek to Latin, refers to the magisterial residence, then the public office where government records are kept. But the archive runs on a passion that is anything but public and which is rarely talked about. Private story-telling dominates all stages of work in the archives. In the beginning, there is the story of a motivation; then the story of a search; then a story about the results. All these involve a subject and a subject's intentions. Yet conventional academic discourse requires that when you write up the results of your archival work, you tell a story about *what* you found, but not about how you found it. The less the seams of your findings show, the better your discoveries lend themselves to use by others. The passion of the archives must finally be used to eradicate all personal stories in the interests of the dry archival report, fit for a public.

Only in what Gérard Genette has dubbed the "para-text," the dedication and the acknowledgements, the list of libraries you worked at, the thank-yous to *x, y, z* for bibliographic wisdom or for access to a collection, is there any room left for you, the archival

YFS 77, *Reading the Archive: On Texts and Institutions,* ed. E. S. Burt and Janie Vanpée, © 1990 by Yale University.

worker, to speak. Were the story of how you got the story really to be told inside the book, it would interrupt or complicate the narrative so much that no results could be understood or even perceived. Every story of success in the archives is emotionally charged, for only the most extreme emotions can drive people to the drudgery, to the discomfort, of sitting and sifting through dog-eared documents, manuscripts, microfilms. To reveal those emotions would not only gum up the narrative, it would threaten its credibility, by showing on what thin strands of coincidence, accident, or on what unfair forms of friendship, ownership, geographical proximity, the discoveries were based.

In this essay, in order to learn something about the forces that seem to be drawing students of literature back into the archives, I will attempt to move through the archival process and recover some of the stories that get deleted in the final scholarly form.

What got me going in the first place, and what kept me going? I once described it to myself like this:

> I had an image of his desk, of the books that were on it when he was writing X, and the more I worked, the more sources I found for his collage of obscure references, the clearer the image became . . . until I began to think of that desk not as an image, but as a memory, rightfully mine.

The convenient distinction made in literary studies between dusty research and speculative theory does not stand up to my tale. Purely imaginary visions like mine are the motive force behind the most empirical kinds of work.

Here, as I imagine them, are the forms that other suppressed meta-archival narratives might take if they were allowed to come to light. There are accounts of motivations, searches, and stories that archivists tell about their results (without giving the results themselves). Details appear in these stories as reality effects. There are libraries, literary genres, and the first initials of authors' names. These are enough to suggest to a reader the number of pages read and to give the flavor of frenzied work; they are not enough to enable a reader to trace the stories back to actual books or people:

1. We were working on an event and needed to compare the reactions of newspaper A, a right-wing conservative daily, with those

of *D*, the anarchist weekly. Interlibrary loan informed us that *A* was available from the Center for Research Libraries but that *D* didn't appear on the National Union Catalogue serials list: there was no way of finding it. So we studied in minute detail *A*'s version of our event, while we had to reconstruct in our own collective political imagination what *D*'s might have been. Of course our own imagination of *D*'s anarchism was highly colored by our own regional history . . . and we felt less constrained by facts.

Oddly enough, and unfairly, the imagined part of our study, evoking *D*, ended up much livelier and much more convincing than the overdocumented section based on our minute study of *A*.

2. I thought my author, *C*, who read all kinds of crazy trash, was probably reading a certain popular magazine in the 1930s, so I went out to the library at Versailles and the one at Nanterre where the few faded copies of the magazine were kept. In one of the issues I found an advertisement for a book to which *C* had referred. Went back to my primary text and sure enough, there were epigraphs and entire paragraphs from the very volume advertised in that tattered old magazine at Versailles. I was furthermore convinced that my author first learned of the book by reading the ad in that bulletin. A week after I made the connection, a colleague—who also works on *C* and who knows the bibliography well—alerted me to an obscure article from 1938, where a certain *Z* made exactly the same connection. My "discovery" had been made fifty years earlier and buried in an insignificant journal which itself had only existed for four years. Making the same connection over again gave me a mystical sense of camaraderie with *Z*; I lost interest in my own discovery but became fascinated with the idea of finding traces of *Z*, who had checked the same facts, sat in the same chairs, turned the same pages, as I!

3. He had been working for days in the police archives in the 5th arrondissement, Place Maubert—some routine administrative reports on petty crimes, the kind that police write for their superiors, just to keep the paper flowing. And after many hours of work, at the end of his rope, he found a single phrase, a gem,

that made him glow for days—an offhand comment made by a policeman in a report on a criminal. One of the policeman's sentences corresponded, both in its casualness and its ingenuity, to everything he had been thinking about the subject of his research. Truer, he felt, in one sentence, than he himself could have been in pages and pages of theory. It lit up in his mind, that sentence, he hummed and whistled it. His goal, in writing, now became nothing more, nothing less than to create the perfect backdrop for that single sentence, the appropriate setting against which to display it. Because when he had told it to his colleagues they frankly didn't see what all the fuss was all about.

Not all the stories can be successes.

4. A professor—a well known scholar in her field—gives you a call number for the National Archives—your key to an important sixteenth-century document on your author, the far from obscure Y. The information people in the front of the archives can't help you, the call number doesn't correspond to anything in the sixteenth-century collections nor to anything catalogued under your author, Y. On a hunch, you figure it out: the number you have been given isn't a call number, it's a date. But it doesn't lead you to your document.

And finally, a "conversion story" about archival research:

5. X had been trained at the U. of Q. in the methodological polemics of her generation. On a fluke—the possibility of a grant to work in an archive in her own University—she undertook what she considered an "old fashioned" biographic study of the recently deceased poet, Y, and found in the University collection the textbooks that Y had studied in grade school. She wrote a series of articles demonstrating the extraordinary influence of these school books on Y's rhetorical imagination. She felt a thrill, an almost guilty allegiance to the empirical realm. "Finally," she told me, "I know when I have a result."

Each of these fables, pulled from behind the scholarly veil, is thick with literature. Each can be analyzed like a text. Their pronouns, for example, change them. In the first tale, "we" carries an institutional charge; a whole team is working on the newspapers (they must be making a report—the project must be huge, and funded). The "I" in the second story garners the most sympathy, falls into a sentimentalism—the lonely "I" finds "Z," the scholar of the '30s, for a companion. The "he" in the police archives is doggedly cheerful, more driven than sentimental; he's something like a miner who has struck gold or found a diamond in the rough. In the fourth story "you," the manipulated reader and graduate student, are a victim of a careless professor's mistake. The fifth story, the conversion, is the most devious, for it involves a slippage from one subject to another. "X" confesses her conversion to the archives to "me" (presumably the author of the story). But it is "me" and not "she" who reports the guilty thrill of empirical research: who is speaking for whom here?

The use of these stories is confidential but they partake of the most public and shared of genre conventions. They are versions of epic, Odysseus's travels, Diogenes' search for the honest man—or the reliable fact. They are redemptive detective fictions with their single problem, their crime, waiting to be solved at the center of the labyrinth. Archival work is an epic, but it is also a dime novel, an adolescent adventure story. It is a mixed up genre whose tropes and figures cross over, multiply, intertwine. The dizziness before the microfilm reader can become that of Theseus in the labyrinth, Oedipus at the crossroads, or Cassandra in the Temple of Athena.

Yet to tell these stories breaks their spell and violates the spirit of the archives. Not just because telling breaks the pact of silence that the researcher makes with herself, but because it directs our attention away from what is in the archives and focuses it on the person who is digging, and whose goal was to disappear behind the glory of her material.

II.

The archives have not always beguiled the literary critic (it was once the author, then the trope), but the special charge and purpose that they now give to literary research is a crucial problem in French studies today. While our sibling rivals in history acknowledge, with more and more frequent reference to our own critical theory, the role of rhetoric in historical narratives, we are turning away from our former self-consciousness about language toward the context of literature, with the curiosity and energetic passion of collectors. It has all happened as though by some process of cross-pollination of desire between historians and literary critics. Anecdotes, marginalia, *"trouvailles"* [finds] of all kinds are finding their way, once again, into the annals of criticism. When Antoine Compagnon's *La Troisième République des lettres* appeared in 1983, it seemed but a reminder of the quaint, distant French literary historical tradition that had been brushed aside by theory. It turned out instead to have announced a new wave of literary history, a "nouvelle érudition" in French letters.

One can no longer, today, speak of erudition in France without mentioning the specific practice known as "génétique littéraire" or literary genetics: the study of the creation of the text. Literary genetics are funded and sanctified by the CNRS, the national French think tank, and are perceived by many as the most prestigious form of literary erudition on the current scene. By analyzing the variants, the *ratures*, the substitutions, within and between versions of manuscripts, the literary geneticists hope to account for the actual process that the author's work with language has taken. There is something blatantly motherbound in this deep nostalgia for the original ("nothing like the feel of a real nth-century text in your hand" . . .), and the nostalgia is only heightened by the disappearance of handwriting in this age of word processors.

Unlike the archivists whose quests I described above, literary geneticists do not make the discovery of the primary text part of their adventure. Manuscript or successive manuscript versions of canonical literary texts are objects whose importance is unquestioned and whose existence is often well documented. It is odd that such manuscripts are cherished now, because they were never meant to be read by a public—only the author, perhaps a typist, and then an editor saw them before they were turned into published text. The analysis of manuscripts may claim to be "materialist" in a literal sense (just as the analysis of successive brush strokes on a painting might be considered highly materialist), but because they have never circulated among a community of readers, manuscripts are not "social" texts.

And to whom are the manuscripts of our canonical authors available? In many cases they are policed by the author's heirs and a few select scholars. The researcher who wants access must penetrate the critical "industry" surrounding that author, and this can be a difficult task for anyone without the right connections. In sanctifying the canonical text, the practice of literary genetics also reinforces a guild system among critics. The pleasure of the literary geneticist is in knowing where the object is, what the object is, and in being among the few to measure its value. It is almost as though literary genetics were trying to cure the archive of what doesn't ail it: its endless field of possibilities, its random objects, its chance finds.

The archive is obviously not a stranger to the process of canonization, for it is often in order to legitimate a given author's work that scholars seek out the archives in the first place. Some authors yield to archival research more easily than others. They've rewritten their every word and filled their margins with speculative notes. Their role in public life has created reams of paper, or their families have saved their laundry lists and grocery bills. If any single author of the twentieth-century French canon can be said to actually demand a recourse, both to public documents and to the line by line study of manuscripts, it is Louis-Ferdinand Céline.

Céline's books drip with obscure references, neologisms, slang, place names, all begging to be footnoted. His complete works, his editor likes to say, are as yet incomplete. Fragments of his manuscripts still appear regularly for sale at auction houses ("in blue ballpoint, heavily revised and corrected, stains from paper-clip at head"); there are even stories of manuscripts found in trunks in the house of his widow. But mostly the stories that send Céline scholars running to do research have been planted by Céline himself, within his own texts, and they are aimed, with a kind of sadistic foresight, at his critics: he writes about the manuscripts he left and lost in his flight from Paris in 1944; he writes primitive versions, and less primitive versions of his books, he carries on legal correspondence, refers to trials, speculates about a missing American lover from the thirties (Elizabeth Craig has just, as I write, been found). He writes about writing, about his editor and his typist and his bills. The personal and political history of Céline are so intricately woven into his narratives that the *Tel Quel* Céline of the fragmented, referent-free subject seems, in our archival moment, almost unfathomable. Céline is a magnet for the new literary history.

I've always felt completely taken in by this Céline who mocks the function of the literary critic even as he plants his text full of obscure references, while I, said literary critic, scramble in pursuit of my own Céline glossary and lexicon.

Completely taken in. And yet, in the case of the antisemitic pamphlets, his trap led me to trap him, through a game of sources. The more stolen words and phrases I could find in *Bagatelles pour un massacre,* the less Céline was its author, the more he was merely a scribe.

My *Relevé des sources et citations dans "Bagatelles pour un massacre"* [Study of sources and quotations in Céline's "Trifles for a Massacre" (Tusson: Editions du Lérot, 1987)], which participates fully in the current rush on the archives, is a report of results. It (not I, as it were) juxtaposes Céline's own prose, page by page, with the popular antisemitic literature that inspired it. Sometimes Céline plagiarizes entire pages of antisemitic propaganda; sometimes he lifts a line; sometimes he copies a piece of text but distorts a word or phrase in the interest of a style with popular appeal: he substitutes "youppin" for "juif" or takes a stock phrase, like this one from a brochure called *The Jewish Conspiracy:* "The Jew Blumenthal could therefore write with reason" [Le Juif Blumenthal pouvait donc écrire avec raison] and teases it out into the more rambling, speakerly: "It all sticks, it is, I think, admirably in concordance with the events taking place right now. So the Jew Blumenthal had every right to write, so that we might know, in the 'Judisk Tidskrift' " [Le Juif Blumenthal était donc dans son plein droit, écrivant pour qu'on le sache.]

I spent three years in eight different libraries uncovering word changes made by Céline on a group of pamphlets published in the general vicinity of his neighborhood that I finally determined were his immediate sources. It was something like being a literary geneticist, except—and the difference is essential—that I had to reconstruct the manuscript in my imagination, by juxtaposing the published text of *Bagatelles* with its sources. The literary geneticist has a set text in front of him, and that text works as a barrier against open-ended interpretation. For me, not having the manuscript provided the energy I needed to imagine how the pamphlet was written. The work of imagination fueled my search.

As I discovered the sources from the array of clues that Céline had left his readers (an author's name in one place, a truncated title in another), I came to see that he had probably cut out pages from newspapers and pamphlets and pasted them onto his manuscript, penning in a word change here and there. The pamphlets that he stole from also consisted of strings of quotations, lifted from yet another generation of antisemitic works. Many of the quotations could be traced back from 1937 to the generation of Edouard Drumont; many showed up in English, Canadian, American, and South African versions. Interlibrary loan gave me a bird's eye view of the regional history of racism: many of the books I needed were available in southern American libraries. The intertexts I was tracking, from Paris to Pretoria, are the pride of the genre: what counts in antisemitic conspiracy literature is the number of people and quotations that can be brought to bear on the question. The textual weight, the repetition of the same borrowed words, takes the place of argument.

The *Relevé des sources et citations* that emerged from this research, as the book's title might indicate, narrates none of the passion for reconstruction and tracking that had motivated me. Passion and polemic had marred the existing work on the pamphlets: critics used the racism in the pamphlets to condemn Céline's fiction, or they used the stylistic flourishes in the pamphlets to laud Céline in spite of himself. Critics asked the moral question—"why had he written it?", but no one had asked how he had done it. Some critics assumed that Céline had invented the antisemitic quotations whole cloth, out of his anger: they admired his verbal invention so much that they wanted even his racism to be the work of imagination.

My own passion existed alongside my empirical zeal. It consisted first in a kind of invented memory of the books on Céline's desk, a partial memory that I struggled to complete—first the desk, then the books, their shape and size, then the titles. . . . This is the image of a desk that I report at the start of this essay. The fable about *C* and *Z* is also my own. *Z* is Georges Zérapha, a Jewish activist in LICA (Ligue Internationale contre l'Antisémitisme) who had published an article on plagiarism and quotation in *Bagatelles* in 1938 in *La Conscience des Juifs*. His article had confirmed my first archival "leads," he became my imaginary archival companion.

From a notebook:

That memory—of Céline's writing table—is getting sharper. I am starting to give names to the books and pamphlets scattered across his desk. I'm trying to figure out where he went to get his antisemitic pamphlets. It isn't arbitrary—he didn't just happen to get them—he had a source. He was a neighborhood kind of guy; a man of habits; everything that everyone ever said about him points to that. Georges Zérapha has already traced a number of his quotations back to a pamphlet factory operated by Darquier de Pellepoix in the 17th arrondissement, the rue Laugier. I dragged my friends there, to the exact building, a Gothic building at number 12, which is in the process of renovation and *looks* antisemitic (how to explain what that means to me—horror film Germanic?). I dreamt about the basement, about cartons of books still there. The whole 17th arrondissement looked, today, the way it probably looked in 1937, 1943, evil, haunted.

But I can't imagine Céline there—he's too much a Montmartois.

. . .

Finally, I've come across a whole other set of the same antisemitic texts published by a different, but collegial group of authors in the 9th, on the rue du Cardinal Mercier, the neighborhood next to Montmartre. This time it was almost midnight when I grabbed the same bewildered friends for a walk through Montmartre, tracing Céline's imagined steps. From the rue Lepic, where Céline lived, we walked down the hill, on the shortest path we could take to the rue du Cardinal Mercier, off the Boulevard de Clichy. The dividing line between Montmartre and Clichy was a cemetery. The cimetière Montmartre, a cemetery full of cats. You walked through it along a bridge that went over it, a baroque village of tombstones on both sides. I felt death, we were walking through death—for Céline it must have been war dead, his veteran's pacifism, fueling his anger as he walked to the antisemitic pamphlet house. The dead, then the dancing girls of the Moulin Rouge, then he heard the honky talk of Clichy, he passed a pool hall, the Académie du Billard, which hasn't changed for fifty years. Finally he went around a corner to a dead-end street, the rue du Cardinal Mercier, with a fountain at the end. The store front where the pamphlets must have been sold was still there, businesslike window and all, only now it has no visible use and the window needs cleaning.

Céline's populism; his neighborhood identity; his hatred of the big daily press; his affection for the little mimeographed spreads. His use of the word "little," every time he wants to laud something. All this comes across in the text of the pamphlets, and makes the walk from Montmartre to the rue du Cardinal Mercier make sense.

I needed my imagination of Céline as a "neighborhood guy" to reject the pamphlet factory in the 17th arrondissement as the final source, and to locate the pamphlet factory that was within walking distance from Céline's apartment on the rue Lepic. I needed to imagine the walk from Montmartre to Clichy in order to recognize that the pamphlets produced on the rue du Cardinal Mercier were worth studying. So it is not the case that these wanderings through Paris, this notebook, make my archival research relative to some personal experience or autobiographical quest. They were a necessary ingredient in the research, they *changed the results of the research*, they made the discoveries possible.

III.

Much of the vulgar antisemitic literature published in 1937, the stuff that Céline cribbed to write *Bagatelles pour un massacre*, is now housed at the Center for Contemporary Jewish Documentation. The C.D.J.C. is located behind an iron gate in the Marais, the old Jewish quarter of Paris (17, rue Geoffroy-l'Asnier 75004: another walk . . .). Your entrance through the courtyard is studied on the security screen in the vestibule. Your purse gets searched (there have been bombings). You pass the holocaust memorial on the first floor; you go up to a small room on the third floor to do your work. No one is anonymous at the Center for Jewish Documentation; no one searches the shelves by themselves, and the organization is such that you really do best to explain your whole project to the librarians, who, willy nilly, bring you papers and books. The correspondence of racial theorist Georges Montandon emerged one day from boxes; the librarians aren't sure how it is that they acquired the correspondence of Montandon in the first place, but it's there and it's numbered: it turned out that Montandon was in contact with Céline.

Along with this exhilarating sense of mystery and chance in the C.D.J.C., one of the things that always flavors work there, more than in any other library where I have worked, is the quantity of people who are there for personal reasons, who are looking for signs of relatives who died in the camps, and who work in an entirely different key than the so-called "disinterested" scholars. The C.D.J.C. has been associated with all of the great postholocaust events—with the Barbie Trial, with *Shoah* (Lantzmann worked there for many years) even with Holocaust revisionism (Robert Faurisson could once be found there, too). Many of the books at the C.D.J.C. are gifts; François Gibault, the biographer of Céline and lawyer of the Céline estate, came in person to offer his three volume Céline biography: *Le Temps des espérances* (1894–1932); *Délires et persécution* (1932–1944); *Cavalier de l'Apocalypse* (1944–1961) (Paris: Mercure de France, 1981–1985). The librarians who work there are reviewers of new literature, they are living bibliographies, they are translators—from the Yiddish and from the German. And they are therapists, depositories of memory.

In 1982 the center receives in the mail the "manuscript testimony" of a woman who, as a child, survived the Grand Rafle du Vél d'hiv. The Vél d'hiv was an indoor sports stadium to which on 16 and 17 July 1942 the French police brought more than 12,000 Parisian Jews destined for deportation to Nazi camps. She remembers in her testimony that the night before the rafle she ate "du boudin avec de la purée," sausage with mashed vegetables. When the officers arrived, as she tells it, her mother decided to fix her younger sister's hair. The arresting policeman told the sister, Annette, that she could go buy a comb at the neighborhood drugstore. Annette went—the druggist told her to run away, " quick," but she ran right back home to her mother and sister, back to deportation, because she was too frightened to run away from home. Incredible, that the police gave Annette permission to go to the drugstore, but the story as her older sister writes it rings true.

A woman walks in, waddling, with difficulty, while I am there, she says to the librarian in a voice that we all hear, a voice that isn't used to whispering in libraries: "Here are my memoirs of Drancy (a French concentration camp in the suburbs of Paris). I'm getting old" [mes mémoires de Drancy, je vieillis].

But the librarian corrects me as we talk: "It's not the deportees who come most often, it's the children and grandchildren who suffer from the silence of their parents. Often they begin a project, then disappear."

"They can't bear it?"

She shrugs. "Maybe they don't need to see it through to an end."

The missing person stories come daily: the library doubles as a detective's office. There is the professor whose children urged her to come to the C.D.J.C. to find out her origins. Her parents had given her to the neighbors in '43 and she had grown up in isolation. She started with the card file marked "children."

Other people come to the C.D.J.C. to consult published lists of the names of the deported. A woman arrives in 1988, she looks through the lists of convoys of the deported, she finds the name of her husband, dead in 1944.

This happens everyday.

In this atmosphere I work on the sources of Céline's antisemitic pamphlet, and I read: fifteen versions of the Protocols of the Elders of Zion, a book called *The Popular Front: Instrument of the Jews*, a diatribe on Jewish-Communist conspiracy by the women's anticommunist league of Montreal called *The Key of the Mystery*, and *The Anti-Jew: France for the French*, a weekly mimeographed sheet.

To the left of the table where I always work in the C.D.J.C. is a framed black and white photo of a fashionable man. An Algerian, rakishly handsome, his hand in his vest pocket like Napoleon, his eye right on the camera. His pocket is embroidered with the yellow star and imprinted with the word "juif." In the 1970s, the man who had modeled for his photograph, no longer young, had come to the C.D.J.C. to offer it as a gift, hugely enlarged. He had kept it, he said, out of admiration for his own youthful beauty. The yellow star really had nothing to do with it, it was but a pretext for vanity's offering. And here I had imagined for the many years I had worked beneath this big photo—another of my private stories—that the photograph had once served as some kind of bizarre propaganda, designed to encourage Jewish residents to put on their stars. Nothing of the kind. "The picture *doesn't belong here*," the librarian tells me, "mais ici on trouve tout"—there's some of everything here.

The archive is constituted by these errors, these pieces out of place, which are then reintegrated into a story of some kind. The story may have nothing to do with the original meaning but it allows work to take place, answers to be found. It's much the same for the fables I began with. The guy in the police archives with the one jewel-like quotation; the conversion story of the woman who thinks she's escaped from polemics; the midnight walk that the critic takes with a dead author: these stories, too, are fragile but necessary contingent ingredients of archival work, they are the private process that is erased as soon as it succeeds in producing a bit of truth. This is perhaps the common denominator of all archival passion—the sense that even the smallest result is "a bit of truth." If there are values to be protected in the archives, they belong to this realm of passion, where intuition and coincidence turn random documents into results. They belong to an archival space where some things don't belong, where you have the right to wander through stacks, flip through the cards, invent a missing piece until you get to the next step, the right to value books of uncertain provenance and unstable value, read texts that are unsigned and reject the dicta of the canon. Usually there is no mother lode, no original manuscript to be retrieved—the gold is all in the dust.

PATRIZIA LOMBARDO

Hippolyte Taine between Art and Science

> To me he [Taine] embodies the last twenty years of criticism; he is
> the ripe fruit of that school which was born on the ruins of rhetoric
> and scholasticism. The new science made up of physiology and
> psychology, history and philosophy blossomed with him. . . . I
> consider him, in literary and artistic criticism, the contemporary of
> the telegraph and the railroads.
> —Emile Zola, *Mes Haines*, 1866

THE *ESSAI SUR TITE-LIVE*, OR HISTORY AGAINST RHETORIC

Disciplines are not ready-made objects, they are historical products.
The result of an interaction between texts and institutions, they
come into existence and die. Subject as they are to changes of name,
object of study, method, area of influence, they can be said to be
situated halfway between the so-called freedom of knowledge and the
struggle for power among institutions and within institutions.

Several texts of the nineteenth century prefigure some of the institutional tensions of today and may help in reflecting on the present-day status of literary studies. After 1850, Hippolyte Taine is a
key figure for understanding the relationship between literature and
history, as well as the role of literary criticism in the century often
defined as the one that invented both history and literature.[1] A short
history of the French institutions with which Taine was in contact
and by which he was often rejected, will provide insight into the
complex network of small events that determine texts and are deter-

---

1. See Roland Barthes, *Le Degré zéro de l'écriture* (Paris: Editions du Seuil, 1972), 7.
Gabriel Monod spoke of the nineteenth century as the "century that is above all the
century of history." See Monod, *Les Maîtres de l'histoire: Taine, Renan, Michelet*
(Paris: Calmann-Lévy, 1894), 41.

YFS 77, *Reading the Archive: On Texts and Institutions*, ed. E. S. Burt and Janie Vanpée,
© 1990 by Yale University.

mined by them. This does not mean that texts are simply produced or explained by facts. The deterministic flavor of the historical approach is and should be continuously jeopardized by the unpredictable games of language. Reading the archives is the best way to ask a question about the status of literature and criticism. It is also the best way to blend erudition and interpretation, formalism and historicism in the very practice of writing.

In 1856 Taine published his *Essai sur Tite-Live* which reads as a manifesto suggesting that modern history should no longer be considered as a great oratorical work [*opus oratorium maxime*], as Cicero defined it, but rather as a science based on documents and facts. For Taine the best moments of Livy occurred when he went "straight to the true fact, the original detail, the authentic word"; the worst moments were the "few traces, not quite erased, of ancient declamations."[2] The last pages of the essay, although praising Livy's beautiful style, affirmed that "only the moderns have given [history] its name and goal" (359). Taine's essay attacking Cicero's definition of history was written for a highly institutional event: a public award to be given by the French Academy. At the moment that German philosophy was starting to be popular in France among the younger generation, the Academy proposed a topic of research reinforcing the classical tradition. It asked in 1854 for a critical and rhetorical study of Livy, whom it defined as the exemplary historical genius of all time. The wording of the subject proposed in the contest suggested that the contestants indicate what a great model he was for antiquity and what a seminal example he could still prove for "the historical art of our century" (i).

At that time, long before he wrote *Les Origines de la France contemporaine* (begun in 1871), long before he was elected as historian to the French Academy (1878), and long before he came to be perceived as a right-wing intellectual, Taine's academic situation was symptomatic of the institutional resistance to modernist attitudes. A brilliant student of the *Ecole normale,* Taine had been trained in the scholarly tradition of the nineteenth century, which consisted in the study of the classical authors and in endless rhetorical exercises. But the *Ecole normale* was a liberal institution, where the students were also free to read modern writers and philosophers, such as Balzac and

2. Taine, *Essai sur Tite-Live* (Paris: Hachette, 1896), 49. All subsequent references to this work will appear in parentheses in the text. All translations from the French are my own.

Hegel. Taine was among the most enthusiastic readers of the German philosopher, encouraged by his director of studies, Etienne Vacherot, who finally was forced to leave the school after he was accused of Hegelianism by the Abbé Gratry.[3] Taine was perceived by his professors as the best student in philosophy, of real promise for the national competition, the *Concours d'agrégation*. In 1851, a scandal broke out when he failed to pass the exam. Prévost-Paradol, Taine's friend at the *Ecole normale*, recounted the whole misadventure in front of the jury, which was mainly composed of members of the *Institut* (the five-part institute in which the French Academy is included). According to Prévost-Paradol, in spite of the rigorous logical construction of Taine's argument, some people in the jury could not accept his dry and scientific thesis in which the role of divine providence was not considered. Moreover they found Taine's reading of Bossuet through Spinoza very dangerous. Taine's disappointment was particularly bitter since, in 1852, the *agrégation* was abolished by Napoleon III, which meant that he could not receive institutional recognition as a philosopher. He would in fact never be recognized as such. In 1855 the Sorbonne rejected his thesis on sensations (*De cognitione rerum externarum*, whose main argument was later taken up in his famous *De l'intelligence*). In this second failure of Taine can be read a tension between two institutions, the Sorbonne and the *Ecole normale*. How could the Sorbonne, so Aristotelian in its approach, accept a thesis on the illusory nature of sensations, which it deemed a dangerous product of the *Ecole normale*'s sophistic and liberal tradition? Adolphe Garnier wrote the thesis report, restating the idea he had stressed after Taine's *agrégation:*

> I saw Mr. Taine at the last *concours d'agrégation*. He is verbally very talented; his rhetorical skills are irreproachable. It is impossible to express oneself with more grace and to be more seductive with an audience; but these qualities are rhetorical, not philosophical. . . . I am convinced that his imagination is too strong for him to become a philosopher. He would exploit more appropriately and more happily his brilliant qualities working with literature and poetry.[4]

---

3. See *Une étude sur la sophistique contemporaine, ou lettre à M. Vacherot* (Paris: Charles Duniol, 1851).

4. Taine, *H. Taine, sa vie et sa correspondance (1847–1853)*, (Paris: Hachette, 1902), vol. 1, 249. Letter by Adolphe Garnier to Victor Le Clerc, Dean of the Faculty, dated 17 May 1852.

The old philosophical tradition that, since Plato, had condemned rhetoric, was protecting disciplinary definitions: the art of discourse is good for the disciplines requiring imagination, like literature and history, but it is bad for reasoning. Each field should be well marked. But any new movement tends to oppose the rigidity of boundaries and to challenge stubborn and comfortable convictions concerning their ability to delimit disciplines. We will see an example of boundaries being overrun in Taine, who was considered too rhetorical to be a good scholar in philosophy, and who, at the same time, did not hesitate to criticize Livy precisely for his oratorical skills. We will see also that Taine was not only imbued with ancient rhetoric but also helped in creating a new rhetoric, the rhetoric of facts.[5]

Now, Taine's *Essai sur Tite-Live* discussed Livy in terms that the Academy could hardly share, since the latter's interest was in maintaining the tradition of rhetoric in historical writing. Taine stated that the Latin historian, who was a contemporary of Cicero and a man surrounded by an entire generation of orators, had an "imperfect idea of history" (27) precisely because he was overwhelmed by Rome's oratorical tradition. Livy's eloquence and his overly learned style blurred the clarity of the facts, even when his documentation was accurate. Moreover, because of his love for Rome, he was not objective and "kept the rhetorical and poetical language of old legends and the greatness of the Roman character" (331). Taine bluntly stated that Livy was nothing but an orator, lacked critical sense, and very often made mistakes in consulting the documents.

Taine defined all the qualities and defects of Livy with the label, or, as he liked to say, formula [la formule], of "historian orator." His formula aimed at the clarity of a geometric definition while it highlighted the impossibility of defining Livy simply as a historian. It

5. Taine dared to criticize ancient rhetoric in a work for the French Academy, the very institution that aimed to maintain the classical tradition. At first, Taine's criticism seemed too severe to the jury of the Academy. The award was not given to anybody in 1854 and Taine was asked to make some corrections, which would allow him to win the award the following year. Compromise is an easy game when the stakes are not high: winning an award is not like being given a state job in the university. In those years Taine had just quit his job as a high school *suppléant* in the provinces. Having refused to sign a document in favor of Napoleon III, he had been moved by the Minister of Education from the teaching of philosophy to "a less dangerous subject of teaching: rhetoric" (*Taine, sa vie et sa correspondance*, vol. 1, 90, letter to Prévost-Paradol, dated 1 July 1849). Taine became a freelance critic in Paris who had no hope of an "academic future in the university" (ibid., 299, letter to Prévost-Paradol, dated 1 August 1852).

sounded almost like a warning for the modern reader who could not expect to read Livy's history as pure history.

Taine's essay did not win the contest on the first try, for the jury found that he had "too little respect for Livy and for great men in general" and "too strong a taste for modern ideas in the field of history."[6] Taine was forced to use cunning when he came up against the demands of the Academy in rewriting his essay. The compromise on Taine's part consisted in an attempt to write a modern manifesto at the same time he sought to save some classical values. Taine wanted to show that modern history was superior to ancient history, and that science was superior to eloquence. He had to advance this thesis carefully: if eloquence was not dead in France, it was thanks to institutional protection. But the spirit of classical rhetoric did not meet the romantic claims of the first century that invented history as a discipline. Already in 1838, Eugène Magne had complained about the mechanical reduction of ancient rhetoric to a useless series of recipes. He believed that the art of discourse "would be dead in France today without the official protection of the university's curricula."[7] The result of Taine's compromise with the Academy was that the *Essai sur Tite-Live* affirmed history to be both art and science. The essay itself is divided into two sections corresponding to the compromise between the moderns and the Ancients: "History Considered as a Science" and "History Considered as an Art." Taine insisted that rhetoric and history had to be separated if history were to be founded as a science, thus opening the way to the more extreme statement of Fustel de Coulanges (who entered the *Ecole Normale* in 1849, one year after Taine): history is and must be a science. Taine's criticism of Livy initiated the positivist historical consciousness that devalued the ancient art of persuasion. He led the way for such statements as the one made by Gabriel Monod in the first issue of the *Revue historique* (1876), where he proclaimed the need for a scientific method "in which every statement would be accompanied by proofs, by references to sources and quotations, while severely excluding vague generalities and oratorical developments."[8]

The Academy wanted to safeguard the merits of rhetoric and the eternal value of the Ancients; from this follows the uneasiness ex-

6. *H. Taine, sa vie et sa correspondance,* vol. 2, 58. Letter to Prévost-Paradol, dated 3 June 1854.

7. Eugène Magne, *La Rhétorique au XIXe siècle* (Paris: Firmin Didot, 1838), 7.

8. Gabriel Monod, "Avant-propos," *Revue historique* 1 (1876): 2.

pressed in its review of the *Essai*. The person who wrote the review was Abel Villemain, elected to the Academy in 1821, at the age of 31, and the author of a *Tableau de l'éloquence chrétienne au IVe siècle*, of several works in the tradition of eulogy (*Eloge de Montaigne, Eloge de Montesquieu, Essai sur le génie de Pindare*), as well as the editor and translator of Cicero's *Republic*. He was therefore one of the most stubborn defenders of the Ancients. (Baudelaire's hatred of him, as is shown in his pamphlet *De l'esprit et du style de M. Villemain*, is well-known.) Because Taine's *Essai* was not a eulogy, but a critique, it puzzled Villemain. The academician par excellence had to write the report assessing the award to somebody who did not enthusiastically prize the Latin historian. In his review, published as a preface to the *Essai*, Villemain did not stress Taine's novelty of method, but tried to recuperate the classical values embodied in Livy while noting the severity of Taine's judgement on Livy. The institutional position was stubbornly maintained, in spite of Taine's questioning of it. Livy was a great man, the greatness of Rome should be an everlasting example for the modern world, history should always be an oratorical work.

A wonderful denegation shapes the pompous style of the academician. Villemain sees Taine's argument without wanting to understand it. He contrasts Taine's dryness with the "astonishment" many critics express when they speak of Livy, as if to state his own regret that Taine did not express a similar astonishment:

> Judging Livy, he [Taine] shows a curious and free attention for many other subjects. Even the epigraph that he chooses, *in historia orator*, and the many pages of his book devoted to justify it, could allow us to believe that, through the title of orator by which he defines Livy, he is not, in the praise itself, completely just toward the great historian. [iv–v]

What Villemain seems to mean without actually saying it, is that he is sure that Taine was not "completely just" toward Livy. To make this point, he feels obliged to reintroduce the classical distinction between oratorical and eloquent language, that is, between bad and good rhetoric, that Taine was contesting. Taine complains about the overly ornate style of the Latin historian, to which Villemain replies that Livy's discourses are "narrative's lovely attire"; they exhibit Livy's greatest qualities, "the beauty of the story he tells"; and they set off "the truth of its characterisation, and, lastly, the passion behind its words . . . ; it is in these features and thanks to them that we find the eloquence of Livy's narrative which, without any oratorical excess, demonstrates the very essence of eloquence" (v). The conservative argument seals the values of morality and aesthetics. The commentary by Villemain provides a perfect example of the display of vague generalities and oratorical developments against which Taine and the positivist generation would consistently fight. Positivism came onto the scene in the second half of the nineteenth century, like structuralism in France in the 1960s, against the decrepit convictions monumentalized in the most respectful institutions. Villemain flatly contradicted the young scholar's judgment on Livy's beautiful style: for Taine the Latin historian was "as exact as one can be, when one is by nature an orator and not a historian" (39). The problem for Taine is that history should be an exact science, while the Academy wants to hold onto the definition of history as oratorical art.

THE ELOQUENCE OF FACT

Taine did not doubt for a moment that all of ancient history was imperfect. For the essence of history is to be found neither in eloquence nor in the persuasiveness of passionate language of which Villemain spoke in his review. The essence of history lies in factual truth, for it provides mute proof and is capable of convincing us by means of its simple existence and evidence. Factual truth is a silent trace, completely free from any oratorical halo. Facts are visible; they can be studied and observed. Their presence alone allows them to speak. History is a science founded on facts. Criticism is also a science that Taine does not distinguish from history, since, as he repeated in his 1858 preface to the *Essais de critique et d'histoire,* both should be based on facts. The move to disregard eloquence because it cannot be exact corresponds to the needs of positivism and its general devaluation of the oral document relative to the written document. Fustel de Coulanges disregards legends and oral traditions; he trusts only written texts. The written document alone is an objective fact, and is therefore characterized by the conditions it must fulfill in order to be true, in order to be an object of science. Taine admits that Livy had that marvellous sparkle of the mind that can be called "historical intuition," next to which an error in data or names was of minor importance. Nevertheless he insists on the necessity of exactness. Scientific truth is exact and quantifiable. Science demonstrates, language persuades. For the positivists, science is objective, while spoken language is always subjective. Scientific language seems to be the language that renounces all the seductive power of language, a language closer to the thing than to the word. A written document is a tangible object and provides visible proof that can be controlled; an oral document evaporates and changes as it is affected by the passion of spoken words, the instability of the audience, and the diversity of voices, legends and traditions.

Sainte-Beuve, the tireless journalist and literary critic of the moment, reviewed the *Essai sur Tite-Live* upon its publication the year after the contest. The *Essai* came like an event upon the Parisian intellectual scene, and was widely reviewed. To the published version of his essay, Taine added a short introduction where he took the opportunity to revenge himself on the backwardness of the Academy and the State juries: he stressed the necessity of a rigorous method, comparing the humanities with the natural sciences, and mentioning Spinoza, who had caused him so much trouble at the *agrégation*.

Much more lucid than Villemain, Sainte-Beuve grasped the real importance of Taine's book. He spoke of the beginning of a new method in history and literary criticism that would have algebraic precision and clarity of formula. Comparable in this to a structuralist of the twentieth century, Taine sought above all a method. His idea of exactness in history is founded on what he calls the dominant forces (*les forces maîtresses*), the main structures linking together the most important events.

Unlike Villemain, Sainte-Beuve did not regret that Taine had not written a eulogy of Livy. He perceived that a new generation had come onto the scene, a generation that wanted facts, that had cut itself off from the blurred discourses of the past, and that had a keen scientific, mathematical insight, amounting almost to cruelty. Sainte-Beuve especially understood that Taine was undertaking to question the value of the oral document in history. He viewed this undertaking with mixed feelings: although he admired the novelty of Taine's approach, he criticized the dryness of its formulas and definitions and recalled that Livy's own text had not been preserved entirely:

> We have, undoubtedly, the admirable Punic war, the Macedonian wars and the first Asiatic war; but all that follows, and that would have been extremely interesting, is missing. We cannot read the fights between Marius and Sylla, the rivalry between Pompey and Caesar, or the true and real political history of those recent epochs that Livy knew perfectly in spirit and detail thanks to the stories of a tradition

close to him, thanks to that animated and live transmission which is like a fecundating breath.[9]

The historian who preferred oral traditions to written documents was Michelet, who felt that spoken stories were what Sainte-Beuve calls "animated and live transmission." The oral tradition provides better proof of historical reality, since it retains the warmth of people's voices and the presence of their bodies. Sainte-Beuve was not a great admirer of Michelet and reproached Taine for sometimes correcting Livy's history of Rome with references to Michelet, whose excessive style he distrusted. But, in spite of himself, Sainte-Beuve shared Michelet's passion for words, a passion that Taine was leaving behind. In two long reviews of Michelet's history of the Renaissance and the Reformation, contemporaneous with the *Essai* and published in Hachette's journal, *La Revue de l'instruction publique* (1855), Taine questioned the value of Michelet's history by suggesting that the same lyricism which makes history sound like a hymn, also hurts its scientific credibility:

> M. Michelet let grow within himself a poetic imagination. It covered or strangled the other faculties which had initially developed together with it. His history has all the qualities of inspiration: movement, grace, insight, color, passion, eloquence. It does not have the qualities of science: clarity, precision, straightforwardness, measure, authority. Michelet's history is admirable and incomplete; it seduces and does not convince. Perhaps, in fifty years time, when people wish to define it, they will say that it is the lyrical epic of France.[10]

Taine thought that history should neither be oratorical, nor be written in a symbolic-poetic language. The type of persuasion characteristic of spoken language—subjective and not objective—irritated Taine, who devalued *elocutio* and *actio*.

As it turns out, the real target of Taine's *Essai* was not actually Livy, but the school of German philology represented by Herder, Niebuhr, and Michelet (whose history of Rome was founded on Niebuhr's history). Taine openly attacked Niebuhr, that "erudite German of the nineteenth century," who spoke "of philology as the mediation of eternity, of a secret tendency that pushed him to guess at

9. Sainte-Beuve, "Divers écrits de M. Taine," *Causeries du Lundi* (Paris: Garnier Frères, 1853), vol. 13, 221.

10. Taine, "M. Michelet," *Essais de critique et d'histoire* (Paris: Hachette, 1908), 95.

what has perished" (107). If Taine could not stand the ancients' oratorical declamations, neither could he accept romantic confusion
and mystical emphasis. Niebuhr's *Roman History* was "horrid reading" for any historian with scientific pretensions:

> Conjectures upon conjectures; discussions of traditions, alterations,
> interpolations; the most minute facts are commented upon, exam-
> ined, restored; a pile of dissertations, demonstrations, suppositions;
> the thorniest, heaviest, most discouraging erudition; a style that has
> been clouded by abstract words and hampered by long sentences, that
> has no clean divisions or evident direction; you would think that you
> were in the depths of the Hartz mines. [108]

Modern history cannot divine the past as the prophets divined the
future. The obscure language of divination is not the language of
history, but of poetry. It does not have the clarity of criticism. Niebuhr discovered the past with a mythical mind, and proved incapable
of restraining his imagination, "so avid for knowledge that he mistakes conceptions for objects themselves, and imagines Rome when
he cannot restore it" (109). Moreover, in order to reconstitute the first
age of Rome, Niebuhr turns to the poetic tradition, the one proper to
the "barbarians and the populace" who "use symbols to express general facts and represent the revolution of states with legends, in the
same way they turn the laws of nature into gods" (109). For Taine,
philology sides with poetry and fables, and not with the kind of
precise history that is based on verifiable facts. Taine was certainly
influenced by Hegel, who distinguished between poetry (or eloquence) and history, and talked of a heroic age of humanity in which
everything was poetry. But Taine also introduces a distinction within
the realm of facts, for in his opinion philology confuses small facts
with important facts.

But from where does Taine's distinction between the important
and the unimportant, and his call for the elimination of confusion,
derive if not from the study of rhetoric and its rules for the organization of discursive material, the rules of *dispositio*? It would be enough
to go back to the sentence in which Taine compares Niebuhr's piling
up of information and conjectures to the darkness of the Hartz mines.
He talks about a style that has been clouded "by abstract words."
Ancient rhetoric fought abstractness, and clarity was the first requirement of Aristotle's rhetoric. Furthermore, Taine's short preface
to the *Essai* calls for the organisation of the argument, the *dispositio:*

"The whole of method consists in the ordering and arrangement of the things that the mind's eye must consider to discover the truth" (3).

Taine insisted on the importance of finding "the main lines" [*les grands traits*], the general *plan* and system underlying history—the philosophy of history:

> History is a living body that is injured when the economy of parts is troubled. To present facts one by one, as they follow one another in time does not mean to preserve such a balance. The memory that displays facts in this way is a bad judge and its truth is not the truth. Only *reason*, the sole interpreter of the *laws*, perceives the natural order that is the causal order; and, by discovering the *plan* of history, it organizes, confirms and completes the work begun with criticism and erudition. [126, my emphasis]

Reason does not interpret prophecies, it interprets laws, and the plan of history recalls, even more than the spirit of Hegel, rhetorical lessons and French compositions as they were practiced at the *lycée* and at the *Ecole normale*. If facts could make history by themselves, it would suffice to accumulate events and details. But just as history involves an *inventio*, the identification of its material—facts being the *inventio* of history—so it also demands a *dispositio*, an organisation of the facts "invented," chosen through the *inventio*. Historians must uncover the *plan* of history which can no longer be considered what Michelet called "a vast depository" [*un vaste dépôt*]." The system of history as Taine conceived it was not actually a philosophical system, but a rhetorical system requiring, like any other system, an argument and a line of argumentation.

The pact between rhetoric and history is Machiavellian, and infinite, for both rhetoric and history are caught between words and things, between the two different orders that are language and reality. We should then be cautious about making any sharp distinction between the realm of facts and the realm of words, the very distinction that brought the positivists to disregard rhetoric, spoken language, and oral documents. Taine opened the way to positivism because he thought that the language of science could exist, free from the subjectivity of spoken language, of words [*verba*], close to the objectivity of reality, of things [*res*]. History is understood as reality, and rhetoric as words, language. A strange blindness forces the positivists to believe that the written document is a thing, a fact, as if it were not made of language. But, of course, language is there, and as pointed out by

Nietzsche, the notion itself of fact is a linguistic notion.[11] Without discrediting totally the notion of fact, we can say that we approach facts and science through the lens of language. History is written on written documents (or on oral documents, for those who accept their value, like the new historians who talk about "oral history"). History cannot help being language, since language is both spoken and written. History is the writing of the past, its language. How can rhetoric be avoided? *Res* cannot exist without *verba*. But what else is rhetoric—a living rhetoric, not just a recipe of figures—if not the history of the present, its discourses, the linguistic form that legitimizes the events, the facts happening around us? The historian inevitably uses rhetorical strategies to write history. History is therefore bound to rhetoric, and rhetoric constructs the opinions which shape and are shaped by contemporary history as it takes place in gestures, events and words. *Verba* cannot exist without *res*.

But the positivist illusion that rises from the ashes of classical rhetoric would have one believe that facts come first and language can only spoil them. As language becomes less oratorical or poetic, literary, it also becomes more exact and the distance between language and factual truth is diminished. Hegel, Taine's inspirer, felt that the historian should tell the story of "what happened and how it happened, lending neither poetic significance nor poetic form to the facts."[12] The historian is better off giving up all pretensions to literariness, all passion. But the point is to choose a style, even if this style seems not to obscure the facts, to be the style in which *verba* are transparent or reflect the *res* like a mirror. Rhetoric, which seemed excluded, comes back in through the main door as stylistic simplicity. Thus Taine was enthusiastic about the style of Xenophon, to whom he devoted not only a number of pages at the end of his *Essai*, but also an entire essay in 1856. Xenophon was never subjective, he never tried to be the subject of his narration; he did not make any "general remarks" that might reveal his opinion of events. He offered

11. See Roland Barthes, "Le discours de l'histoire," *Le Bruissement de la langue. Essais critiques 4* (Paris: Seuil, 1984), 164. See also the essay "L'effet de réel," *Le Bruissement de la langue*, 167–74. On the theme of history and rhetoric see Hayden White, *Tropic of Discourse. Essays in Cultural Criticism* (Baltimore: The Johns Hopkins University Press, 1978).

12. Hegel, *Poétique*, translated by Charles Bénard, (Paris: Joubert, 1855), 14. Bénard was Taine's professor at the Collège Bourbon, and had introduced him to the reading of Hegel before he entered the *Ecole normale*.

to the reader "only facts, shown with equal naïveté and concision."[13] In the *Essai,* Taine judged Xenophon's narrative to be perfect, since it was "neither embellished with ornaments nor agitated by oratorical passions, nor formulated as praise" (338). In the 1856 article he admired the lack of figures, turns of phrase, and "everything that can be called invention."[14] But Taine himself could not resist falling into the trap of rhetoric. A war with tropes, Hugo's "guerre aux tropes," cannot be declared without tropes. Having expressed his distrust of figures and his admiration for Xenophon's severe and stripped language, Taine represents the clarity of discourse with an image. The Greek historian's language can be expressed "with an image," he explains: "one should compare it to water at the source of a stream, still, pure, light, and clear."[15]

But positivism is obsessed with the evidence proved by facts. Taine wants facts alone to speak, as they do in Guizot's *Histoire de la révolution d'Angleterre.* In another article of 1856 Taine emphasized the coldness of Guizot's style and his liking for quantitative history: "only circumstantial, naked facts express quantity."[16] Taine greatly admired the coherent ethic of the austere historian of England's revolution who went so far as to minimize even the passion of certain documents and anecdotes by deleting striking adjectives and expressions from the texts of the period under study:

> Together with his curiosity, he [Guizot] suppressed his own passion. He has but one tone and one style. Always cold and austere, it seems that he withdraws from history and looks at events from above, without feeling them. He banishes expressive words, violent indictments, eager praises, sharp banter. He does not penetrate into human souls, he does not take part in joys, sorrows, fierce hatred, enthusiastic devotions, feelings. He does not commit himself, he is not an artist: when Cromwell passes through Ireland, he marks the number and type of massacred people, and that's all.[17]

Guizot went straight to the object of his book, the English revolution and its political history. He was, in Taine's words, always "master of his subject," as a man of science is master of his experiments.

---

13. Taine, "Xénophon," *Essais de critique et d'histoire,* 152.
14. Ibid.
15. Ibid., 152.
16. Taine, "M. Guizot," *Essais de critique et d'histoire,* 134.
17. Taine, ibid., 135.

Even better, he came close to the essence of facts, to actions as they were taking place: "Macaulay writes about events like an orator, pleading his cause. M. Guizot writes about events like a statesman, as they are enacted [*comme on les fait*]."[18] The literary quality of historical narrative is an ornament, a luxury. This idea has continued to define history into the twentieth century: it became the institutional conception that defines the limits of the discipline. Fustel de Coulanges affirmed, as mentioned above, that history "is and must be a science" whose object is man: "It does not consist in pleasurable narration or in profound discourse. It consists, like any science, in the notation of facts, in their analysis, comparison, and interconnection."[19] In 1911, Henry Berr, the founder of the *Revue de synthèse*, did not hesitate to declare: "History is one of many ways of seeking truth: it is not a literary genre."[20] The idea that the critic and the historian should give up literary quality was one of Lanson's favorite arguments: literary history had to be based only on the true, renouncing the beautiful.[21]

But Taine does not go so far as Guizot, however much he admires the latter's sobriety. Taine does not advocate history as a pure science, and that is not only the result of an institutional compromise. Taine expresses the moment at which history and rhetoric, or history and literature, start to be separated within a critical discourse, but have not yet taken on the distinctness of two disciplines within an academic institution. In the midst of all his personal problems and movements among institutions, he is the thermometer indicating a critical temperature. With all his oscillations between the moderns and the ancients, between rhetoric and logic, between art and science, he represents critical consciousness before its institutional integration.

In this sense, Taine is close to Barthes's position in the twentieth century, as one of the founders of structuralism in France. Barthes's criticism was attacked by the Sorbonne, by the institution that has become a bastion of literary history: as is well known, the Sorbonnard, Raymond Picard, called Barthes's critical enterprise, which is

18. Ibid., 144.

19. Fustel de Coulanges, "Une leçon d'ouverture et quelques fragments inédits," *Revue de synthèse* 6 (May–June 1901): 3.

20. Henri Berr, *La Synthèse en histoire* (Paris: Albin Michel, 1953), 226.

21. See Gustave Lanson, "Introduction" to Sainte-Beuve's *Causeries du lundi* (Paris: Garnier Frères, 1909), 46.

informed by linguistics and semiology, *Nouvelle critique, nouvelle imposture.* But there is another reason why we can associate Barthes and Taine. Taine, the modernist, fought against rhetoric, but ended up being the most rhetorical historian of the second half of the nineteenth century. After having fought for critical modernism, at the very moment that the French state recognized the new science of semiology and created, in 1978, a chair of semiology for Barthes at the Collège de France, Barthes pronounced and wrote a very unexpected *Leçon* that embodies the sadness produced by a liberal world capable of absorbing or integrating everything. There he talked about the necessity of abjuring, of passing through intellectual conversions, in order to escape to some extent the pervasiveness of power and its ability to recuperate everything in its institutions. In a liberal society, power embraces subversive instances. His inaugural lecture at the Collège de France has Barthes no longer defining semiology in the dry jargon of linguistics, but in the language of nostalgia. What he mourned was the loss caused by time: things, ideas, people, movements change and lose their freshness. A subversive thinking becomes discipline, institution: literary semiology is now recognized by schools and universities. Therefore, Barthes does not want to call it the science of literature, as he did in the sixties; instead he redefines it as a journey in the deserted land of literature.[22] Barthes's semiology becomes then the swan's song of literature in a world where there is little space for literature.

I do not mean to establish an exact parallel between Taine in the nineteenth century and Barthes in the twentieth century (moreover, all of Taine's texts with which I dealt were early works, while *Leçon* is a text of the later Barthes). I only aim to indicate the ambiguity between the modern and the classical, between a theoretical project and an internal, almost hidden desire. Taine's modernism ends at the moment when he reestablishes rhetorical strategies in the heart of the notion of fact. Barthes's modernism crumbles when he feels nostalgia for the death of literature in our pragmatic society. Taine was more affected by classical rhetoric than Abel Villemain; Barthes is more in love with literature than the Sorbonnards defending literary history. Baudelaire, the poet par excellence of modern life, started one of his most powerful poems of the metropolitan landscape, "Le Cygne," with the exclamation: "Andromaque, je pense à vous." Texts,

22. See Roland Barthes, *Leçon* (Paris: Seuil, 1978), 40–41.

institutions, authors, movements, disciplines: they all swarm with decisions, provocations, big fights, small betrayals, irremediable and wonderful contradictions.

The contradiction between a gesture and a desire is continually at work. Does Taine really admire Guizot so completely? An unexpected remark drops almost inadvertently off his pen just after he praises the sober historian of the English revolution for marking only the number and type of people massacred by Cromwell in Ireland, and undermines his tough recommendation of historical severity and objectivity: "*Pourtant quels beaux massacres!*" [But what beautiful massacres!]

The desire for art, for a beautiful picture is there, wrapped in all the positivist ideology of facts. It is as if Taine were telling us that facts can only strike us when their history is well written. Taine concluded his *Essai* with a rehabilitation of Livy:

> The moderns give too much to science and to specific details; Livy gives too much to art and to general features. But in this exchange of teachings, Livy, thanks to his eloquence, gives the most. Because the essence of eloquence is to reproduce human passions in a perfect style. Passions, since they constitute the causes of events, are the very substance of history. We tend to forget it too often today: questions of finance, strategy, politics, administrations, details of dogma, philosophy, arts, science, all features must be included in the picture of human life, of human passions. And the real object of history is the soul. But a picture of passions, without perfect expression, is false or cold. In order to be a historian, one has therefore to be a great writer. [359–60]

The conclusion is more than a bow in the direction of the classical Academy. It represents Taine's divided position as he stood torn between two cultures that he wished to unify—the modern and the ancient, the literary and the scientific. In spite of his devotion to facts and the programmatic character of his *Essai*, Taine believes also that history is a literary genre that chooses human events as the argument of its fiction. Taine does not treat history from the perspective of a historian, but as a literary critic.

At the beginning of the second half of the nineteenth century, Taine's *Essai*, together with the group of articles quoted above, constituted a text challenging some institutional constraints, opening the way to the positivist division between literature and history, at the same time as it also inaugurated a critique of the positivist notion of fact. Taine wanted to found a new history and literary criticism that would get rid of both the rhetorical education coming from the French system, and the romantic vein coming from his own intellectual formation. This could be done by insistently talking about science. The famous 1858 preface to the *Essais de critique et d'histoire*, where he collected the above mentioned articles on Michelet, Guizot, and Xenophon, and that proved so important for Emile Zola's founding of his naturalist school, is nothing but a summary of the main themes of the *Essai*. It takes the same prescriptive, sharp tone as the *Essai:* "The aim of history is not to draw in the multitude of details . . . , but to reach the master force, to lock it up in a formula for every century."[23] The preface also ends, as does the *Essai*, with the praise of art. Behind Taine's scientific method, behind the chain of causes and effects, can be heard "that invisible choir, mentioned by the old poets, that circulates through all things and through which the eternal universe throbs." These are the traces of Taine's past culture that will function in resistance to his own positivistic ideology and to the later institutionalization of positivism. Lanson, the father of literary history, who represents this institutionalized position, could not accept Taine's *Histoire de la littérature anglaise* as a work of literary history: he claimed that it was written with too much stylistic concern, and mixed together the works of poets, writers, historians, and philosophers.

When Taine becomes a historian—like Renan after the Commune, to help save the country from what the former called the horror of revolutions—he is perceived in the way he himself perceived Livy and Michelet. In 1885 Ferdinand Brunetière reviewed his *Origines de la France contemporaine* (the volume on the French Revolution): "The nature of M. Taine explains, and does not justify, but at least softens his excessive partiality. M. Taine's talent is altogether ingenuous and violent; ingenuousness forms its basis, violence its master quality: M. Taine therefore has very intense impressions and his manner of conveying them exaggerates their intensity."[24]

23. Taine, "Préface de la Ie édition," *Essais de critique et d'histoire*, 9.
24. Brunetière, "Un historien de la Révolution Française," *Revue des Deux-Mondes*, (15 September 1885): 393.

III. Reading Legacies

BARBARA SPACKMAN

Machiavelli and Maxims

No text can be read without taking into consideration the layers of interpretations it has engendered, but Machiavelli's *Prince* is a lesson to the critic who would attempt a reading of a text in its "original" purity. From a single seed, planted on different soil, have grown various forms of Machiavellism and antimachiavellism, monarchist readings and populist ones, reactionary interpretations and Marxian rewritings. For Jean-Jacques Rousseau, *The Prince* was the republican's manual; for Antonio Gramsci, the blueprint for the modern political party. For Leo Strauss, *The Prince* was the work of an evil man; for Innocent Gentillet, that of the devil. Intuitively, one might attribute such long-lived radiation to the explosive content of the text itself, to a "truth" unveiled. Yet while it would be foolish to deny that *The Prince* touches upon "something essential," none of the "truths" that might be drawn from the text seems adequate to explain its unique status, especially at such a historical distance.[1] As the first voice to have proclaimed the autonomy of politics from ethics, Machiavelli has surely earned an honored place in the history of thought, but does this in itself cause continuing controversy? Does the scandal of bringing private practices to public notice spark ever new readings? Or does the text's volatility lie perhaps in some formal characteristic

1. Typical is Claude Lefort's response to this inevitable problem: "in order to justify our research, it will suffice to recall that no work has ever captured an audience's attention for such a long period of time, elicited such varied and extensive commentaries, or even found itself at the origin of a mythical representation, without touching upon something essential." Claude Lefort, *Le Travail et l'oeuvre: Machiavel* (Paris: Gallimard, 1972), 315. My translation.

YFS 77, *Reading the Archive: On Texts and Institutions*, ed. E. S. Burt and Janie Vanpée, © 1990 by Yale University.

of the text itself? I would like to suggest that, rather than originating in the text's themes or in its presumed analytic rigor, the peculiar openness of *The Prince* is an effect of a particular rhetorical form, the maxim, and of a particular rhetorical trope, irony.[2] Readers of *The Prince* have been both inscribed in, and expelled from, Machiavelli's text by the redefinitions of terms effected by the maxim, and by the discursive doubleness of irony.

The "maximatic" approach is not unproblematic, for it is drawn from the antimachiavellian tradition. Already in 1576 a voluminous countertext to Machiavelli was published in which the category of maxim is employed as organizing principle and focus of attack: *Discours sur les moyens de bien gouverner et maintenir en bonne paix un Royaume ou autre Principauté: Contre Nicolas Machiavel Florentin*. There, Innocent Gentillet draws upon both *The Prince* and *The Discourses* to extract fifty of the *sententiae* most offensive to his Calvinist orthodoxy, his opposition to the French Catholic court, and the Italian presence in France—most pointedly, the presence of Catherine de' Medici, then queen mother.[3] These maxims (and more than a few are either not to be found in Machiavelli's texts or are malevolent distortions) are used as titles for Gentillet's own impassioned chapters. His specific counterarguments are more interesting for the history of antimachiavellism than for an analysis of Machiavelli's maximatic discourse, for by 1576 we are dealing with a response to Machiavellism, or to what Gentillet perceives as such, in a France ruled by an Italian and torn by power struggles between Protestants and Catholics. But Gentillet's opening criticisms of the use of the maxim as a rhetorical strategy are remarkably shrewd, and will serve as an organizing principle for my own discussion.

It is the maxim's claim to universality, its absolute and transhistorical pretension that most disturbs Gentillet, and appears to him to need most urgent debunking. "General rules" may occasionally be expedient in political theorizing, but Gentillet cannot grant them the status of eternal truths; to argue against maxims is to argue that history is change:

> For the circumstances, implications, consequences, and antecedents
> of each particular case are most often completely different and op-

2. I am indebted to John Freccero for the suggestion that the study of the maxim might illuminate Machiavelli's text.

3. For a lucid account of the historical situation, see Antonio d'Andrea's article "The Political and Ideological Context of Innocent Gentillet's *Anti-Machiavel*" in *Renaissance Quarterly* 23, no. 4 (Winter 1970): 397–411.

posite, in such a way that however much two cases may be similar, they must not therefore be conducted and determined according to the same rule or Maxim, on account of the diversity of accessory facts. And in fact, experience teaches us that what is good in one time is not so in another, and what is appropriate for some nations is not so for others, and so on for other circumstances.[4]

In a broad sense, this is a predictable enough denial of Machiavelli's explicit claim in both *The Prince* and *The Discourses* that human nature and political dynamics have not changed so greatly since Classical Antiquity that general truths might not be drawn from history. It is, as well, an assertion of the nonapplicability of Italian models to the French situation. Yet Gentillet's comment also implies that the maxim, as a form, is improper to historical discourse. In one section of this essay, I will examine the syntactic and grammatical characteristics that define the maxim and give it its transcendent force.

A second section will elaborate upon a rather offhand and typically venomous comment in which Gentillet refers to *The Prince* as the Koran for French courtiers—Koran, of course, because Gentillet, himself embroiled in a political dispute where religious matters were of central ideological importance, never tires of berating Machiavelli for his lack of piety nor of referring to him as the "Italian atheist." This epithet (as well as Machiavelli's Anglo-Saxon nickname, "Old Nick," the devil incarnate) might be shorthand for several elements of interest: *The Prince* comes to be equated with an anti-Bible, a guide to an antimorality. Putting equal emphasis on both the prefix "anti" and the formal characterization of the text as "manual," we may move in two directions: toward the idea of *The Prince* as a handbook of strategies for acquiring and maintaining power and secondly, toward an analysis of maximatic discourse as a rhetoric of negation, directing new movements on an older field—whether of battle or of semantics—of political praxis. What is striking about this particular manual is not only the absence of detailed manoeuvres by which an overall strategy might be executed, but also that the text does not, by a most conspicuous absence, indicate univocally the agent who should carry out a strategy. As a rhetorical form, the maxim both lends itself to appropriation by, and at the same time creates, an "absent subject."[5]

4. Innocent Gentillet, *Discours contre Machiavel*, ed. A. D'Andrea and P. D. Stewart (Florence: Casalini, 1974), 10. All references will henceforth appear in the text.

5. This absence has been incisively noted by Michael McCanles: "The prince never *is* this or that, he *uses* this or that quality, or rather he has this or that quality

Gentillet's third criticism alludes to an area that is a consequence of the aforementioned ones. Gentillet questions fleetingly the relation of the proffered examples to the maxims that presumably illustrate, support or prove: "the Maxims and general rules of the art of politics . . . are nevertheless not as certain as the Maxims of Mathematicians; rather, they are rules that would be very dangerous if one were not to accommodate them to, and make them serve current matters, rather than accommodating matters to such Maxims and rules" (Gentillet, 9–10). Here we can take Gentillet quite seriously: does the text prove, exemplify, illustrate, or even contradict the *sententiae* that it surrounds? What sort of accommodation is at work between maxim and "example"? The third section of this essay examines the relation of example to maxim, and proposes that the relation between maxim and example is, particularly in the case of Cesare Borgia, an ironic one.

FROM ABSOLUTENESS TO TIMELINESS

Because Machiavelli's maximatic discourse has been the site of controversy, it is worthwhile to define the constraints that mold those pithy statements that we recognize as maxims and to see to what extent they may apply to Machiavelli's text. Commonsensical descriptions seem to emphasize their lapidary quality: maxims are "gem-like," well-honed, have a particular "ring" or resonance.[6] Descriptions that aim toward more rigid criteria seem to concur on two main characteristics: the maxim announces a universally applicable statement describing a rule of morality or conduct, and appears in didactic discourse.[7] Grammatically, the subject of the sentence is

---

predicated of him by others: a discourse that is full of predicates but lacks a subject, a substantive person. A void at the center of *Il Principe* marks the absence of the prince himself. . . . The prince exists only to the extent that he is the grammatical subject of sentences that are uttered and written about him." McCanles, *The Discourse of Il Principe* (Malibu: Undena Publications, 1983), 106. This excellent study includes McCanles's earlier article "Machiavelli's *Principe* and the Textualization of History," *MLN Italian Issue* 97, no. 1 (1982): 1–18.

6. Mary Zeller's lengthy introduction to her dissertation, *New Aspects of Style in the Maxims of La Rochefoucauld* (Washington D. C.: The Catholic University Press, 1954), provides an extensively footnoted catalog of such impressionistic descriptions and attempts to distinguish the maxim from related forms such as aphorism, apothegm, proverb, etc.

7. Most of the available literature on maxims, even as a general linguistic form, either draws upon or directly concerns *Les Maximes* of La Rochefoucauld. In my

frequently "humanity," an abstract noun or moral quality, or the sort of "absent subject" provided by the impersonal *on* in French or the *si* in Italian. The generality of such statements leaves interpretation and application open to discussion. The didactic aspect of maximatic discourse is realized in several ways in *The Prince:* grammatically, by the use of the modal and exhortative verb "ought to" [*dovere*], so that the greater number of *sententiae* seem to pattern themselves on the following construction: "one should never [*non si debbe mai*] allow chaos to develop in order to avoid going to war, because one does not avoid a war but instead puts it off to his disadvantage" (87).[8] Such didactic intent is corroborated by the narrator-reader relation which, as an effect of such discourse, becomes that of teacher-student, giving a rather ironic twist to the power relations obtaining between the exiled Machiavelli and the supposed addresses of *The Prince,* the ruling Medici. Machiavelli, as narrator, claims a privileged Archimedean point from which absolute statements are possible when, in his dedication to Lorenzo, he asserts that, "to know well the nature of the people one must be a prince, and to know well the nature of princes one must be of the people" (78). Machiavelli, who presumably knows well both natures, is in neither camp. Though in the subsequent phrase the narrator humbly reassumes his position in "these lowlands" in order to exalt Lorenzo (and perhaps to identify himself politically with the people), his claim is clearly to omniscience.

A corollary distinctive feature of the maxim is that its main verb is almost always in the durative present tense, in a present tense that summarizes and absorbs the past and excludes the possibility of a future differing qualitatively from the present. Philip Lewis has aptly written that this present tense marks "not the discontinuous character of experience, but the continuity of permanence; not the fullness of presence but the emptiness of absence" (Lewis, 20). This "emptiness of absence" seems to be one of the qualities of these

---

discussion of maxims, I draw upon two of these studies, as well as upon Aristotle's remarks in *The Rhetoric:* Serge Meleuc's "Structure de la maxime" in *Langages* (March 1969): 69–98, and Philip Lewis, *La Rochefoucauld: The Art of Abstraction* (Ithaca: Cornell University Press, 1977). Page numbers will be cited in the text.

8. Translations of both *The Prince* and *The Discourses* have been drawn from Peter Bondanella and Mark Musa, ed. and trans., *The Portable Machiavelli* (New York: Penguin, 1979). Page numbers will be cited in the text. I have slightly modified several of the translations in order to render them more literal, and have included, when necessary, the original Italian as it appears in Niccolò Machiavelli, *Il Principe,* in *Opere,* ed. Ezio Raimondi (Milan: Mursia, 1969).

sententiae that allows us (or Gentillet) to pillage texts from them, to lift them from their context and "fill" them by placing them in new frames. Always true, even banally so, they are never specific. A part of their nonspecificity is attributable, according to Serge Meleuc, to the absence of adverbial modifiers (especially adverbs of time) that would transform the maxim into a reflection, a judgment qualified by details that would cancel the maxim's fundamentally transhistorical character. When adverbs do appear, they simply underscore this latter quality (*always, never, everywhere*); nor are modifying adjectives included except to indicate an entire class of agents. Machiavelli's pronouncements on human nature typically assume such a form: "And men in general [*in universali*] judge more by their eyes than their hands; for everyone can see but few can feel [*sentire*]" (135). Indeed, the absence of modifiers is here underscored by the presence of "in universali." We might say that adverbial and adjectival modifiers are added only when the maxim is put into practice; otherwise, as Lewis suggests, the maxim seems to have not only a deliberately cryptic quality and enigmatic effect, but "a real conceptual obscurity can be glimpsed in 'umbrella words' or in '*mots-mana*,' in abstract notions such as interest or vanity that include or explain so much they verge on equivocation" (Lewis, 39). The shiftiness of the terms "virtue" [*virtù*] and "fortune" [*fortuna*], of the "prince" and the "people," would seem to fit this description of "umbrella words," as does the Machiavellian elaboration of the Ciceronian metaphor of the lion and the fox. Though the metaphorical status of the terms lion and fox, wolf and traps, adds a second order of difficulty, the statement that "it is therefore necessary to be a fox in order to recognize the traps and a lion in order to frighten the wolves" (134) seems to exemplify the conceptual obscurity of which Lewis speaks. Indeed, history has passed its time filling in the space beneath the "umbrella" with glosses of this last maxim, from Shakespeare to Gramsci.

Both Mary Zeller in *New Aspects of Style in the Maxims of La Rochefoucauld* and Meleuc in his generative grammar analysis point out that the structure of the maxim is typically bipolar, and juxtaposes or equates two members so that "surface structure" may appear as an antithesis, as a juxtaposition (A Machiavellian example: "Everyone sees what you seem to be, few perceive what you are," 135), or as a syntactic or lexical inversion, especially as an inversion utilizing active and passive forms of the same verb. This last construction is well-exploited by Machiavelli in his definition of social classes: the two classes hold desire in common, but their desires are at odds and are expressed by a play on the active/passive use of "to command" and "to oppress": "the people do not wish to be commanded or oppressed by the nobles, and the nobles desire to command and to oppress the people" (107). Indeed, while Federico Chabod and Fredi Chiappelli might have applied the term "structure of dilemma" [*struttura dilemmatica*] to many of the preceding examples, it is increasingly clear not only that their rhetorical complexity exceeds the use of diaeresis, but also that analytic rigor is subordinated to their rhetorical form.[9] The above example of inversion is in fact a chiastic reversal. The form itself appears to have a symbolic function: this sort of digital on-or-off construction would seem to be an attempt to eliminate any grey area of indecision between two poles, or at least to diminish its importance. The juxtaposition of two absolute alternatives rhetorically excludes the validity of a middle way of circuitous reasoning, and, as Chabod suggests, is implemented as an affront to the "middle way" followed by Florentine politicians with, for Machiavelli, disastrous results.[10] In terms of symbolic action, then, the choice of maximatic discourse can be seen as the critical and corrective response to Florence's temporizing politics. We might go even farther and suggest that its binary structure creates a rhetoric of crisis by limiting choice to two alternatives, one of which is clearly unacceptable.[11]

In the chapter on conspiracy in the third book of *The Discourses*, we find a passage that could serve as a metamaxim concerning the strategic necessity for this sort of absolutism: "Let me say, then, that nothing disturbs or impedes the actions of men more than to have to change a plan quickly, without sufficient time, and to modify it from what had been planned earlier. And if change creates confusion in

9. See Federico Chabod, *Scritti su Machiavelli* (Turin: Einaudi, 1964), Fredi Chiappelli's *Studi sul linguaggio del Machiavelli* (Florence: Le Monnier, 1952), *Nuovi studi sul linguaggio del Machiavelli* (Florence: Le Monnier, 1969), and *Machiavelli e la lingua fiorentina* (Bologna: Massimiliano Boni, 1974). On the "scientificity" of Machiavelli's style, see also Rafaello Ramat, *Per la storia dello stile rinascimentale* (Messina: G. D'Anna, 1953), especially 117, as well as Mario Pozzi, *Lingua e cultura del Cinquecento: Dolce, Aretino, Machiavelli, Guicciardini, Sarpi, Borghini* (Padua: Liviana, 1975).

10. See Chabod's remarks on Machiavelli's "procedure of dilemma" [*procedere dilemmatico*] in "Metodo e stile di Machiavelli" in *Scritti su Machiavelli*, 372–73.

11. See Jacques Derrida's brief article, "Economies de la crise," *La Quinzaine littéraire* 399 (August 1983): 4–5, for a discussion of the relation of "a binary situation" to the rhetoric of crisis.

anything, it does so especially in matters of war and in things similar to those of which we are speaking" (369). Here a need for "absoluteness" is brought together with the *moment* of political action, with the crucial moment. For Machiavelli, politics concerns not only the acquisition and maintenance of power, but above all a shrewd sense of the right moment to seize that power. In *The Prince* the topos of "timeliness" is all important: it is only a sense of timeliness that brings together "virtù" and "fortuna" and opens up the possibility of effective action. The final *exhortatio* of *The Prince* is, indeed, a demonstration and enactment of this topos that appears throughout the text and is, finally, amplified as the narrator announces that the moment is ripe for the implementation of a program that has been sketched in maximatic form. The maxim becomes a command to act when a deictic adjective is added: "One must not therefore allow *this* opportunity to pass by" (165, my emphasis). If action is not taken, the alternative is clear and despicable: remain in "this barbarian dominion" (166). "He who hesitates, fails" might be extrapolated as the underlying maxim. If we can encapsulate the contemporaneous political rhetoric in the commonplace "to put time on your side" [*godere el beneficio del tempo*], as does Machiavelli himself, then the very form of the maxim in *The Prince* seems designed to combat that rhetoric, for that form creates a crisis by transforming the maxim as abstract rule into the maxim as command. The final chapter is but the staging of the crisis implicit in the binary form of the maxim.

THE KORAN FOR COURTIERS

Having outlined the grammatical characteristics of the maxim, we may move on to examine its more properly rhetorical function. Indeed, Serge Meleuc suggests that maximatic discourse often functions as a rhetoric of negation insofar as it responds to a preestablished code (and often exhibits that preexistent code within itself) in order to redefine its configurations. The preestablished code is the material upon which the maxim works, so that a former antithesis may be transformed into an identity, or a former identity split to become an antithesis in the "new" code. This metalinguistic function of the maxim seems of particular interest, and it may be useful to illustrate it with Meleuc's own example from *Les Maximes* of La Rochefoucauld: "Poverty is not a vice." This maxim refers us to an ideologically weighted code in which poverty is synonymous with vice, thereby implying a corollary identity of wealth with virtue. La Rochefoucauld's maxim emits a semiotic judgment on the relations obtaining in the presumed code of the reader, rearranges the interpretants and shifts the ideological weight. It is this paradoxical move that best characterizes both *Les Maximes* of La Rochefoucauld and maxims as a general category.[12] It is hardly surprising that we should discover a similar rhetoric of negation in the text like *The Prince* in which the topos of paradox, of speech against the *doxa,* is so prevalent, and employed in an aggressive and sometimes brutal form. The move of redefinition associated with the maxim is employed in less explicit form in Machiavelli's text than in that of La Rochefoucauld, and yet is the source of the many transformations worked upon previous categories of political and ethical theorizing. We have already cited one exemplary maxim: "one should never allow chaos to develop in order to avoid going to war [*per fuggire una guerra*], because one does not avoid a war but instead puts it off [*si differisce*] to his disadvantage" (87). "Fuggire" is here redefined so that the very possibility of avoiding a war is cancelled by the new interpretant assigned the word: "to put off or to defer." Again, in the discussion of "generosity and miserliness," traditional categories initially presented as opposites, Machiavelli transmutes one verb into the other:

> A prince, therefore, unable to use this virtue of generosity [*questa virtù del liberale*] in a manner which will not harm himself if he is known for it, should, if he is wise, not worry about being called a miser, for with time he will come to be considered more generous [*sempre più liberale*]. [128]

Machiavelli's double perspective allows the two terms to coexist in an unprecedented way: the prince may be miserly, but will be held to be "generous," indeed *because* he is miserly, he will be considered generous. No longer antithetical, generosity and miserliness are now a single term viewed from different points in space and time. The relation between them is not one of opposition but, linked together temporally ("with time"), of cause and effect.[13]

This strategy is repeated in the chapter "On Cruelty and Mercy"

---

12. See Meleuc, 96.

13. McCanles masterfully analyzes the entire passage on generosity and miserliness and notes the dialectical process whereby "we have signs that gradually shift into their opposites, and do so as reciprocal functions of each other." McCanles, 108–09.

[*De crudelitate et pietate*]; cruelty can have compassionate results as in the case of Cesare Borgia, while compassion can have cruel results, as in the case of the Florentine people whose compassion caused the destruction of Pistoia: "Therefore, a prince must not worry about the reproach of cruelty when it is a matter of keeping his subjects united and loyal; for with a very few examples of cruelty he will be more compassionate [*piestoso*] than those who, out of excessive compassion [*per troppa pietà*] permit disorders to continue" (130). The two "antithetical" terms now coexist as cause and effect. Machiavelli himself underscores this strategy when he asks if it is better to be loved than feared: "I reply that one should like to be both one and the other; but since it is difficult to join them together [*accozzarli insieme*], it is much safer to be feared rather than loved when one of the two must be lacking" (131). "To join them together" is precisely the strategy adopted to redefine terms in *Il Principe*. Here the difficulty encountered is overcome by means of the move of redefinition seen in the case of "fuggire": "A prince must nevertheless make himself feared in such a manner that he will avoid hatred, even if he does not acquire love; since to be feared and not to be hated can very well be combined" (131–32). The question of "being loved" has been replaced by that of "avoiding hatred."

Surely the most striking transformation of a former, classically established antithesis into a quasi-identity in *The Prince* is worked upon the pair "virtù"-"fortuna" in order to minimize drastically the importance of fortune. There is no maxim in *The Prince* that states "fortune is nothing other than a lack of virtue," and yet the rhetorical structures of the text itself encourage and support the formulation of such a maxim. Already in Chapter 6 fortune undergoes a reduction in status:

> And examining their deeds and their lives, one can see that they received nothing but the opportunity [*la occasione*] from Fortune [*fortuna*], which then gave them the material they could mold into whatever form they desired; and without that opportunity [*occasione*] the strength of their spirit [*la virtù dello animo loro*] would have been extinguished, and without that strength [*virtù*] the opportunity would have come in vain. [93]

Fortune is first reduced to "occasione," (a term that carries its own history of figuration as fortune's young companion); then an interdependence between "virtù" and "occasione" is established such that the two exist in dialectical relation to one another.[14] Were the reduction of fortune to end here, then we could agree with Michael McCanles that "virtù" and "fortuna" are bound together by analytic implication. But the relation of "virtù" and "fortuna" is immediately reformulated in Chapter 7 where it seems that "fortuna" has been restored to its traditional status of autonomous force. At the beginning of Chapter 7, Machiavelli can find no cause for blame in Cesare Borgia's failure for "if he did not succeed in his plans, it was not his fault but was instead the result of an extraordinary and extreme instance of ill fortune" [estrema malignità di fortuna] (97). This statement appears to be contradicted by the conclusion of the chapter, a contradiction considered by some critics to be yet another of Machiavelli's inconsistencies.[15] For after repeating his assertion that no blame can be laid upon Borgia, Machiavelli attributes his downfall not to "fortuna" but to Borgia's error, to his lack of foresight and hence to a failing in his "virtù": "One can only censure him for making Julius Pope; in this he made a bad choice. . . . The Duke then erred in this election, and it was the cause of his ultimate downfall" (102–03). Unable to make this puzzling inconsistency dialectical, McCanles dialogizes it and turns to the notion of free indirect discourse in The Prince: the opening appeal to "fortuna" would thus be Cesare's voice, Cesare's own rationalization of his failure, while the concluding judgement would be Machiavelli's own. Though this is an intriguing reading, there appears to be little justification for the introduction of the category of free indirect discourse into this chapter: no linguistic tags mark its appearance. What McCanles names, however, is a kind if discursive doubleness in the text that might instead be attributed to irony. If Chapter 6 witnesses the reduction of "fortuna" to "occasione," Chapter 7 ironically revives "fortuna" only to obliterate it entirely and does so precisely in the chapter that Garrett Mattingly has used as foundation for his argument that The Prince is not "political science" but "political satire."[16] If read ironically, the doubleness would be accounted for not by the presence of Cesare's voice

14. A useful catalog of the changing guises of fortuna and occasione is to be found in Hannah Fenichel Pitkin, Fortune is a Woman: Gender and Politics in the Thought of Niccolò Machiavelli (Berkeley: University of California Press, 1984), 138–69.

15. See, for example, Gennaro Sasso, "Coerenza o incoerenza del VII capitolo del Principe, La Cultura 10 (1972): 1–35, and McCanles, 73.

16. See Garrett Mattingly, "Machiavelli's Prince: Political Science or Political Satire," The American Scholar (Autumn 1958).

in the text, but by the movement of semiotic critique and redefinition associated with maximatic rhetoric. The dissonance between the opening and the conclusion of the chapter would thus be attributed to the redefinition of fortune. No longer a metaphor referring to an autonomous force outside the subject, fortune is redefined as that which is produced by an error of "virtù," as a metaphor for a lack. Fortune is, in other words, simply an excuse, an alibi, for the failed virtue of a subject.

The shift in the reference of the metaphor *fortuna* comes to a climax in Chapter 25 where two conflicting metaphors for fortune appear: that of the "ruinous river" and that of fortune as a woman.[17] But here again, rather than marking an inconsistency in Machiavelli's text, the dissonant metaphors appear to perform a relay of properties that deals the final blow to fortune. The violent destructiveness of the "ruinous river" is located above all in its "impetuousness": "everyone flees from them, everyone yields to their onslaught [*ognuno cede allo impeto loro*] unable to oppose them in any way" (159). Provision can be made to protect oneself against this violence so that "their impetus will not be either so disastrous or so damaging" (159) [*l'impeto loro non sarebbe nè sì licenzioso nè sì dannoso*] (63). So it is with fortune, which shows its power where there is no *virtù* to resist it, "she directs her impact [*e sua impeti*] where she knows that dikes and embankments are not constructed to hold her" (159). "Impetuousness" is the pivotal term, and at this point Machiavelli turns to a discussion of the various ways in which men conduct themselves: "one by caution [*con respetto*], another with impetuousness [*l'altro con impeto*]; one through violence, another with guile; one with patience, another with its opposite" (160). These qualities are quickly reduced to two, "respetto" and "impeto," and Pope Julius II is put forth as an example of one who "acted impetuously [*impetuosamente*] in all his affairs" (161) and "with his impetuous action" [*con la sua mossa impetuosa*] (161) succeeded in his aims, while "the cautious man" [*l'uomo respettivo*] inevitably fails. Machiavelli concludes: "I

17. This conflict is the subject of Pitkin's chapter on fortune. Her resolution of the "inconsistent shifting figures" of fortune is not only reductive but not even true on the most literal level: "The suggestion of this study, however, has been that they are, as a group, of central importance to Machiavelli's thought and that they are close to interchangeable because fundamentally they are all versions of a generalized feminine power against which men struggle." (Pitkin, 169). There is nothing specifically feminine about the river metaphor, and its implications are certainly different from those of fortune as a woman.

am certainly convinced of this: that it is better to be impetuous than cautious" (162). This (partial) conclusion seems logical enough, for both fortune and men appear to succeed insofar as they are "impetuous." But what of the relation between fortune and man's "virtù"? What will be the outcome of this clash of impetuous forces? The outcome is, figuratively speaking, the relay of "impetuousness" from "fortuna" to "virtù" as the *vir* behind "virtù" steps forth: "because Fortune is a woman, and it is necessary, in order to keep her down, to beat her and to struggle with her. And it is seen she more often allows herself to be taken by men who are impetuous than by those who make cold advances; and then, being a woman, she is always the friend of young men, for they are less cautious, more aggressive, and they command her with more audacity" (162). What was, in the beginning of the chapter, "disastrous impetuousness" of fortune has become the literally licentious impetuousness of "virtù." The juxtaposition of two conflicting metaphors for fortune, then, both effects a relay of properties and underscores the fact that "fortuna" is, first and foremost, a metaphor for lack or error of "virtù."

This "literary" turn is linked to the change in tone of the final *exhortatio*. We need not resort to chronological explanations nor to notions of "deterioration" to explain this change: Machiavelli is, in chapter 26, being Machiavellian in the pejorative sense (that is to say, using the fox) and simulating the five qualities befitting the prince: "all mercy, all faithfulness, all integrity, all kindness, all religion. And there is nothing more necessary than to seem to possess this last quality" (135).[18] Indeed, the unexpected use of theological language and Christian typology seems to be a demonstration of the prescribed persuasive technique: it is a simulation of the fullness of time. In the most "literary" chapter of The Prince, the ripe moment, "the oppor-

---

18. Thomas M. Greene suggests that the "desperate urgency" of the final chapter may be due to "deterioration of the writer's enterprise." The literariness of the chapter is thus an "admission that the book had begun by misrepresenting its own character and that it truly belongs to that flow of cultural production it had initially wanted to repudiate." See "The End of Discourse in Machiavelli's *Prince*," *Literary Theory/Renaissance Texts*, ed. Patricia Parker and David Quint (Baltimore: The Johns Hopkins University Press, 1986), 75–76. Greene seems to locate this repudiation in Machiavelli's opening denial that this text contains rhetorical flourishes, and thereby falls victim to the rhetoricity of antirhetoric. That is to say, Machiavelli's disavowal of rhetoric is itself rhetorical, and couched in language that flaunts that rhetoricity. For a discussion of the rhetoric of antirhetoric, see Paolo Valesio, *Novantiqua: Rhetorics as Contemporary Theory* (Bloomington: Indiana University Press, 1980), 42–60.

tunity", is offered as a literary topos, almost a fiction that must be believed in order to mobilize "virtù." "Fortuna" exists as literature that is instrumentalized to spur the prince (the people?) on to action, much as religion is described in the *Discourses* as a means to facilitate the introduction of arms.

A similar strategy of realigning antitheses seems to be employed with the terms "principe" and "populo." Again, though Machiavelli never formulated the maxim "the prince is nothing other than the people," the text encourages this formulation. If the prince exists in the eyes of his beholders (his "seeming" must be seen by someone), then the people play an all-important observer's role.[19] The interdependence of the two terms and resultant shiftiness in definition allows absolute monarchists and Marxist-Leninists to offer interpretations that are at odds with one another, and yet seem justified by the text. When read in relation to its own historical context, the referent to be assigned to the prince is even more problematic. The text is written around an essential absence, just as maxims create an absent subject: Italy has no monarch, and the text evokes the presence of "its redeemer" to fill the slot of agent of political action. Are we truly to believe that Machiavelli hoped the Medici, who had imprisoned and exiled him, would become that longed-for agent? Garrett Mattingly, a defender of the republican Machiavelli, thinks not, and remarks with refreshing candor:

> I suppose it is possible to imagine that a man who has seen his country enslaved, his life's work wrecked and his own career with it, and has, for good measure, been tortured within an inch of his life should thereupon go home and write a book intended to teach his enemies the proper way to maintain themselves, writing all the time, remember, with the passionless objectivity of a scientist in a laboratory. It must be possible to imagine such behavior, because Machiavelli scholars do imagine it and accept it without a visible tremor. But it is a little difficult for the ordinary mind to compass.[20]

While seemingly based upon a commonsensical notion of human nature, Mattingly's argument that *The Prince* should be read as a

19. See also Michael McCanles, "Machiavelli and the Paradoxes of Deterrence," *Diacritics* 14, no. 2 (1984): "People will respond to the power textualized in discourse only as long as they believe that such an entity as power distinct from discourse really exists, and remain ignorant that the prince, being always an emperor with no clothes on, becomes powerful only when they dress him in that power."
20. Mattingly, 485.

satire is also based upon textual evidence; indeed, he notes that "the number of times its princely reader is reminded . . . that his people will overthrow him at last is quite remarkable."[21] And yet if a collective group were to supply leadership and free Italy of foreign domination, where might Machiavelli have found such a group? Is it not too radical a reading to suggest that Machiavelli is advocating a popular uprising? Or, since we find ourselves once again puzzling over the final chapter, are we simply to accept the view that, in Felix Gilbert's words, the last chapter "cannot be regarded as the end for which the previous parts of the treatise were designed?"[22] Might we not say that Machiavelli is indirectly encouraging the Florentine people to mold their leader by expressing their assent or dissent to their leader's "semblance"? In that case, the movement of redefinition in Machiavelli's text would be so radical as to replace his opening title, *The Prince*, with a concluding title, *The People*.

"IT WOULD HAVE WORKED . . ."

I have suggested that the use of maximatic discourse, when considered as a rhetoric of negation, underscores the status of *The Prince* as the morality of antimorality. A sort of lay catechism, it serves as a substitute for an outmoded system of moral precepts and is the met-

21. Mattingly, 490. As Mattingly remarks, "To read the *Prince* as a satire not only clears up puzzles and resolves contradictions; it gives a new dimension and meaning to passages unremarkable before." Though McCanles cites Mattingly's well-known work on Renaissance diplomacy, he nowhere cites this article and seems unaware of it. Thus though he repeatedly remarks that Machiavelli appears "coolly ironic" (46), "sardonic" (51), and detects "keen irony" (52) and "mockery" (27), he does not arrive at Mattingly's conclusion and therefore must go to considerable lengths to account for some of the puzzles to which Mattingly refers. Mattingly reads Chapter 5 as bitter irony directed at the Medici who were indeed attempting to rule a former republic. McCanles instead notes that "such discourse is not illogical; it is only perverse" (28) and finally attributes the oddness of the chapter to Machiavelli's "pessimism" and concludes that: "the capacity of well-formed discourse to produce the bizarre paradoxes of Chapter Five is something inherent within all those restrictions, rules, and guidelines that supposedly keep human discourse rational and human actions therefore sane. The disruptions that human discourse and actions suffer do not come from outside itself; rather, they lie latent within the very rules of textual well-formedness that are intended to guard human discourse and human action against these disruptions" (28). McCanles's model for the text is a grammatical (as opposed to rhetorical) one, and thus contains the disruption that occurs in this chapter within logical categories, while Mattingly attributes that disruption to the rhetorical mode of the text, irony.

22. Felix Gilbert, *Machiavelli and Guicciardini: Politics and History in Sixteenth-Century Florence* (Princeton: Princeton University Press, 1965), 183.

alinguistic critique of a previous lexicon of commonplaces, both moral and political, in much the same way as Nietzsche's aphorisms (a rhetorical form related to the maxim) constitute a later counterphilosophy. However else we wish to read Machiavelli's claim to speak of the "effective truth of the matter," we must read it as a claim to speak a truer truth, as the substitution of a new *"dover essere"* for an outmoded one. Yet up to this point, we have been speaking of maxims as a form in isolation, as though we were dealing with La Rochefoucauld or even Guicciardini, neither of whom fills the white space between their maxims. Those of Machiavelli, however, occur in a text that presents itself as a meditation on history, that seems to be drawing examples from history and analyzing inductively from specific case to general principle. What, then, of the text that supports the *sententiae?*

In *The Rhetoric,* Aristotle divides maxims into two categories: those that state nothing that runs counter to common opinion and may consequently stand alone, and those that are paradoxical (against the *doxa*) and should therefore be followed by an example or some third member that would complete the enthymeme. The latter formulation would seem to describe Machiavelli's text. Gentillet's instincts were correct when he questioned the relation of maxim to example, though the thrust of his argument was misguided when he aimed to erode the maxim's "foundation" by reinterpreting its illustrations. The supporting text, in fact, seems more aptly characterized by Perelman and Olbrechts-Tyteca's description of illustration as a form that "increase(s) its presence to the consciousness," whereas examples are designed to *establish* a rule.[23] For Machiavelli is not arguing from example, inducing from particular case to particular case in order to arrive at generalizable truths. If that were so, it would be possible to argue with invalidating examples, as is Gentillet's strategy. Instead, the text surrounding the maxims is filled out with illustrations, dramatic enactments of stage directions, enactments that merely concretize an abstract rule. Such a reading concurs with that of Bàrberi Squarotti who, in *La forma tragica del Principe,* discusses the "gnomic structure" of Machiavelli's text and suggests that the *exempla* are necessary only insofar as absolute statements about human nature

---

23. Charles Perelman and L. Olbrechts-Tyteca, *The New Rhetoric: A Treatise on Argumentation* (Notre Dame: University of Notre Dame Press, 1969), 357.

may require explanation and elaboration in more concrete form.[24] Thus maxims appear as names for paradigms, rubrics under which are subsumed demonstrations drawn from a history that then becomes, Bàrberi Squarotti suggests, a pool of archetypes. While the most effective course in argument by example would be to use radically different examples, Machiavelli often offers illustrations that mirror each other. Bàrberi Squarotti notes that such is the case in Chapter 8 where, in illustration of the maxim "injuries should be inflicted all at the same time, for the less they are tasted, the less they offend; and benefits should be distributed a bit at a time in order that they may be savored fully" (107), Machiavelli discuss the histories of Agathocles the Sicilian and Oliverotto of Fermo. Both men are of lowly birth, both move through the ranks of the military to become heads of their respective armies, both by "wickedness" [sceleratezza] expand their power—and it is the same wickedness, for both collect their opponents in a single place, then withdraw to discuss matters of state (so they say), leaving their guests to be slaughtered. Both emerge in control of a city's government. In but one respect do they differ: Oliverotto's reign was less long-lived. Bàrberi Squarotti notes that this detail is rendered grammatically as a hypothetical construction, while the preceding specular narratives had been rendered in the indicative. The text reads" "His expulsion would have been as difficult as that of Agathocles if he had not permitted himself to be tricked by Cesare Borgia" (106). It is as though, when events fall short of adherence to the directions given by the maxim, the fault is in reality, in history itself. As long as the episode concurs with the maxim, the narrative moves along in the indicative, but when it encounters "deviant" events it moves into a hypothetical construction so that adequation might be possible. Again, when Machiavelli cites the examples of Hannibal and Scipio in *The Prince*, he does so with a slightly different emphasis than that of the *Discourses*. In the latter work, the similarity of the end result of Hannibal's and Scipio's actions is crucial to Machiavelli's argument that the end justifies the means. But in *The Prince* the two are used in illustration of another maxim: "it is much safer to be feared than to be loved," and Scipio is admonished for "his tolerant nature." Once more a hypothetical construction is used to fit the illustration to the maxim: "Such

24. Giorgio Bàrberi Squarotti, *La Forma tragica del Principe* (Florence: Olschki, 1966), 191–92.

a nature would have, in time, damaged Scipio's fame and glory if he had maintained it during the empire; but, living under the control of the senate, this harmful characteristic of his not only concealed itself but brought him fame" (133). In fact, some of the illustrations have been so tailored to suit the maxims that they are little more than the addition of a named agent, a named scene of action, and the past tense of the verb. Francesco Sforza, for example, is cited under the rubric "On New Principalities Acquired with the Arms and Fortunes of Others." Sforza appears as the counterexample to Cesare Borgia (to whom more extensive space is allotted) and the entire passage regarding him reads: "Francesco, through the required means and with a great deal of ingenuity (*virtù*), became Duke of Milan from his station as a private citizen, and that which he had acquired with a thousand efforts he maintained with little trouble" (96). No extraneous details are recounted, as though Sforza's name sufficed as a label for a series of actions toward which the text points but does not expose. We might say that the maxim here functions as a *fabula*, in the Russian Formalist sense of a skeletal series of terms that may or may not be fleshed out with elements of plot. Or we might consider them as titles, following Kenneth Burke's essay "What Are the Signs of What?", in which Burke suggests that language is a means of entitling, of "summing up the nonverbal context of the situation to which it is applied" in ever more abbreviated form until an overall god-term is reached.[25] Burke suggests that "details could be treated as the exfoliation in time of the eternal now that was contained in the rational seminality of the title." This "exfoliation" would describe both the relation of illustration to maxim in Machiavelli's text, and the trajectory through time along which *Il Principe* has passed.

This relation of "god-term" to illustration is, however, particular to the satirical pamphlet known as *The Prince*. Indeed, it is by analyzing this relation that the satirical edge suggested by Mattingly shines forth. In the most notorious Machiavellian example, that of Cesare Borgia, the hypothetical construction I have discussed above takes on the ironic coloring of a Dantean subtext: Guido da Montefeltro's "it would have worked" [*giovato sarebbe*] in Canto 27 of the *Inferno*. As John Freccero has pointed out, Guido da Montefeltro is a proto-Mach-

25. Kenneth Burke, "What Are the Signs of What?", *Language as Symbolic Action* (Berkeley: University of California Press, 1966), 370.

iavellian character, schooled in the ways of the fox.[26] In Guido's case, of course, it couldn't have worked: his mistake was to have believed that absolution could be given in advance for sins yet to be committed; he thought the favor of the pope could win him favor with God. But the pope's promise was faulty with respect to divine logic, and Guido lost his gamble. Cesare Borgia, too, relied upon the favor of a pope ("he would have quickly succeeded in this if Alexander had lived" [100]) and relied as well upon French troops for assistance. However he may have tried to correct his mistakes, that faulty premise was the cause of his ruin. "The contradiction that does not allow it" [la contradizion che nol consente], as Dante puts it in Canto 27 is, in Machiavelli's text, not in relation to God's word, but to a "god-term": the Machiavellian maxim that no one relying upon the arms and fortunes of others can succeed in maintaining power: "Such men depend solely upon two very uncertain and unstable things; the will and the fortune of him who granted them the state; they do not know how and are not able to maintain their position" (96). It is not that Borgia's case is an inadequate illustration, which would create an irony undercutting the validity of the maxim. Rather, the maxim stands intact, and the Dantesque irony is directed instead, as Mattingly suggests, toward Giuliano de' Medici, brother of a pope, and the Medici family who had reentered Florence with the aid of Spanish troops. The analogy is seductive: the future will reenact the past and the Medici, having begun from faulty premises will (Machiavelli seems to be saying) be with Guido and Cesare, muttering to themselves: "it would have worked."

---

26. John Freccero pointed out the connection between Canto 27 of the *Inferno* and Machiavelli's *Prince* in "Political Sexuality in Machiavelli," a lecture given at Northwestern University, November 1988.

JANIE VANPÉE

Rousseau's Emile ou de l'éducation: A Resistance to Reading

I know that your Council states in its replies that "according to the author's intention, *Emile* must serve as a guide to fathers and mothers:" but this statement is not excusable since I revealed in the preface and several times in the book a very different intention. This book is about a new educational system whose blueprint I offer to the scrutiny of the wise, and not about a method for fathers and mothers, which I never thought of. If at times, by way of a common enough figure of speech, I seem to speak to them directly, it is either to make myself better understood, or to express my thoughts in fewer words.

—J.-J. Rousseau, *Lettres écrites de la montagne*

Rousseau's masterpiece, *Emile ou de l'éducation*, gives priority to one of the most fundamental problems of all pedagogical discourses—the problem of transmission, and in particular, of their own transmission. What knowledge, skills, and traditions should be saved and passed on and by what criteria should they be selected; how should this transmission best be realized; and how should the means of transmission be themselves taught or handed down—these are the questions that Rousseau's work problematizes repeatedly. For example, the very foundation of Rousseau's pedagogical enterprise is predicated on the recognition of the failure of transmission between parent and child. His work begins as an attempt to mend or repair the break in the "natural" channels that exist between father and son, mother and child, and that society has disrupted. Rousseau's text is first of all a stopgap measure, an attempt to fill the breach and to keep some channel open through which a given legacy could be passed on in an education. Until a repair has been effected, questions such as what knowledge or traditions will be handed down, and by what means, are moot. But since such a repair is, at best, a substitute for the real channels between parent and child,

YFS 77, *Reading the Archive: On Texts and Institutions,* ed. E. S. Burt and Janie Vanpée, © 1990 by Yale University.

the text's second and true aim is to transfer its own function of transmitting back to those who had abdicated that responsibility, and thereby to restore the original and "natural" order of transmission.

The text conveys its pedagogical mission in at least two modes: as a story describing the process by which an orphaned child will be educated to take the place of both father and tutor and thus become the ideal pedagogue of his own offspring; and as a performative discourse enacting the very process it describes and implicating the reader as the agent by whose means its transmission proceeds. As is evident from this second mode, Rousseau's pedagogical discourse calls upon the reader's active involvement and participation in transmitting its mission. A glimpse at the history of *Emile*'s reception, however, reveals that most readers have ignored the effects this discourse on teaching produces on them and have thereby avoided the fundamental issues raised concerning their role in the transmission and mastery of teaching. Rather than attend to the performative dimension of the text, readers and critics have most often privileged its constative dimension, seeking to understand the knowledge and ideas it imparts in both its theory on education and its fictive narrative about an education.[1] They have read for the information and knowledge that Rousseau's pedagogy articulates, or to put it another way, for its meaning, and they have ignored the text's presentation of pedagogy as a complex polyphonic discourse between theory and narrative, master and pupil, text and reader, cognition and performance, description and prescription. By not taking into account the text's discursive presentation, indeed, by placing themselves in an "objective" position outside the field of tension where the different discursive modes converge, readers have remained untouched by the text's potential to teach them. It could be argued that the text's particular knowledge about the transmission of knowledge has failed to be transmitted and that, therefore, its pedagogical mission remains un-

---

1. See, for example, the following studies which focus on the pedagogical knowledge and information that Rousseau communicates in *Emile:* Jean Château, *Rousseau: Sa Philosophie de l'éducation* (Paris: J. Vrin, 1969); Peter D. Jimack, *La Genèse et rédaction de l'*Emile *de J.-J. Rousseau: Etude sur l'histoire de l'ouvrage jusqu'à sa parution,* in *Studies on Voltaire and the Eighteenth Century,* 23 (Geneva: Institut et Musée Voltaire, 1960); André Ravier, *L'Education de l'homme nouveau; Essai historique et critique sur le livre d'*Emile *de J.-J. Rousseau* (Lyon: M. and L. Riou, 1941); Francisque Vial, *La Doctrine de l'éducation de J.-J. Rousseau* (Paris: Delagrave, 1920). For a more complete pedagogical bibliography, see Pierre Chanover, "Rousseau: A Pedagogical Bibliography," *The French Review* 46, no. 6 (May 1973): 1148–58.

fulfilled. The controversial work that originally sparked violent debate has slipped instead into the quiet realm of history. Hence, today we tend to read *Emile* as a fundamental document in the history of pedagogy or of literature, to trace the sources and influences of Rousseau's pedagogical and literary ideas, to mark the work's place in his philosophy, or to situate it in the philosophical tradition of the period.[2] The work has been reduced to a cultural artifact, important to be sure in the history of ideas, but denied its continuing power as a text to affect its audience. Such approaches cast the text's pedagogy as the reader's object of study; they dismiss the more intriguing possibility that the reader might be subject to its teachings, that the transmission of knowledge that it problematizes might also be operative; in short, that the reading of this work might constitute an education in itself.

This lesson, however, cannot be taught or passed on to be taught in the future if the means by which it transmits its teachings are deliberately unrecognized or repressed. For Rousseau is concerned first of all with the conditions that enable the transfer of knowledge to occur and not so much with the actual content of that knowledge. In other words, what is fundamentally at stake in Rousseau's pedagogy is not so much the truth of its theory or the practical usefulness of its narrative, as most critical analyses would have it, but *how* the theory and story are read and how this reading, then, effectively realizes, or performs, the text's teachings. Rehabilitating the pedagogical thrust of Rousseau's work requires examining the dynamic complexity of the reader's engagement with the text's teachings and the function and integration of his reading in the aims of the text's pedagogical program.

Rousseau's repeated use of apostrophe to address the reader draws attention to the modalities of the pedagogical discourse and ideally prevents the reader from forgetting the discourse in reference to the message or meaning it conveys. The use of this common rhetorical figure in *Emile* differs from its more conventional use in fiction because the book's subject of pedagogy invokes a particular situation

---

2. An example of a study that approaches the pedagogical theory and practice outlined in this work as an object of analysis rather than as an engagement that implicates the reader/critic in the dynamic encounter of pedagogical effects would be E. Durkheim's interpretation "La Pédagogie de Rousseau," in *Revue de Métaphysique et de Morale* 26 (1919): 153–80, in which he argues for the scientific basis of Rousseau's theory and for its seminal influence on the founding of cognitive psychology.

governed by the specific conventions of the pedagogical institution, conventions that the reader will recognize to be those of a master/student relationship and to involve the transference of something commonly called knowledge or mastery. By virtue of its discursive presentation and its pedagogical subject, the text confers a special status upon the reader. He is not just any reader coming to terms with any text; he is a reader cast in the role of pupil to the text's role of master. Moreover, he is not just an objective observer and student of a pedagogical theory and practice; he is positioned in the center of a pedagogical situation and thus subject to its conventions. He will not just read a theory of how knowledge is transmitted and mastery achieved; as the student, he is the recipient of that knowledge, the one targeted to achieve that mastery, and the one through whom it will be transferred.

The history of the book's reception and criticism, however, shows that readers have failed to assume their prescribed role as participants in the transmission of the text's pedagogical lesson. But their failure should not come as a surprise, for by all accounts, including, as we've seen, Rousseau's, the pedagogy that he describes and performs courts failure. A brief overview of the earliest interpretive moves, from those of the most public and official critics to those of the most private readers, should make the case in point.

Because the reactions of both state and church institutions to the book's publication were so dramatic, their interpretive failures are perhaps the easiest to chart. Even in a period of such widespread and institutionalized censorship as was the mideighteenth century in France, the official state and church responses stand out as extreme.[3] The work met with exceptional resistance despite its publication through familiar channels developed and widely used to circumvent the official censorship system.[4] The condemnations of the *Parlement*

3. Within a week and half of its sale and distribution on 27 May 1762, the *Parlement* de Paris seized and confiscated *Emile* (3 June), condemned it (9 June), and burned it (11 June). Rousseau was threatened with a "prise de corps" and was forced to leave France on 9 June, thus beginning what would be an eight-year exile and peregrination across Europe. This first quick response was soon followed on 7 June by the Sorbonne's decision to censor the book, although the official document was not drawn up until 20 August. In Geneva both *Emile* and *Le Contrat social* were confiscated (9 June), condemned, and burned (19 June). In Holland permission to publish *Emile* was revoked (29 June) and *Le Contrat social* was prohibited (20 June).

4. A February 1723 *arrêt du conseil et état du roi* had codified all aspects of the book trade in the "Réglement pour la librairie et imprimerie de Paris," from approval and editing of manuscripts to their publication, distribution, and sale. Put briefly, for a

de Paris, the Sorbonne, and Christophe de Beaumont, the Archbishop of Paris, effectively censored the book retroactively. There are, of course, plausible explanations for the hyperbolic refutations, as several critics have argued persuasively.[5] For instance, Christophe de Beaumont's refutation, which was one of the most forceful and cogent, focused on the "Profession de foi du Vicaire Savoyard," excising it from the rest of the work for special scrutiny. In light of his official position and religious point of view, his critique of the "Profession"

book to be published officially in France, it had to be submitted for approval by an appointed censor. Once approved, the book was given the royal privilege, printed clearly on its title page. The privilege authorized it to be published and sold in France and also protected the publisher's rights to the work. By midcentury, however, a second type of approval had come into practice. The tacit permission was also granted by a censor, but no written record of it was kept, thereby always putting into doubt its official status. This second, parallel system allowed controversial works to be published but in no way guaranteed them the government's protection once published. Authors who published with a tacit permission risked reprisal if, as in the case of *Emile*, public reaction was hostile.

Rousseau's publisher for *Emile*, Duchesne, and his patron, Mme de Luxembourg, were familiar with the intricacies of the censorship system. They succeeded in getting a tacit permission from Malesherbes, the Directeur de la Librairie. However, despite a letter of reassurance from Malesherbes himself, Rousseau insisted that the work be published abroad, as his other works had been since the *Discours sur l'inégalité*. Publishing abroad was the most secure way to avoid problems with censorship later. According to Rousseau's account of his transactions with Duchesne and Mme. de Luxembourg in *Les Confessions*, they assured him that *Emile* was, indeed, being published in Holland. Later Rousseau was to discover not only that *Emile* was being published clandestinely in France but that Duchesne had never had the intention of publishing abroad. By then it was too late to stop publication, and Rousseau turned his attention and anxieties to producing as accurate an edition as possible. See Rousseau's version of the events in Book 11 of *Les Confessions*, vol. 1, 534–88. For an overview of the institution of censorship under the *ancien régime* see William Hanley, "The Policing of Thought: Censorship in Eighteenth-Century France," in *Studies on Voltaire*, vol. 183 (1980): 265–95 and N. Herrmann-Mascard, *La Censure des livres à la fin de l'ancien régime 1750–1789* (Paris: Presses Universitaires de France 1968).

5. The following studies assemble the correspondence, the *Confessions*, and the correspondence of others involved (i.e., Malesherbes) to analyze the events that triggered the violent official reaction; Marcel Françon, "La Condamnation de l'*Emile*," in *Annales Jean-Jacques Rousseau*, (Geneva: 1946–49) vol. 31, 209–45; André Ravier, *L'Education de l'homme nouveau: Essai historique et critique sur le livre de l'*Emile *de J.-J. Rousseau*, 2 vols. (Lyon: M. and L. Riou, 1941), especially Chapters 1 and 2, 1–105; Peter D. Jimack, *La Genèse et rédaction de l'*Emile *de J.-J. Rousseau: Etude sur l'histoire de l'ouvrage jusqu'à sa parution*," in *Studies on Voltaire and the Eighteenth Century*, vol. 23 (Geneva: Institut et Musée Voltaire, 1960), 44–68; Gustave Lanson, "Quelques documents inédits sur la condamnation et la censure de l'*Emile* et des *Lettres écrites de la montagne*," *Annales J.-J. Rousseau*, (Geneva: 1905), vol. 1, 95–140; P. M. Masson, *"La Profession de foi du Vicaire Savoyard" de J.-J. Rousseau*, édition critique (Fribourg and Paris: 1914).

from a traditional hermeneutic perspective was justified. Clearly the Church had to contest the vicaire's spiritual uncertainties and unorthodox approach to faith and to defend its own orthodox understanding of revelation. Furthermore, given that the "Profession de foi" is in some ways a reflection upon the shortcomings if not the impossibility of the traditional hermeneutic interpretation of God and man's relationship to him, it stands to reason that the Church should have felt particularly vulnerable. The "Profession" put into question not only the content of the Church's teachings and dogma concerning revelation, but much more radically, its way of interpreting it. It is important, however, not so much to locate the motivating reason for the Church's partial interpretation, in both senses of the word, but rather to recognize that such a predictable, because institutionally determined, response established the prototype of subsequent interpretations.[6] For, as it turns out, such official and public interpretations as the Church's were forceful or persuasive enough to transmit a kind of reading practice or cliché that was easily repeated.

Indeed, one of the strongest legacies in *Emile ou de l'éducation*'s critical tradition has been precisely the pattern of selecting only part of the text to interpret. This pattern is apparent even in the most private and personal of interpretations, those of parents who read Rousseau with an eye to practical guidance in their roles as parents and educators to their children. Traces of such interpretations can be found in Rousseau's correspondence with those parents who wrote to him for further elucidation on the practical matters of his pedagogy.[7] These are readers who, in their hunger for the secure knowledge of information and facts that can be verified and applied to their empirical situation, read the text in the most literal of ways as an educa-

6. See Ravier, op. cit., who argues persuasively that overreaction to the "Profession" impeded more impartial interpretations: "It is the 'Profession de foi' in *Emile* that upset catholic theologians and protestant ministers. The rest of the book was criticized and judged only indirectly. All the attacks targeted the "Profession de foi du Vicaire savoyard." And this single-minded view warped the judgment of the book as a whole" (vol. 1, 105).

7. See, for instance, Rousseau's correspondence during the course of 1763–64 with Louis Eugène Prince of Wurtenberg, in which the prince solicits Rousseau's advice on the education of his daughter, Sophie, *Correspondence complète*, vols. 17–23, ed. R. A. Leigh, (Geneva: Institut et Musée Voltaire, 1965–1980). See also "Letter 1967" (June–July 1762) vol. 11, where Rousseau is offered the position of preceptor. In this case, not only are Rousseau's theories interpreted literally, but Rousseau's actual identity is confused with that of the author, the narrator, and the character, Jean-Jacques, of his work.

tional manual. Identifying themselves with the fathers and mothers that Rousseau's text apostrophizes, and their child with the fictive character, Emile, they read very much as Emile first does. For them, as for Emile when he begins to read, the text operates mimetically in relation to the empirical world; it is a script that proleptically describes the world as it can come to be if its instructions are followed to the letter, if, in other words, its knowledge is successfully transmitted to the future. Hence, their anxious appeals to Rousseau to clarify certain points should be understood as a need to verify that their interpretations are "right," that they have correctly identified and understood what is to be handed on. Such a need for a confirmation, however, reveals that they have remained untouched by the text's lesson. Far from securing their transformation into the master pedagogues capable of understanding and judging their own reading, their identification with the character of the pedagogue reveals the unbridgeable difference that exists between them and the projected ideal. By reading so literally for the referential knowledge that must be passed on and by identifying with and imitating the characters of the text's story, these readers fail to reflect upon how the text teaches them by engaging them in the process of transmitting its knowledge. They cast themselves in the role of tutor without reflecting either upon their problematic identification or the difference between the role and the actual identity. In that lack of reflection, in the blind repetition, the crucial difference between the literal and the figural is lost. Because of this blindness to the text's figurative dimension, these readers succeed only in repeating the story, without, however, the story's ironic self-reflection upon the failure that such repetition indicates. They confuse repetition and imitation with transmission, failing to understand how the text's reflection upon the process of transmission implicates them in that very process.

While the motivation of the official bureaucracies may have been different than that of these more "impartial" critics and readers, the effect of their interpretations was the same. Public institutions, sensitive to doctrinal issues, censored what deviates from or exceeds established doctrine; parents censored the theoretical aspects that tend to interfere with the text's use value. Thus both private and public responses generated a canon of critical gestures that preclude an integral reading and promote a censoring of some aspect of the text. Later critics, like these first readers, have tended to focus on one particular aspect of the text, most often on its pedagogical content, unknowingly repeating the gesture of overlooking what is precisely most pertinent to them as the teachers and students of pedagogy whom this text addresses. Paradoxically, then, the legacy that this text transmits from the beginning is not that of its own lesson on transmission but rather that of a repeated failure to realize this lesson.

Certainly, such contradiction is symptomatic of the underlying oppositions at work in, and around the margins of, this text. The most explicit conflict takes place around the struggle for power to determine what is selected to get passed on, which traditions and values, and to control the means of its transmission. For Rousseau's text not only puts into question the content of an education—his is, after all, a negative education, one which blatantly rejects and refuses to pass on what society and its institutions have valued—but it also subverts the conventional ways by which society conveys its educational practices. For instance, Rousseau criticizes the long established public institutions of "collèges," as well as the private practice of putting servants in charge of a child's education. Given these critiques, it is completely understandable that Rousseau's pedagogy should be perceived as a threat that must be contained and defused. And although the official attacks of the government and the Church do not admit to the real nature of the struggle for power in which this text engages them, the rigor of their attack, the arsenal they call upon to prevent the distribution of the book and the transmission of its pedagogy— banning it, burning it, censoring it, threatening Rousseau with a "prise de corps," and forcing him into exile—all this suggests the seriousness of the stakes in the struggle.

This exterior struggle between author and authorities to control the text's content and diffusion is repeated within the text in the struggle to master its interpretation. The resistance to reading *Emile* from the scripted vantage point in the text, that is, as a reader subject to its teachings, could thus be understood as a refusal to relinquish the critic's role as the master of interpretations. The repeated critical gesture of privileging meaning and knowledge in *Emile* over the production of and reflection upon knowledge could then be explained in terms of the struggle for mastery at stake in the reading of this text. To read it exclusively for its meaning would circumvent and subvert its pedagogical intent of making the reader conscious of the reading process and how it generates meaning by drawing him into a text which problematizes the transmission of meaning. Indeed, dismissing the troubling ambivalence of reading a complex polyphonic discourse in favor of seeking a fixed interpretation provides an effective means of controlling the text's meaning and its production of meaning. The reader/critic retains his mastery, but only at the expense of forsaking the text's master lesson of learning how to read it. The victory is empty and paradoxically meaningless.

But is contradiction the only way to interpret this configuration of critical responses and the impasse it leads to? In other words, is there any way to read the critical failures to which the text's contradictions lead as a necessary step in a process rather than as a dead end? Instead of blocking the transmission of a legacy, could the failures be a constitutive part of the epistemological process that the text imposes? Could a reading of the text from the premise that it carries within itself the blueprint of its own interpretations both elucidate the critical reactions and provide a model for reading the book? And what would the connections be, if any, between a text that produces its own misreadings and the pedagogical theory that it articulates?

If, as I am suggesting, learning to read, or relearning to read, as the case may be, is both the end and the means of Rousseau's pedagogical program, then what can the example of Emile's passage from illiteracy to literacy teach us about reading? How can we read Emile's story, not as an example to imitate or reproduce blindly, but as a figure of our own lesson? Although Rousseau suggests provocatively that books will be proscribed from Emile's education, "At twelve Emile will hardly know what a book is,"[8] Emile will of course read. In fact, it could be argued that reading, defined broadly as the deciphering of signs, subtends all of his education and functions as a master metaphor at every stage of his cognitive development. Viewed in this way, Emile's education could be understood as an extended reading lesson, where the different parts of the learning process, carefully identified and separated, correspond to the different cognitive models that govern his development. What, then, are the different models that the reading lesson follows and how do they parallel and program the reader's own reading apprenticeship?

The first model that structures both Emile's education and his

8. *Emile ou de l'éducation, Oeuvres complètes* (Paris: Gallimard, Bibliothèque de la Pléiade, 1969), vol. 4, 357. The English translation is from Allan Bloom (New York: Basic Books, 1979), 116. Page references to both the French edition and the Bloom translation (in that order) will henceforth appear in the text.

reading is a mimetic one. This model recognizes two contradictory impulses in the young child—the indiscriminate capacity to repeat and imitate everything he sees and hears around him and the concomitant inability to judge and understand what he so easily mimics. Rousseau compares the child's skill at memorizing and imitating to a mirror; it is a passive mechanical device that engages neither the intellect nor the powers of will and concentration, without which no change in understanding, and hence no learning, is possible. "Their brains, smooth and polished, return, like a mirror, the objects presented to it. But nothing remains; nothing penetrates. The child retains the words; the ideas are reflected off of him. Those who hear him understand them; only he does not understand them" (4, 344; Bloom, 107). One of the foremost tasks of the educator, then, is to discriminate for the child suitable actions to imitate. Until the child internalizes the faculty of judgment, it is the tutor's purview to censor the situations and subjects whose imitation does not contribute to Emile's development. This model thus acknowledges the need to incorporate censorship in the learning process.

What can Emile first learn and understand? For Rousseau, the young child's world is purely material and sensual. His learning is limited to his immediate experience and surroundings. He can only understand what he sees, hears, and touches; he cannot yet make judgments concerning what he imagines. The tutor must thus censor situations and subjects that do not relate to the child's immediate sensorial experiences. This necessarily transforms the traditional curriculum; history, geography, foreign languages, poetry are eliminated. Emile will be encouraged to imitate acts and gestures that he witnesses rather than discourses that refer to absent and perhaps unknown, and therefore imaginary, experiences. For example, Jean-Jacques will allow, indeed, guide Emile to imitate the gardener, Robert, in planting a garden. It is by literally putting his hands in dirt and physically working, in imitation of Robert, that Emile will come to conceive and understand the very abstract concept of property.

The child's innate ability to mimic books and texts is potentially more pernicious for it puts into play his imagination. Because he does not distinguish clearly between imagination and reality, fiction and the empirical world, Emile believes words and stories to be exact and true reflections, even extensions, of the world. Since he mistakenly conceives that the world around him is coextensive with its representations, he identifies with and enacts what he reads just as easily as he imitates what he sees. Reading, it seems, inevitably leads Emile to err, to confuse an action that only exists in language with its referent. But if the child's imaginative capacity cannot be stopped—it is, after all, what makes him human—it can, however, be contained, and the errors he makes as a result of his imagination can be controlled. Therefore, just as the mimetic model governs the tutor's choices of what Emile can and cannot imitate, so will it determine his selection of what Emile can read in *Robinson Crusoe,* and what and how he cannot read in La Fontaine's fables—according to the text's potential for literal interpretation. Can Emile be guided to enact what he reads as literally as possible so that his inevitable mistaking of actions in literature for empirical actions will, on some level, be true? To insure that fiction and reality coincide, the tutor must choose texts whose literal interpretation will conform to Emile's experience and be determined by his referential understanding. Recognizing what he reads, Emile will thus imitate what he already knows and has experienced. His reading will remain firmly anchored to his immediate present and past experience and the imagination's dangerous potential of projecting a future will be deferred, at least for a while.

In both the cases of what the mimetic model allows and forbids the child to read, it exercises censorship openly. Emile cannot read La Fontaine's fables because he would interpret literally what is a thoroughly figurative discourse, and thereby misunderstand the ethical issues at stake. Nor can he read *Robinson Crusoe* in its totality. His reading must be limited to the parts that he can interpret univocally without any ambiguity. Because he will already have experienced the difficulties of claiming property and of laboring over a garden, he will recognize Robinson Crusoe and easily reincarnate him. As Rousseau remarks, "I want him to be busy with his mansion, his goats, his plantations . . . I want him to think he is Robinson himself . . ." (4, 455; Bloom, 185). This example illustrates perfectly how, for Emile, the text operates as a mirror of his knowledge and experience and therefore conforms to his understanding of books as accurate reflections of the world. Conflating performative and cognitive elements of the text, he will learn what he enacts of Robinson's story. The text and Emile's interpretation thus mirror each other infinitely and, as in a house of mirrors, it proves difficult to find one's way out. "I want it to make him dizzy" says Rousseau (4, 455; Bloom, 185). But for this "mimetic" interpretation to succeed and reflect at least some aspect of the text's truth, the text must be pruned or censored. The historical setting, the literary frame and references, and the allegorical dimensions of the novel are carefully deleted, lest Emile imitate what is inimitable. Thus, at this first stage of the child's education, censorship controls his mimetic interpretations, limiting them to the literal where his understanding will coincide with his enactment. Censorship here acknowledges openly the child's limitations and, modeling itself on these limitations, acquiesces mimetically. The mimetic model, therefore, is not determined by censorship, but, on the contrary, governs censorship.

What does this model suggest in terms of the reader's approach to the text? It would suggest that the reader, like Emile, is initially tempted into a mystified identification with the story he is reading and blind to the text's knowledge of its own artifice. It would explain the tendency first to read *Emile* literally, without regard to the figurative dimension such artifice points to, and second of all, referentially, as an educational manual with immediate application and pertinence to the practical world. It would also predict the many interpretations that have been paraphrases, or uncritical repetitions, of its pedagogical theories. Furthermore, it would assume a partial understanding, based on the necessary censorship at work in a literal interpretation. Hence, this model offers an understanding of the mechanisms of repetition and censorship operating at the core of *Emile*. It does not, however, explain why such repetition and censorship might be a necessary part of the educational process.

For such an explanation we must turn to another model, less obvious in that it does not at first pertain directly to reading, but more pertinent, I believe, in demonstrating why reading functions at the center of this text's pedagogical insights, both thematically as a crucial moment in Emile's education and heuristically, as a programmed step in the reader's contact with the text. I am referring to a contractual model. I propose to trace the development of this contractual model: first, as it very literally structures the dominant relationship between master and pupil in the story that the text narrates, and second, as it unfolds a program of cognition that guides both Emile's reading of the signs and discourses he encounters and the reader's reading of the text.[9]

The story of Emile's education provides a consistent illustration

9. In the preface to Jacqueline Givel's and Robert Osmont's *Index de Rousseau juge de Jean-Jacques* (Geneva: Librairie Slatkine, 1977), Michel Launay traces the evolution of what he calls Rousseau's "contractual writing" with his reader, from its

of an education initiated, developed and fulfilled in terms of a contract. In fact, the relationships among the main characters of the story are articulated solely and repeatedly in a series of contracts that are renegotiated as the terms of the relationships change. The first contract takes place between the tutor, Jean-Jacques, and the father of the future pupil, Emile. The father surrenders his rights as tutor to the preceptor.[10] In exchange, he regains his freedom. This first agreement merely prepares the situation for the basic contract or exchange between tutor and child at the foundation of Emile's education. The economics of the contract are spelled out clearly in an accounting of profits and losses: Jean-Jacques will lose his present freedom but form a man capable of taking care of him when he grows old, thereby assuring himself of a secure future; Emile will unknowingly lose his father and his freedom but will gain an education and a friend.[11]

Although the relationship between the tutor and the child is modeled to seem "natural" to the child, Rousseau emphasizes that this is an appearance, a masquerade for the child's benefit and security. More significantly, Emile's education is scripted to play naturally because once the natural channel of transmission between parent and child has been broken the natural can only be reinstated by being simulated artificially. Artifice, symbolized and achieved by the contract, is the foundation of this most "natural" of educations. Yet much as the tutor censored Emile's reading to correspond to the child's under-

---

ambivalent introduction in the *Contrat Social*, its repudiation in the *Lettres écrites de la montagne*, and its transcendence in the *Rêveries*. Launay's analysis of the introductory pages of these texts focuses on the direct and indirect relationships to the reader that Rousseau articulates formally. Launay's study, however, fails to include how the texts' subject matter might affect the development of a "contract" between author and reader. This omission might explain why he excludes *Emile*. According to the formal criteria Launay uses, *Emile* does not present a clearly defined moment in the development of "contractual writing," but rather serves as a draft for the mature articulation of the contract in the *Contrat social*.

10. "Emile is an orphan. It makes no difference whether he has his father and mother. Charged with their duties, I inherit all their rights. He ought to honor his parents, but he ought to obey only me. That is my first or, rather, my sole condition" (4, 267; Bloom, 52).

11. "But when they regard themselves as people who are going to spend their lives together, it is important for each to make himself loved by the other; and by that very fact they become *dear* to one another. The pupil does not blush at following in his childhood the friend he is going to have when he is grown. The governor takes an *interest* in concerns whose *fruit* he is going to *harvest*, and whatever merit he imparts to his pupil is an investment [*un fond qu'il place au profit*] he makes for his old age" (4, 268; Bloom, 53; emphasis added).

standing, so will he censor the actual contract that binds the two together and thereby hide the fundamental artifice that governs their relationship. It is part of Rousseau's pedagogical strategy that the two systems—the tutor's artificial, manipulative planning of Emile's education and the child's naive belief in "natural" occurrence—operate separately yet simultaneously so that all others but the child be aware of the artifice. The censorship is to operate selectively for the child only. Rousseau has been criticized for promoting such a double standard—honesty, directness, transparent correspondence between cause and effect, between intention and act, for Emile, and duplicity, indirectness, manipulation for Jean-Jacques. But Rousseau does not value one system over the other; on the contrary, each system unmasks the other as inadequate and illusory. In fact, their coexistence, which models the duplicity of the pedagogical situation, is necessary for any demystification to occur. To interpret this strategy as insincere, then, is to ignore the unavoidable artifice of the pedagogical situation and to interpret as univocal what is necessarily double. Such interpretations, favored by the "partial" and literal-minded readers described earlier, either repeat Emile's naive error of believing in "natural" correspondence between will and action, between the world and its signs, or Jean-Jacques' self-deception in his belief that he controls the will of others.

It follows that while the contract between father and tutor is openly recognized by both parties involved, the contract between tutor and child goes unacknowledged at first, under the pretense of a "natural" relationship. The true nature of his relationship to his preceptor is to remain concealed until he is old enough to recognize it for the conventional agreement that it is. Hence, this first contract between Jean-Jacques and Emile must be made by proxy. The father substitutes for Emile, as yet incapable of independently engaging himself in a contractual situation, which Rousseau describes as an "agreement made in advance," (4, 268; Bloom, 53). From the beginning the father thus participates in two contracts, one for himself in which his child Emile functions as the object of the exchange, and one for the child in which he substitutes for Emile as subject. Likewise, the tutor participates in two contracts, one with the father and one with Emile.

It is important that neither father nor tutor reveal the arrangement to the child. As Rousseau makes clear, the tutor must carefully erase from his discourse and his behavior all allusions to such a contract. From its inception, then, the contract between tutor and child institutionalizes censorship. Not only is the tutor to exercise self-censoring by not revealing his true role and his motives, but he must also censor Emile's curiosity and questions by redirecting them, or by willfully misunderstanding them. In a way, the tutor must make himself deaf to the real sense of Emile's queries and must actively refuse to give him the knowledge he requests. Rousseau explicitly thematizes the need to gloss over what is really at stake and to defer interpreting the relationship between J.-J. and Emile and the debt that structures it: "Until it is time to treat him like a man, *let the issue be never* what he owes you but what he owes himself. To make him docile, leave him all his freedom; *hide* yourself so that he may seek you. Lift his soul to the noble sentiment of gratitude *by never speaking to him* of anything but his interest. *I did not want him to be told* that what was done was for his good before he was in a condition to understand it" (4, 522; Bloom 234; emphasis added).

Is this censorship necessary? As we have seen with the mimetic model of the reading lesson, it is, for the child does not yet understand the way texts or discourses signify, the conventions they presuppose, the multiple, and sometimes contradictory, meanings they generate. At this stage in his development, he can only understand such texts and discourses literally. Another way of putting it would be to say that he seeks an exact correspondence between text or discourse and a real referent in the world he knows through previous experience. For him, texts and discourses are not governed by either social, intertextual, or linguistic conventions; they can have but one fixed meaning, and that meaning is at the service of the world to which they refer. Were Emile to be aware of the contract that governs his relationship to his tutor, he would be incapable of hearing, let alone understanding, its conventional and figurative dimensions. Instead, he would interpret it as the master/slave relationship it appears to be and whose terms he has been tricked into accepting. He would rebel, refusing to honor the terms of a contract that would appear to authorize the loss of his will and freedom. Emile's interpretation and consequent action would be hasty and superficial. The unfortunate result would be the foreclosure and premature failure of his education.

The tutor's objective in structuring the child's education as a contract is precisely to lead him beyond the uncritical and repetitive mimetic model of understanding the world and its signs to the recognition of the contractual or conventional nature of those signs and his relationship to them. The most effective way to provoke this understanding is to make Emile see that the identity he derives for himself from his relationship to his tutor is not the natural one he believes it to be, but rather a conventional one, determined arbitrarily by contract. Although the tutor takes great care to prepare for this moment of recognition, it is the child, and not the tutor, who must unmask the "natural" appearances and dismantle his former interpretation to reach a truer understanding. This second understanding of his situation will not be constituted by the abstract knowledge of what a convention or contract is, but rather by a reinterpretation of his identity as a role he has been acting out all along with his tutor. Only then will Emile recognize by himself and at the right moment that his relationship to his tutor can be understood as a contract beneficial to both. Only then can he choose willingly to continue under its terms: "I did not want him to be told that what was done was for his good before he was in a condition to understand it. In this speech he would have seen only your dependence, and he would have taken you only for his valet. But now that he begins to feel what it is to love, he also feels what a sweet bond can unite a man to what he loves; and in the zeal which makes you constantly busy yourself with him, he sees a slave's attachment no longer but a friend's affection" (4, 522; Bloom, 234).

The contractual model structures understanding to evolve temporally. Its sequence unfolds a first moment of knowing empirically and uncritically through immediate experience followed by a second moment of understanding critically through the re-cognition or the self-consciousness of the experience, which, in turn, leads to its reinterpretation. Emile comes to understand himself and his relationship to his tutor at the exact moment that he steps away from himself to reflect upon it. Thus, Emile's discovery of the contract governing his relationship to Jean-Jacques can only take place if he is first kept in ignorance of it, or allowed to misinterpret it. The censorship at the heart of the contract proves to be a necessary, albeit paradoxical, prelude to revelation. Rousseau's remarkable pedagogical insight is that error is not the opposite of knowledge; it is, rather, constitutive of the very structure of knowledge.

The child's re-cognition of his situation marks the triumphant moment in his education. In choosing to understand love rather than self-interest to be the motivating force of his preceptor's behavior, Emile unveils and inaugurates his newfound ability to "see" figuratively, that is, to reinterpret his former misinterpretation. Note, however, that this second interpretation is not necessarily truer than the first one. For who can say with certainty that either love or self-interest is more the true meaning of the tutor's actions? Indeed, self-love and love of the other are inextricably fused and confused in both Emile's and his tutor's attitudes to one another; each motivates and grounds the other to such an extent that it is impossible to determine which is which. But whereas before Emile's understanding was limited to the one interpretation that was most apparent, he is now aware of the two, equally plausible interpretations, neither one of which is necessarily or clearly the "right" one. This is a cognitive act of immediate and irremediable consequences: it simultaneously authenticates the pedagogical method and proves its success; it lends authority after the fact to the original proleptic and clandestine contract; it is the necessary condition for the openly acknowledged contract to function; it repays the preceptor's initial risk; and finally, it liberates both Emile and Jean-Jacques from censorship. At the very moment Emile recognizes the contract and could free himself from it by refusing to accept the terms in which he had no part, he voluntarily abdicates his newfound autonomy and places himself back in the contractual situation: ". . . I do not doubt for an instant that he will come by himself to the point where I want to lead him, that he will eagerly put himself in my safekeeping, . . . and will say to me with all the warmth of his age, 'O my friend, my protector, my master! Take back the authority you want to give up at the very moment that it is most important for me that you retain it. You had this authority up to this time only due to my weakness; now you shall have it due to my will. . . . I want to obey your laws; I want to do so always. This is my steadfast will. . . .' " (4, 651; Bloom, 325).

In renewing this relationship with his teacher, Emile proves that he is no longer the innocent pawn or object of an exchange, but rather, a subject consciously participating in the exchange. And this time the preceptor does not disguise the language he uses to describe the agreement; he explicitly compares it to a formal and written contract: "When the moment has come, and he has, so to speak, signed the contract, then change your language. Make your dominion as gentle as you had indicated it would be severe" (4, 653; Bloom 326).

Although Rousseau openly calls the agreement a contract, he also calls attention to its figurative dimension. The agreement between Emile and Jean-Jacques is not literally articulated in a contract, but rather is *like* a contract, "so to speak" [*pour ainsi dire*]. The extent of what the child's misunderstanding would have been, had he prematurely discovered the true role of his tutor, is now revealed. Emile would have interpreted literally and univocally what must be understood figuratively. Emile's enlightenment, however, originates in his newfound awareness, carefully prepared by his tutor, of the possibility of language's figurative dimension. Once this possibility is conceived, any univocal interpretation will appear limited, if not false. Understanding that language and the texts it generates allow the coexistence of multiple interpretations where none necessarily prevails, but where all play off of each other, is the necessary condition of reading. It is this sudden ability to read the world and those of its signs previously given a univocal interpretation that frees Emile to recognize and to understand his tutor, himself, their relationship and the conventions of the "contract" that binds them. Having learned to read the contract figuratively, Emile can now conceive of nonreferential, figurative language and actions; he can make the symbolic gesture of ratifying the contract with his "signature," thereby acting upon his newly discovered understanding. And Jean-Jacques can now safely "change his language" [*changez alors de langage*], knowing that Emile will be attentive to the figurative dimension of his "gentle authority" [*mettez autant de douceur dans votre empire*] and not be fooled by either its gentleness or authority.

The double lesson of Emile's sudden understanding of language's ambiguity and Rousseau's self-consciously figurative language should not be lost on the reader. Since the contract functions as the text's dominant pedagogical model, the reader reads the story of its inception, repression, and eventual discovery and reading as proleptic of the story of his own illumination. In other words, just as Emile's understanding derives from his newfound ability to read the contract and thus understand its figurative dimensions, so must the reader's comprehension of the text depend on his capacity to read it other than literally. He must read Emile's story not as a model to apply referentially to the practical world, but as an allegory of his own evolving understanding. Moreover, just as Emile's enlightenment is predicated on an ignorance and a series of deliberate misinterpretations carefully managed by his tutor's authority, so does the reader's understanding of the text proceed from an initially censored understanding programmed by the text's ambiguous authority split formally between two different types of discourse—one fictive and the other theoretical, one cognitive and the other performative. Such a split in effect encourages the reader to follow myopically only one path or direction through the text, blinding himself to that path's relation and convergence with the other paths and directions. The allegorical reading will gradually emerge out of the reader's recognition and re-reading of his previously limited interpretations, out of his reading of both discourses each as the figure of the other.

If the reader submits to the text's directives and its embedded pedagogical program, the story of Emile's education and his relationship to his tutor, commonly interpreted as an illustration or the pedagogical example of Rousseau's theory, operates instead as a reflection on and of the reader's discursive relationship to the text. What Emile's story describes and narrates, the reader's reading actually mimics or performs, with, however, a critical difference. The difference between Emile's first mimetic reading of texts and the reader's is that the act of reading Emile's story as his own should make the reader self-conscious of the mimetic process, and in so doing, transform a blind, unknowing identification into a recognition of its figurative dimension. In the final account, then, it is the reader's willingness to recognize and accept the text's performative effect on him and how it teaches him to read the text as an allegory of his own learning to read that allows the pedagogical program to be realized. Paradoxically, it is only through an allegorical reading of Emile's reading lessons that the text might literally transmit its lessons on reading.

In light of the double story of Emile's and the reader's learning to read, it is now possible to reread the history of *Emile ou de l'éducation*'s recurrent censorship in its various guises and discover an epistemological cause to the historical pattern. For, if the story of the contract's repression postulates that censorship is a necessary moment in reading, then *both* the child's and the reader's misinterpretations are anticipated and scripted in the epistemological presuppositions of Rousseau's pedagogy.

Such a reading of the contractual model would point to a happy conclusion, to the eventual success, after a series of epistemologically programmed failures, of the pedagogical mission, the repair of the broken-down channels, and the restoration of the father as rightful and natural pedagogue who would then guarantee the transmission of the pedagogical legacy to the future generations of his children. As we have argued, the conclusion of Emile's education seems to uphold the possibility of such a success. Emile himself marks the closure of his education when, about to become a father, he recognizes this event as the moment of transmission of authority. In a long speech to his tutor, he authoritatively makes the decision to take on the responsibilities of both father and tutor to his child. In so doing, he exerts the authority that proves that his tutor Jean-Jacques, has successfully transmitted that authority and responsibility to him. The tutor, it would seem, has succeeded in restoring the link between parent and child that best assures the transmission from one generation to the next.

Yet, it is precisely at this crucial moment of transferring authority that the transmission is once again disrupted. In the hiatus between the speech that closes both Emile's education and the book and *Emile et Sophie, ou les solitaires,* the sequel in which Emile recounts to his tutor the errors and failures of the life he led after he triumphantly asserted his authority and independence, something goes wrong. Having failed at his marriage, Emile repeats his father's abdication of responsibility and abandons his own children. The purpose of Emile's education, which was to transcend this pattern by substituting for and eventually reestablishing the "natural" means of transmission between father and son, remains unrealized. Emile's jubilant identification with his tutor proves to have been false. His education thus ends exactly as it began—in a failure to transmit. It does not transform him into the ideal pedagogue who will, in his turn, form future pedagogues. Instead of transmitting the ability and right to transmit to future generations, Emile's tutor has only succeeded in allowing the possibility of repeating the attempt to transmit. The contractual model of education, which had promised to supplement the failings of the mimetic model, proves to be just as lacking. With the sequel, *Emile et Sophie ou les solitaires,* Rousseau reads his previous interpretation of pedagogical models, and provides a critique of *Emile.* Ironically, it is by following *Emile's* pedagogical insights to the letter, that is, by rereading the mimetic and contractual models, that he is led to put into question and reject the pedagogical models he so rigorously constructed in *Emile.* Rousseau's final reading, although unfinished, would suggest that the pedagogical model of the contract that he sets forth in *Emile* provides both a model to read it *and* to misread it, to transmit its lesson *and* to block the transmission. In the long run, then, it would seem that the operative figure in this story of an education is not metaphor, which would posit the transformative possibilities of education through the student's or reader's eventual identification with his master, but rather repetition and ironic reversal, which insist on the impossibility of such transformations and the delusion of such identifications.

PAUL DE MAN

Roland Barthes and the Limits of Structuralism[1]

Despite the refinements of modern means of communication, the relationship between Anglo-American and continental—especially French—literary criticism remains a star-crossed story, plagued by a variety of cultural gaps and time lags. The French have only just gotten around to translating an essay by Empson,[2] and by the time American works of literary theory or literary criticism appear in Paris they often have lost much of their youthful freshness. There is more good will and curiosity in the other direction, yet here too a mixture of misguided enthusiasm and misplaced suspicion blurs the actual issues. Even some of the most enlightened of English and American critics keep considering their French counterparts with the same suspicion with which English-speaking tourists might approach the café au lait they are being served for breakfast in French Provincial hotels: they know they don't like it but aren't entirely certain whether they are being imposed upon or if, for lack of some ritualistic initiation, they are perhaps missing out on a good thing. Others are willing to swallow French culture whole, from breakfast coffee to Mont Saint Michel and Chartres, but since intellectual fashions change faster than culinary tastes, they may find themselves wearing

1. [The manuscript of this essay appears to date from 1972. It was commissioned by the *New York Review of Books* as a review of extant translations of Barthes's work into English but was never published. Correspondence indicates that there were differences between de Man and the editors over whether the vocabulary of the essay was too technical for a general readership. All text in brackets is supplied by the transcriber and editor, Thomas Pepper, who also wishes to express his thanks to E. S. Burt and Janie Vanpée for their help and patience. Thanks are also due to Mrs. Paul de Man for making this article available.]

YFS 77, *Reading the Archive: On Texts and Institutions*, ed. E. S. Burt and Janie Vanpée, © 1990 by Yale University.

a beret and drinking Pernod at a moment when the French avant-
garde has long since switched to a diet of cashmere sweaters and cold
milk. The *Critical Essays*[3] of Roland Barthes that have just become
available in excellent English translations date from 1953 to 1963;
Mythologies goes back to 1957 and appears in a regrettably abridged
version.[4] I cannot help speculating about all the things that could go
wrong in the reception of texts that now combine a nostalgic with a
genuine but out-of-phase revolutionary quality. Perhaps the most
useful function for an American-based view of Roland Barthes may be
to try to anticipate unwarranted dismissal as well as misplaced enthusiasm for the aspects of the work with which Barthes himself may
no longer be so pleased. Barthes has been introduced to Americans as
possibly "the most intelligent man of our time"[5] and any man needs
and deserves protection from the expectations raised by such hyper-
bole.

For despite the emphasis on structure, code, sign, text, reading,
intratextual relationships, etc., and despite the proliferation of a technical vocabulary primarily derived from structural linguistics, the
actual innovations introduced by Roland Barthes in the analytic
study of literary texts are relatively slight. Even in his more technical
works, unfortunately not yet available in English, such as *S/Z* (the
analysis of a brief narrative text by Balzac), and the various articles on
narrative technique published in *Communications*,[6] the contribution to practical criticism is not as extensive as the methodological
apparatus would lead one to expect. The work of "pure" structuralists
such as the linguist Greimas and his group or of some among Bar-

2. It should be added, in all fairness, that *Poétique* has also published recent
American work. [See, for example, the following essays, all published in *Poétique* 2
(1971): Seymour Chatman, "Henry James et le style de l'intangibilité"; William Empson, "Assertions dans les mots"; and Northrop Frye, "Littérature et mythe."]

3. [Roland Barthes, *Essais critiques* (Paris: Seuil, 1964), trans. Richard Howard,
Critical Essays (Evanston: Northwestern University Press, 1972).]

4. [Roland Barthes, *Mythologies* (Paris: Seuil, 1957), trans. Annette Lavers, *Mythologies* (New York: Hill and Wang, 1972).]

5. By Susan Sontag. [She writes in her preface to *Writing Degree Zero* (New York:
Hill and Wang, 1968), vii: "Still, I would argue that Barthes is the most consistently
intelligent, important, and useful critic—stretching that term—to have emerged anywhere in the last fifteen years."]

6. [*S/Z* (Paris: Seuil, 1970), trans. Richard Howard, *S/Z* (New York: Hill and Wang,
1974). Some of the essays first published in *Communications* have been reprinted in
Roland Barthes, *L'Aventure sémiologique* (Paris: Seuil, 1985), and in English in Roland
Barthes, *Image-Music-Text*, trans. Stephen Heath, (New York: Hill and Wang, 1977).]

thes's most gifted associates, such as Gérard Genette or Tzvetan Todorov, is more rigorous and more exhaustive than Barthes's—though it is only fair to point out here its avowed indebtedness to him. Hence the risk of disappointment or overhasty dismissal for the wrong reasons. Barthes is primarily a critic of literary ideology and, as such, his work is more essayistic and reflective than it is technical—perhaps most of all when the claim to methodological precision is most emphatically being stated. The close integration of methodology with ideology is an attractive characteristic of European intellectual life ever since structuralism became a public issue in the sixties—and, for better or worse, French writers on literature are still much closer to being public figures, committed to articulate positions, than their American counterparts. Barthes played an active part in the recent Battles of the Books and his work bears the traces of his involvements. It has to be read and understood as an intellectual adventure rather than as the scientifically motivated development of a methodology. He is at least as interested in the reasons for advocating certain technical devices as in their actual application; hence the polemical, proselytizing tone of many of his essays, hence also the many interviews, pamphlets, position papers, etc. His work should be read within the context of the particular situation within which it is written, that of the ideological demons underlying the practice of literary criticism in France. This situation is idiosyncratically French and cannot be transposed *tel quel* (*c'est le cas de le dire*) to the American situation. It does not follow however that the story of Barthes's intellectual itinerary is without direct interest for American readers. American criticism is notoriously rich in technical instruments (but much poorer in understanding the rationale for their use); but it is frustrated, as well it might be, in its attempts to relate particular studies and findings to larger historical, semantic, and epistemological questions. That such difficulties exist is by no means a sign of weakness; it only becomes one if the very awareness of the larger context is lost or if the broader inferences of a method are misunderstood. Regardless of its regional peculiarities, the configuration of Barthes's enterprise is of wide enough significance to have paradigmatic value for all students of literature willing to put the premises of their craft into question.

A somewhat euphoric, slightly manic tone runs through Barthes's writings, tempered by considerable irony and discretion but unmistakably braced by the feeling of being on the threshold of major discoveries: "A new anthropology, with unsuspected watersheds of meaning is perhaps being born: the map of human *praxis* is being redrawn, and the form of this enormous modification (but not, of course, its content) cannot fail to remind us of the Renaissance."[7] This statement dates from 1966, but one still finds similar trumpet blasts, only slightly muted, in recent utterances. It is the tone of a man liberated from a constraining past, who has "the earth . . . all before (him)," and who looks about "with a heart/Joyous, not scared at its own liberty."[8] The exact nature of this liberation can best be stated in linguistic terms, in a formula justly borrowed from Barthes himself: it is the liberation of the signifier from the constraints of referential meaning. In all the traditional polarities used throughout the ages to describe the inherent tension that shapes literary language—polarities such as content/form, logos (that which is being said) and lexis (the manner of saying it), meaning/sign, message/code, *langue/parole*, *signifié/signifiant*, voice/writing (and the sequence could be continued)—the implicit valorization has always privileged the first terms and considered the second as an auxiliary, an adjunct in the service of the former. Language itself, as the sign of a presumably nonlinguistic "content" or "reality," is therefore devalorized as the vehicle or carrier of a meaning to which it refers and that lies outside it; in the polarity man/language, it seems commonsensical enough for us humans to privilege the first term over the second and to rate experience above utterance. Literature is said to "represent" or "express" or at most, "transform" an extralinguistic entity or event which it is the interpreter's (or critic's) task to reach as a specific unit of meaning. Whatever the shadings used in describing the relationship (and they are infinite), it remains fundamentally best expressed by the metaphor of the *dependence* of language (literary or not) on something in whose *service* it operates. Language acquires dignity only to the extent that it can be said to resemble or to partake of the entity to which it refers. The Copernican revolution heralded by Barthes consists not in turning this model simply around (and thus claiming that, instead of being the slave of meaning, language would now become its master) but in asserting the autonomy of what the

7. [See Roland Barthes, *Critique et vérité* (Paris: Seuil, 1966), 48; in English, *Criticism and Truth*, trans. Richard Howard, (Minneapolis: Minnesota University Press, 1987), 66.]

8. [See the opening of Wordsworth's *Prelude*, ll. 15–16.]

linguist Saussure was the first to call the signifier, i.e., the objective properties of the sign independent of their semantic function as code, such as, for example, the redness of a traffic sign as optical event, or the sound of a word as acoustic event. The possibility for the signifier to enter into systems of relationship with other signifiers despite the constraint of the underlying or, if one prefers, over-standing or transcendental, meaning proves that the relationship between sign or word and meaning is not simply one of dependence; it suggests that this metaphorical language of polarized hierarchies and power structures fails to do justice to the delicate complexity of these relationships. The science that sets out to describe the functions and the interrelationships of signifiers (including reference, one among others) is called semiology, the study of signs independent of their particular meanings, in contrast to *semantics*, which operates on the level of meaning itself. Barthes is one of the leading representatives of this science, not so much as its initiator—he is the first to acknowledge his debt to Saussure, Jakobson, Hjelmslev and others—but as one of its most effective advocates.

Why is it that ideas about language leading to the science of semiology acquired such a polemical vigor in the hands of Barthes? They had been around for quite a while, not only in the field of linguistics, but in various philosophies of language and in the formalist schools of literary criticism that dominated the scene in most countries—with the possible exception of France. It is true that the French have a way of taking hold, often belatedly, of other peoples' ideas and suddenly rediscovering them with so much original energy that they are positively re-born; this happened, in recent years, with Hegel, Heidegger, Freud, and Marx and is about to happen now with Nietzsche. In this case however there is more to it than mere Gallic energy. Barthes's deliberate excursion into the realm of ideology is typical of the development summarized under the catch-all term of "structuralism" and of all his books, the early *Mythologies* is perhaps best suited to illustrate the process I am trying to describe.

Barthes is a born semiologist, endowed with an innate sense for the formal play of linguistic connotations, the kind of eye and mind that notices at once how an advertisement for a brand of spaghetti seduces the onlooker by combining, in the picture of the *red* tomatoes, the *white* spaghetti and the *green* peppers, the three colors of the house of Savoy and of the national Italian flag—thus allowing the potential consumer to taste all that makes Italy Italian in one single bite of canned pasta.[9] He has used this gifted eye not only to scrutinize literature, but social and cultural facts as well, treating them in the same manner in which a formalistically oriented critic would treat a literary text. *Mythologies*, a book that remains remarkably fresh although the facts it describes belong to the bygone era of pre-Gaullist France in the early fifties, undertakes precisely this kind of semiocritical sociology. The undisputed masters of the genre are Walter Benjamin and Theodor Adorno and, although Barthes was an early exponent of the work of Brecht in France, I doubt that he knew Benjamin or Adorno well when he wrote the *Mythologies*. The common ancestry is nevertheless apparent from reference, in the important concluding essay on history and myth, to Marx's *German Ideology*, the model text for all ideological demystifications.

Almost any of the *Mythologies* can be used to illustrate Barthes's main insight. Take, for instance, the opening essay on catch-as-catch-can wrestling as an example of the contrast between a referential, thematic reading and the free play of signifiers. The point is not that, in the world of catch-as-catch-can, all the fights are rigged; this would not make the event less referential but merely displace the referent from the theme "competition" to that of "deceit." What fascinates Barthes is that actors as well as spectators fully acquiesce to the deceit and that all pretense at open contest has been abandoned, thus voiding the event of content and of meaning. There only remains a series of gestures that can be highly skillful at simulating the drama of competition (the triumph of winning, the abjection of loss, or the drama of peripeteia or reversal) but that exist purely formally, independently of an outcome that is no longer part of the game. Catch is not a game but a *simulacrum*, a fiction; Barthes calls it a "myth."

Myths of this type abound in the fabric of any society. Their attraction is not due to their actual content but to the glitter of their surface, and this glitter in turn owes its brilliance to the gratuity, the lack of semantic responsibility, of the fictional sign. This play is far from innocent. It is in the nature of fictions to be more persuasive than facts, and especially persuasive in seeming more "real" than nature itself. Their order, their coherence, their symmetry is possible

9. [See "Rhétorique de l'image," in *Communications* 8 (1964), trans. Stephen Heath, "Rhetoric of the Image," in Roland Barthes, *Image-Music-Text* (New York: Hill and Wang, 1977). De Man inflects the same example differently in "Sign and Symbol in Hegel's *Aesthetics*," in Paul de Man, *Aesthetic Ideology*, ed. Andrzej Warminski, (Minneapolis: Minnesota University Press, forthcoming).]

because they are accountable only to themselves, yet these are pre-cisely the qualities wistfully associated with the world of nature and necessity. As a result, the most superfluous of gestures are most likely to become the hardest to do without. Their very artificiality endows them with a maximum of natural appeal. Fictions or myths are addictive because they substitute for natural needs by being more natural than the nature they displace. The particular shade of perver-sity and bad conscience associated with fiction stems from the com-plicity involved in partial awareness of this ambivalence coupled with an even stronger desire to resist its exposure. It follows that fictions are the most saleable commodity manufactured by man; an adman's dream of perfect coincidence between description and pro-motion. Disinterested in themselves, they are the defenseless prey of any interest that wishes to make use of them. When they are thus being enlisted in the service of collective patterns of interest—in-cluding interests of the "highest" moral or metaphysical order—fic-tions become ideologies. One can see that any ideology would always have a vested interest in theories of language advocating the natural correspondence between sign and meaning, since they depend on the illusion of this correspondence for their effectiveness whereas theo-ries that put into question the subservience, resemblance or potential identity between sign and meaning are always subversive, even if they remain strictly confined to linguistic phenomena. Barthes's *My-thologies* are fully aware of this; they bring the subversiveness into the open by exposing the structure of the social myths as well as their manipulation. The political results are clearly visible as *Mythologies* moves from the relatively innocent mystifications of catch as catch can or the Tour de France to consumer goods (e.g., the Citroën DS, steak pommes frites or the singing style of the baritone Gérard Souzay, etc.) to reach finally the domain of the printed word and image as it appears in the movies or in *Paris-Match*. After having been the target of a heavy handed and vicious attack by Raymond Picard, a Sorbonne Professor of French literature whose field of specialization is the life of Racine, Barthes wrote perhaps his best *mythologie* in the first part of the counterattacking pamphlet entitled *Critique et vé-rité*, in which the ideological infrastructure of French academic crit-icism is revealed with masterful economy and without an ounce of personal spite.

The demystifying power of semiology is both a source of strength and a danger. It is impossible to be so completely right at the expense of others without some danger to oneself. The perfect convergence between Barthes's social criticism, including the criticism of academic traditionalism, and the means used in accomplishing this highly desirable aim engenders its own mystification, this time on the level of method rather than of substance. The very power of the instrument used creates an overconfidence that generates its own set of counterquestions. In this case, the questions have to do with the claim of having finally grounded the study of literature in foundations epistemologically strong enough to be called scientific. The heady tone alluded to earlier occurs whenever this claim appears on the horizon. It is accountable for some of his most powerful influence. Putting it into question nowise means a desire to turn the clock back—a foolish wish at best, for there can be no return from the demystifying power of semiological analysis. No literary study can avoid going through a severe semiocritical process and there is much to be said for going through these fires with as urbane, surefooted, and entertaining a guide as Roland Barthes. At stake is the status of structuralism, a methodological blueprint for scientific research that, like Rousseau's state of nature, "no longer exists, has perhaps never existed and will probably never come into being" but which we nevertheless cannot do without.[10]

As in Barthes's social myths, the referential, representational effectiveness of literary language is greater than in actual communication because, like his catch-as-catch-can wrestlers, it is so utterly devoid of message. Literature overmeans, as we say of bombs that they overkill. This referential suggestiveness, which accounts for the fact that one responds with stronger emotion to a fictional narrative than to an actual event, is of course illusory and something for which a science of literature (whether we call it stylistics or literary semiology or whatever) should account without being taken in by it. The classical way of dealing with the question is to bypass it, as when Roman Jakobson rightfully asserts that, in literature, the language is auto-telic, i.e., "focus[sed] on the message for its own sake"[11] rather than on its content. By getting rid of all the mess and muddle of

10. [Jean-Jacques Rousseau, *Du contrat social*, in *Oeuvres complètes* (Paris: Gallimard, 1964), vol. 3, 123. De Man's translation. Cf., also Paul de Man, *Allegories of Reading* (New Haven: Yale University Press, 1979), 136.]

11. [See Roman Jakobson, "Closing Statement: Linguistics and Poetics," in his *Selected Writings*, "Poetry of Grammar and Grammar of Poetry," ed., Stephen Rudy, (The Hague: Mouton, 1981), vol. 3, 25.]

signification, the formula opens up a heretofore undiscovered world of scientific discourse, covering the entire field of literary syntax, grammar, phonology, prosody, and rhetoric. With the inevitable result, however, that the privileged adequation of sign to meaning that governs the world of fiction is taken as the ideal model towards which all semantic systems are assumed to tend. This model then begins to function as a regulatory norm by means of which all deviations and transformations of a given system are being evaluated. Literature becomes, to borrow a phrase from the title of Barthes's first book, a degree zero of semantic aberration. We know that it owes this privileged position to the bracketing of its referential function, dismissed as contingency or ideology, and not taken seriously as a semantic interference within the semiological structure.

The seduction of the literary model has undoubtedly worked on Barthes, as it has to on all writers endowed with literary sensitivity. Up through *Mythologies* it takes at times rather naive forms, as when, in the concluding essay of that book, literature is held up, in opposition to ideology, as a "transformation of the sign into meaning: its ideal would be . . . to reach, not the meaning of words, but the meaning of the things themselves."[12] More technical versions of the same myth appear in various texts, as when, in an article on names in Proust (whose planned title for the concluding section of his novel is known to have been at some point, "The Age of Things") he speaks of literature as [that which "would be defined by a Cratylian consciousness of signs and the writer would be the mouthpiece of an age-old myth which decrees that language imitates ideas and that, contrary to the specifications of linguistic science, signs are motivated"].[13] Unqualified assent to such propositions would be an example of misplaced enthusiasm for the most debatable aspect of Barthes's enterprise.

In the manifesto *Critique et vérité* (1966) in which the vocabulary is more transformational than structural, closer to Chomsky than to Jakobson, the position is more complex but not essentially different. It now takes the form of a three-pronged, hierarchized approach to

---

12. [See *Mythologies* (Paris: Seuil, 1957), 241.]

13. [Quotation supplied by the editor from Roland Barthes, "Proust et les noms," in *Le Degré zéro de l'écriture* suivi de *Nouveaux essais critiques* (Paris: Seuil, Collection Points, 1953, 1972), 136. For the English translation of the essay, see Roland Barthes, *New Critical Essays*, trans. Richard Howard, (New York: Hill and Wang, 1980), 68. De Man refers to a previous passage from the same essay in "The Resistance to Theory," in *The Resistance to Theory* (Minneapolis: Minnesota University Press, 1986).]

literature in which a distinction is made between literary science, literary criticism, and literary reading. The controlling authority of the first discipline, the only one to be free of the error of semantization and to lay claim to truth, is beyond question. "If one is willing to admit the textual nature of the literary work (and draw the proper conclusions from this knowledge), then a *certain type* of literary science becomes possible. . . . Its model will undoubtedly be linguistic. . . . Literary science will have for its object, not to explain why a certain meaning has to be accepted, nor even why it has been accepted (this being the task of the historians), but why it is acceptable. Not in terms of the philological rules of literary meaning, but in terms of the linguistic rules of symbolic meaning." [*Critique et vérité* 57–58, de Man's translation.] By emphatically drawing attention to its own methodological apparatus, *S/Z*, Barthes's most systematic piece of literary analysis to date, allows itself to be taken as a first exemplary move in the elaboration of such a science. The impact of this program on literary studies has been and will remain considerable. It will not do to dismiss the methodological claims as a hoax or as ironic window-dressing used by a writer of more traditional literary virtues. We cannot reassure ourselves by stressing the elegance, the sensitivity, the strongly personal, even confessional element that is part of Barthes's distinctive tone and that makes him into one of the "best" writers at work today in any genre, in the most traditional sense of this qualitative epithet. The theoretical challenge is genuine. It has to be taken all the more seriously since the particular quality of Barthes's writing is due to his desire to believe in its theoretical foundations and to repress doubts that would break its stability.

The unresolved question is whether the semantic, reference-oriented function of literature can be considered as contingent or whether it is a constitutive element of all literary language. The autotelic, nonreferential aspect of literature stressed by Jakobson cannot seriously be contested, but the question remains why it is always again and systematically being overlooked, as if it were a threat that had to be repressed. The first quoted passage from *Critique et vérité* laying down the directives for the literary science of the future is a good example: one can see Barthes fluttering around the question like a moth around a flame, fascinated but backing away in self-defense. All theoretical findings about literature confirm that it can never be reduced to a specific meaning or set of meanings, yet it is always being interpreted reductively as if it were a statement or message. Barthes grants the existence of this pattern of error but denies that it is the object of literary science to account for it; this is said to be the task of historians, thus implying that the reasons for the pattern's existence are not linguistic but ideological. The further implication is that the negative labor of ideological demystification will eventually be able to prevent the distortion that superimposes upon literature a positive, assertive meaning foreign to its actual nature. Barthes has never renounced this hope; in a recent interview, despite many nuances and reservations, he still talks about "the ultimate transparency of social relationships"[14] as the goal of the critical enterprise. Yet, in the meantime, his methodological postulates have begun to erode under the impact of the question which he delegated to other, more empirical disciplines.

That literature can be ideologically manipulated is obvious but doesn't suffice to prove that this distortion is not a particular aspect of a larger pattern of error. Sooner or later, any literary study, no matter how rigorously and legitimately formalistic it may be, must return to the problem of interpretation, no longer in the naive conviction of a priority of content over form, but as a consequence of the much more unsettling experience of being unable to cleanse its own discourse of aberrantly referential implications. The traditional concept of reading used by Barthes and based on the model of an encoding/decoding process becomes inoperative if the original master code remains out of reach of the operator, who then becomes unable to understand his own discourse. A science unable to read itself can no longer be called a science. The possibility of a scientific semiology is challenged by a problem that can no longer be accounted for in purely semiological terms.

This challenge reached Barthes from the somewhat unexpected quarters of philosophy, a discipline that earlier structuralists had dismissed in favor of the so-called sciences of man: psychology, anthropology, and linguistics considered as a social science. This dismissal proved to be premature, based as it was on an inadequate evaluation of the specifically philosophical ability to put the foundations of philosophy into question, in a self-destructive manner that no science could ever dare to emulate. The work of Michel Foucault and especially of Jacques Derrida—whose determining impact on literary

14. [See Roland Barthes, "Réponses," in *Tel Quel* 47 (Fall 1971), special issue on Roland Barthes, 107.]

theory is confirmed by the recently published book *La Dissémination*—thematizes the problem of linguistic delusion in a manner which semiological critics of Barthes's persuasion cannot afford to ignore, all the more since it reveals that the challenge had never ceased to be present in a philosophical and literary activity that structuralists tried to ignore. One thinks of certain recurrent misreadings of Rousseau's, Hegel's, and especially Nietzsche's (as well as Heidegger's) attitude towards literature and also of Barthes's cryptic remark during a recent discussion that "A criticism of Lautréamont, for example, is probably not possible," a remark that could be read as an abdication of semiology when it confronts the language of poetry.[15]

Barthes's intellectual integrity is apparent in his reaction to this philosophical challenge. For the moment, it has taken the form of a retreat from the methodological optimism that still inspired *S/Z*. More recent theoretical papers (not other recent books such as *L'Empire des signes*, inspired by a trip to Japan, or *Sade, Fourier, Loyola*, in which the semiological euphoria is allowed to reign undisturbed)[16] sketch out a much less ambitious program that sounds like a return to a pragmatic collecting of literary data, and are sharply aware of the inability of semiology to account for the stylistic tension between written and spoken language. One of these papers available in English translation invites us to embark on "the search for models, of patterns: sentence structures, syntagmatic clichés, divisions and *clausulae* of sentences; and what would inspire such work is the conviction that style is essentially a citational process, a body of formulae, a memory (almost in the cybernetic sense of the word), a cultural and not an expressive inheritance. . . . These models are only the depositories of culture (even if they seem very old). They are repetitions, not essential elements; citations, not expressions; stereotypes, not archetypes."[17] Traces of the reading of Derrida, Gilles Deleuze, Foucault (and perhaps also of the Columbia-based stylist, Michael

15. [See, for example, the second part of *Critique et vérité*, (65), where Barthes addresses the problem of the confrontation of criticism with lexically esoteric texts, and refers to Lautréamont.]

16. [Roland Barthes, *L'Empire des signes* (Geneva: Skira, 1970), trans. Richard Howard, *The Empire of Signs* (New York: Hill and Wang, 1982); *Sade, Fourier, Loyola* (Paris: Seuil, 1971), trans. Richard Miller, *Sade, Fourier, Loyola* (New York: Hill and Wang, 1976).] I suspect that some of these essays may in fact be of earlier date but have no information to confirm this.

17. [See Roland Barthes, "Style and its Image," in *Literary Style: A Symposium*, Seymour Chatman, ed. (London: Oxford University Press, 1971), 9–10.]

Riffaterre) are noticeable in these sentences. They cannot however represent a definitive position. The mind cannot remain at rest in a mere repertorization of its own recurrent aberrations; it is bound to systematize its own negative self-insight into categories that have at least the appearance of passion, novelty, and difference. There is every reason to suppose that Barthes's future work will participate in this development as he participated in the development that led up to it. The avant-garde review *Tel Quel*, whose attitude toward orthodox structuralism has always been healthily uncomplacent, recently devoted an entire issue to Roland Barthes,[18] thus creating the misleading impression that they were trying to erect a monument of a man who is about as monumental as a Cheshire cat. I doubt that *Tel Quel* was trying to kick Barthes upstairs into some kind of Pantheon of unchanging forms; whoever assumes this to be possible would seriously misjudge the resilience of one of the most agile and resourceful minds in the field of literary and linguistic studies.

As far as American criticism is concerned, its reaction to Barthes is not yet clear. The recent translations are a useful but still inadequate first step in introducing his work into English. The *Critical Essays*, mostly prefaces written for commercial editions, stem from the period that precedes the development of semiology—roughly 1963—and are mostly interesting in showing Barthes's discontent with the prevailing methods of literary study during the fifties in France, and his delight at discovering the new perspective opened by his readings in linguistics. They create the somewhat misleading impression that his main interests are confined to the theater of Brecht and to the novels of Robbe-Grillet and they should certainly not be taken as a fair sample of his accomplishments. There is more semiological finesse to be gathered from the *Mythologies*, including several not included in this selection, than from the *Critical Essays*. How the availability of his more important theoretical books (*On Racine, Critique et vérité, S/Z*, various theoretical papers)[19] might influence American criticism can be inferred from the reactions of some American specialists who are familiar with his work and show a fundamental resistance. In a recent essay entitled "On Defining Form," even as knowledgeable a scholar as Seymour Chatman, who

---

18. [*Tel Quel* 47 (Fall 1971).]

19. *On Racine*, which was translated in 1962, raises the entire question of Barthes's relationship to psychoanalytical criticism, a question too complex to be treated here. [See Roland Barthes, *On Racine* (New York: Hill and Wang, 1964).]

has already done a good deal in bringing together continental and American studies of literature, takes Barthes to task for putting the referential function of literary language into question: "It is difficult to understand," he writes, "why one should deny that there are, ultimately, contents or *signifiés* referred to. . . . The content of a literary work is not the language but what the language stands for, its reference. . . . The language is a mediating form between the *literary* form (structure-texture) and the ultimate content."[20] Barthes's point never was that literature had no referential function but that no "ultimate" referent could ever be reached and that therefore the rationality of the critical metalanguage is constantly threatened and problematic. I have suggested that Barthes was being all too hopeful in having believed, for a while, that the threat could be ignored or delegated to historians. At least, the scientific self-assurance thus gained is productive and has a negative validity, as far as it goes—and now that it seems to know its horizons, it remains a necessary fact of any critical education. To return to an unproblematic notion of signification is to take two steps backward, a step backward into a pseudo-science in a domain in which no science is possible, and a step backward into a pseudo-science that, unlike Barthes's semiology, is too remote from its object to be demystified by it. As long as the "libération du signifiant" is being resisted for the wrong reasons, Barthes's criticism will have little to teach American students of literature.

20. [In *New Literary History*, 2 (1971), 218–26.]

IV. Subverting Texts

ANDRZEJ WARMINSKI

Monstrous History: Heidegger Reading Hölderlin

PREFATORY NOTE

A sure way to ignore or to mistake what texts *as* texts "have to say about the institutions set up to transmit them" and about how they may or may not "escape institutional strictures" is not to read them.[1] Among the many strategies of nonreading, perhaps none is quite as effective, at least these days, as the easy historicizing move that would defuse and neutralize a genuinely critical thought by placing it in "historical context." This is where the recently celebrated "cases" of Martin Heidegger and Paul de Man—in themselves very different—have a great deal in common. In both cases, gossip about the putative "historical context" and the biographies of individuals has taken the place of reading. This is, of course, no accident. For a reading of these texts would discover that they have much to say about history and the relation between "author" and "work," and that what they say amounts precisely to a critique of the presuppositions behind such crude historicizing. If we read the texts, we find that we can no longer inscribe them in the same old "histories" of "philosophy" or of "theory," or even less in the pseudohistories that are nothing so much as the symptoms of institutional (e.g., academic) attempts to contain thinking that tampers with the axiomatics of the institution.[2] In

1. I quote from the project proposal for this volume.
2. Most of what has been written in the United States about something called "deconstruction" can be taken as such a defensive and reactive attempt at containment. Jacques Derrida's reminders are always therapeutic in this regard: ". . . politics does not take only the conventional distribution along an axis running from left to right. The reproductive force of authority can get along more comfortably with declara-

YFS 77, *Reading the Archive: On Texts and Institutions*, ed. E. S. Burt and Janie Vanpée,
© 1990 by Yale University.

short, reading the texts means having to tell new, different, other histories—more heterogeneous and more differentiated (i.e., more *textual*) histories that, as such, render more difficult if not impossible the reassuring activity of putting up theses and taking political positions pro and con. The "context" is also—always—already—a text and hence in need of being read rather than presupposed as given.

A good example of a text's refusal to be turned into "context"— i.e., its insistence on the necessity of being read—occurs in the infamous *Spiegel* interview with Martin Heidegger. The interviewer quotes a passage from Heidegger's Nietzsche lectures of 1936–37:

> **SPIEGEL:** A propos of Hölderlin, we ask your indulgence to quote your own writings. In your Nietzsche lectures you said that the "widely known opposition between the Dionysian and the Apollonian, between the sacred passion and sober presentation, is a hidden stylistic law of the historical destiny of the Germans and we must be prepared and ready one day to be formed by it. This opposition is not a formula with whose help we describe "culture." With this opposition, Hölderlin and Nietzsche have put a question mark before the Germans' task to find their being historically. Will we understand this sign, this question mark? One thing is sure. History will take revenge upon us if we don't understand it."[3]

The interviewer has high hopes of finally pinning Heidegger down. Here is a statement that in 1936–37 assigns a special task and a special destiny to "the Germans." Its distasteful nationalism and its reprehensible politics, especially "in context," are clear enough and would seem to require some explanation, if not justification or apology, in 1966. The interviewer clearly thinks he is on the track: "**SPIEGEL:** So, would you clarify this a bit? It leads us from generalities to the concrete destiny of the Germans." Heidegger explains and clarifies by talking about how thinking can be transformed only

---

tions or theses whose content presents itself as revolutionary, provided that they respect the rites of legitimation, the rhetoric and the institutional symbolism which defuses and neutralizes whatever comes from outside the system. What is unacceptable is what, underlying positions or theses, upsets this deeply entrenched contract, the order of these norms, and which does so in the very *form* of works, of teaching or of writing." See Jacques Derrida, "The Time of a Thesis: Punctuations," in Alan Montefiore, ed. *Philosophy in France Today* (Cambridge: Cambridge University Press, 1983), 44.

3. "Only a God Can Save Us: Der Spiegel's Interview with Martin Heidegger," *Philosophy Today* (Winter 1976): 281. The interview took place in 1966 but was not published until shortly after Heidegger's death in 1976 (*Der Spiegel*, 31 May 1976).

by a thinking that has the same origin and calling, but he does not mention "the Germans." This does not satisfy the interviewer: all this talk threatens to let Heidegger get off the hook and off the track. He pursues: "**SPIEGEL:** You assign in particular a special task to the Germans?" Heidegger's reply stops the pursuer in his tracks: "Yes, in the sense of the dialogue with Hölderlin." In order to continue his pursuit of the "concrete," the interviewer would have to *read:* he would have to find out who "the Germans" are, and he cannot do that until he finds out who "Hölderlin" is, or at least who Heidegger *thinks* he is in his dialogues with Hölderlin. That the interviewer reaches a dead end here, at the name of Hölderlin—and now has to change directions—is appropriate, for it is only in Heidegger's dialogue with Hölderlin that we can begin to think what Heidegger means by history, *our* history, and "the Germans." Why? Because Hölderlin's poetry decides who we are historically; it *founds* our historical Being. And it does so in dialogue with or, better, *by translating* Greek and "the Greeks." This translation is, as always, decisive: "Tell me what you think of translation," writes Heidegger, "and I will tell you who you are."[4] The question remains whether "Hölderlin" is indeed who Heidegger thinks he is. In the following very compact reading of one moment in Heidegger's dialogue with Hölderlin—what he thinks of translation of Greek into German and the translation of *German into German,* i.e., Hölderlin into Hölderlin—we would ask whether Hölderlin is who Heidegger translates him into or whether Hölderlin does not always remain someone else.[5]

Heidegger's lectures on Hölderlin's late hymns—his third and last lecture course on Hölderlin, given in the summer of 1942 and published in 1984 as volume 53 of the *Gesamtausgabe*—follow a path from and back to a commentary on Hölderlin's "Der Ister" by way of a

4. Martin Heidegger, *Hölderlins Hymne 'Der Ister'* (Frankfurt am Main: Vittorio Klostermann, 1984), 76. This is volume 53 of the *Gesamtausgabe* of Heidegger's works. All further page references to this volume will be indicated in the body of the essay.

5. The paper was written for a special session on Heidegger's and Benjamin's readings of Hölderlin at the 1985 MLA convention in Chicago. I publish it here unchanged—despite the recent furor over the "cases" of Heidegger and de Man—since the nonreading of academic journalism does not change anything, at least as far as the work (and the necessity) of reading is concerned. In short, as something that does not happen (and hence is not historical), gossip about texts can make no difference.

long excursus on the Greek determination of man's essence in Sophocles' *Antigone*. This excursus to Greece—and hence Heidegger's entire interpretation of Hölderlin—turns, as always, on a translation from the Greek. Here it is the well-known second choral ode of *Antigone*, in particular one word in its opening, which Heidegger renders as follows:

> Vielfältig das Unheimliche, nichts doch
> über den Menschen hinaus Unheimlicheres ragend sich regt.

And which Ralph Manheim in turn translates as: "There is much that is strange, but nothing that surpasses man in strangeness."[6] This opening is something of a riddle—why is it, how is it, that man is stranger than strange, more uncanny than the uncanny?—and the lines that follow could hardly be taken as an answer: man goes out on the sea and on land, masters the earth and the animals, teaches himself language and thought, cures illnesses, and yet comes to nothing, for he cannot escape death. Whatever the "answer" to the riddle of man, it has to do with what he can do and what he cannot do anything about, his living and his dying. Heidegger's translation of the Greek words *deinon* and *deinataton* by *unheimlich* ("uncanny," say) is already an answer to the riddle: an account of man's living and dying, his always going out to that which is different and his always coming back to the same. But before going over to Heidegger's "answer"—to his determination of man's essence as the most uncanny of that which is uncanny—we should note that it is a little different from, not quite the same as, Hölderlin's own "answer." That is, Hölderlin translates the opening of the choral ode by rendering the Greek not as *unheimlich* but as *ungeheuer:*

> Ungeheuer ist viel. Doch nichts
> Ungeheuerer als der Mensch.

> Much is monstrous. But nothing
> more monstrous than man.

Heidegger is, of course, well aware of this difference and the apparent strangeness of interpreting Hölderlin's dialogue with Sophocles and yet not using Hölderlin's own translation of Sophocles: "Since Hölderlin himself translated the whole of Sophocles' *Antigone*, it would

6. In Martin Heidegger, *An Introduction to Metaphysics* translated by Ralph Manheim (Garden City, New York: Doubleday, 1961), 123.

seem appropriate to listen to this choral ode in Hölderlin's own translation. Nevertheless, this translation (*Übersetzung*) is comprehensible only on the basis of the Hölderlinian translation (*Übertragung*) in its entirety and this in turn only in the immediate proximity of the original Greek word" (70). In other words, Heidegger does not quote Hölderlin's own translation because he does not want to quote it out of context. But the "context" of Hölderlin's translation in its entirety is not to be understood in any ordinary sense. As many scandalized philologists have pointed out, Heidegger has no trouble whatsoever quoting Hölderlin out of context—indeed, some would say that his whole project of interpreting Hölderlin rests on arbitrarily ripping lines out of context and making them mean something other than what they mean "in context." No, Heidegger means more than that by "only on the basis of Hölderlinian translation in its entirety" (*nur aus dem Ganzen der Hölderlinschen Übertragung*)—as the switch from *Übersetzung* to *Übertragung* suggests. He means that Hölderlin's translation of the choral ode would be understandable only on the basis of our already having understood Hölderlin's entire project of translating—carrying over—Greek and the Greeks: that is, only on the basis of our already having understood Hölderlin's interpretation of the Greeks' historical specificity and our ("Hesperian") historical specificity in their sameness and their difference. In other words, the real reason for Heidegger's not quoting Hölderlin's translation here is the nature, the essence, of translation itself. Translation, according to Heidegger's "Note on Translation" which he interposes directly after his quotation of the choral ode, is not the substitution of a word in one language by a word in another language as though one could coincide with the other. All translation has to be interpretation (*Auslegen*), not the preparatory step to interpretation but always the result of interpretation. "But the reverse also holds," continues Heidegger, "every interpretation, and everything that serves it, is a translation. For translation moves not only between two different languages, but rather there is a translation within the same language. The interpretation of Hölderlin's hymns is a translation internal to our German language" (75). Heidegger summarizes: "All translation is interpretation. And all interpretation is translation. Insofar as it is necessary for us to interpret works of thought and of poetry of our own language, this indicates that every historical language in itself and for itself is in need of translation and not only in relation to a foreign language. This in turn indicates that a historical people is at home in its own language not of itself, that is, not without its contribution (its act in addition, *Zutun*). Hence it can happen that we indeed speak "'German' and yet talk in nothing but 'American' " (79–80). (And to talk "American" is according to these lectures of 1942 the worst thing one can do. What the lectures call *Amerikanismus* is bereft of history (*geschichtslos*) and un-historical (*ungeschichtlich*), and even "Bolshevism" is only a degenerate form (*Abart*) of *Amerikanismus*.) If this is the case, if translation is not confined to what takes place *between* different languages but rather is what (always already) takes place *within* "one" and the same language, then it is no wonder that Heidegger, in his attempt to interpret the Greeks and Hölderlin, to interpret the dialogue of Hölderlin and the Greeks, does not (indeed cannot) use Hölderlin's "own" translation but rather has to re-translate both Sophocles' Greek and Hölderlin's German. For Hölderlin's German is not his own, is not truly German, *is* not in an authentically historical sense, except in dialogue with Greek—just as "a historical people *is* only on the basis of the dialogue of its language with foreign languages" [*Ein geschichtliches Volk* ist *nur aus der Zwiesprache seiner Sprache mit fremden Sprachen*] (80). Hence when Heidegger re-translates the Greek word, the x of the Greeks' determination of man's essence, with his *unheimlich* [uncanny] rather than Hölderlin's *ungeheuer*, it is no arbitrary substitution but an interpretation that would say the same thing as Hölderlin. For to say the same [*das Selbe*] is not to say the merely identical [*das Gleiche*]: "The same is truly the same only in the differentiated" (155), says Heidegger. In order to *think* the same of what Hölderlin says, it is necessary to say what he leaves *un*-said, in other words, to say it differently, to say it otherwise. This is why Heidegger says *unheimlich* and not *ungeheuer* (i.e., *unheimlich* says the same thing as *ungeheuer* but [precisely *because*] it says it in its difference). As is clear, all the weight of Heidegger's thinking—of the same and the identical, of *Dichten* and *Denken*, of dialogue as *Auseinandersetzung*, etc.—and what Philippe Lacoue-Labarthe calls its "hyperbologic"—in shorthand, the more it differs, the more it is the same— could be brought to bear in order to justify this re-translation. Nevertheless, questions remain. For one, it remains to be asked whether Heidegger's *unheimlich* preserves the internal difference proper to *ungeheuer*, whether his re-translation translates the word's self-translation. What happens when the x of the Greek, the x of the Greek*s*—their determination of the essential nature of man—is translated as *unheimlich* and not as *ungeheuer*? And since the question of the Greek *x* is precisely the question of translation—that is, going out to the different and returning to the same—this question also asks: what happens when the *x* of translation—the translation of translation, as it were—is translated as *unheimlich* and not as *ungeheuer*?

Heidegger would, of course, have no trouble solving the riddle: what happens is that we begin finally to understand Hölderlin. In other words, Heidegger's retranslation of the choral ode is thinking more Hölderlinian than Hölderlin—just as in order to understand the Greeks we have "to think more Greek than the Greeks themselves" [*griechischer denken als die Griechen selbst*] (100)—and many commentators have pointed out that in his re-translation of the Greek Heidegger only follows a path already marked out for him by Hölderlin's own translation: that is, in the direction of a "pessimistic" reading of the choral ode—not as a hymn to the glory of man but as a putting into question of man as monstrous in his excesses as wielder of *Technik* when thought against the background of his essential finitude. How is *unheimlich* instead of *ungeheuer* more Hölderlinian than Hölderlin? Heidegger thinks man's essential "uncanniness" [*Unheimlichkeit*] on the basis of what he calls the law of history, or, better, "the law of historicity" [*das Gesetz der Geschichtlichkeit*]. This law is to be thought as "the altercation of that which is foreign and that which is one's own" [*Auseinandersetzung des Fremden und des Eigenen*] which is "the grounding truth of history" [*die Grundwahrheit der Geschichte*] (61). If man is *unheimlich*—the most *unheimlich* of all that is *unheimlich*—it is because his essence consists in "coming to be at home" [*Heimischwerden*]; and if his essence is "coming to be at home" [*Heimischwerden*], then this means that it is at the same time "not *being* at home" [*Unheimischsein*]. "Coming to be at home" [*Heimischwerden*] and "not *being* at home" [*Unheimischsein*] are mutually implicated, mutually determine the essence of man: if man has to *come to be* at home, then he *is* not at home; if man *is* not at home, then he has to *come to be* at home.

> Coming to be at home in that which is one's own [*Das Heimischwerden im Eigenen*] is the only concern (or "care," *Sorge*) of the poetry of Hölderlin that has entered the form of the 'hymn,' whereby of course 'hymn' means no fixed literary and poetic schema, but rather determines its essence on the basis of the saying of coming into that which is one's own. That which is one's own [*das Eigene*] is the native

[*das Vaterländische*] of the German. That which is native itself is at home with the mother earth. This *coming to be* at home [*Heimisch*werden] in that which is one's own includes in itself that man first of all and for a long time and sometimes for always is not at home. And this in turn includes that man mistakes and denies and flees the at home [*das Heimische*], perhaps even has to deny it. Thus coming to be at home [*das Heimischwerden*] is a passing through that which is foreign. [60]

This "law of historicity"—the mutual implication and intrication of not being at home [*Unheimischsein*] and coming to be at home [*Heimischwerden*]—is given an ontological interpretation by Heidegger—i.e., in the terms of the fundamental ontological project of *Sein und Zeit*. That is, man's uncanniness [*Unheimlichkeit*] is grounded in his homelessness [*Unheimischkeit*] and this homelessness in turn has its hidden ground in man's relation [*Bezug*] to Being. In short: "The uncanniness of man has its essence in homelessness, but this homelessness is what it is only through this, that man is at home at all in Being" [*Die Unheimlichkeit des Menschen hat ihr Wesen in der Unheimischkeit, diese aber ist, was sie ist, nur dadurch, daß der Mensch überhaupt im Sein heimisch ist*] (113–14). It is this reading of *Unheimlichkeit* on the basis of *Unheimischkeit* and in turn on the basis of man's relation to Being that allows Heidegger to interpret the choral ode in terms of the ontological difference between Being and beings, *Sein* and *Seiendes*. That is, man goes out and seeks his home in beings [*Seiendes*], masters it through his technology, but is always called back to the same nothing by his essential finitude, his death, and this nothing is the nothing *of* Being—the only place he can *be* at home. In short, man's *Unheimlichkeit* is grounded in his essential *Unheimischsein* [not *being* at home] and *Heimischwerden* [*coming to be* at home], and Heidegger has little trouble interpreting Hölderlin's *ungeheuer* as meaning the same as *unheimlich*: "The monstrous is at the same time and properly speaking the unfamiliar. The familiar is the intimate, the at home. The monstrous is the not at home" [*Das Ungeheure ist zugleich und eigentlich das Nicht-Geheure. Das Geheure ist das Vertraute, Heimische. Das Ungeheure ist das Un-heimische*] (86). If *unheimlich* means *unheimisch* and *ungeheuer* means *unheimisch*, then *ungeheuer* means *unheimlich*. Hence Heidegger can justify his re-translation: "In that we translate *deinon* with 'unheimlich', we think in the direction of the not familiar" [*Indem wir das* deinon *mit 'unheimlich' über-*

setzen, denken wir in die Richtung des Nicht-geheuren) (87). In short, Heidegger translates Hölderlin's going over and coming back on the basis of the essence of going over and coming back and this means by himself going over and coming back: from Hölderlin to the Greek(s) and back. Hence it is no wonder that Heidegger also has no trouble in interpreting the enigmatic lines of "Der Ister":

> Der [the Ister] scheinet aber fast
> Rukwärts zu gehen und
> Ich mein, er müsse kommen
> Von Osten.
> Vieles wäre
> Zu sagen davon.

> But it [the river Ister] seems almost
> To go backwards and
> I mean, it must come
> From the East.
> Much could
> Be said about this.

If the Ister—the Greek name for the Danube [*Istros*]—seems to hesitate at its source and origin in Germany before resuming its West to East itinerary and thus seems almost to go backwards (i.e., East to West, as thought it had come from the East), it is not just on account of the difficulty (for a demi-god) of forgetting the source. Rather it is also because the river Ister fulfills the law of historicity—in short, coming to be at home by going out to and back from that which is foreign, the altercation of *Unheimischsein* and *Heimischwerden*—has always already fulfilled the law of history at its source, at its origin, by having invited the Greek Hercules as a guest [*den Herkules zu Gaste geladen*], as the second strophe puts it, when he came from the hot isthmus [*vom heißen Isthmos*] to the shady source of the Ister looking for the shady olive tree to plant it in the shadeless festival arena of the Olympic games. "The Ister," writes Heidegger, "*is* the river, for which that which is foreign is a guest and present already at the source, the river in whose flowing the dialogue of that which is one's own and that which is foreign always speaks" [*Der Ister ist jener Strom, bei dem schon an der Quelle das Fremde zu Gast und Gegenwärtig ist, in dessen Strömen die Zwiesprache des Eigenen und Fremden ständig spricht*] (182). If the Ister at its source seems almost to go backward, as though it had come from the East, it is because its foreignness is *at* the source, it has always already at its source gone out to the foreign and come back to the fatherland. The Ister does not want to go East because it has always already at its source gone to the East and come back to the West—thus fulfilling its authentically historical destiny, its essence as *Halbgott,* and hence as essentially poetic [*dichterisch*], etc.

This brief and insufficient sketch of Heidegger's interpretation *of* going over and coming back *by* going over and coming back should nevertheless indicate the "law" governing his interpretation of Hölderlin. That "law" is the law of history itself—"according to which that which is one's own is the most distant and the path to that which is most one's own is the longest and most difficult" [*derzufolge das Eigene das Fernste und der Weg zum Eigensten der längste und schwerste ist*] (179)—and it is grounded in an ontological interpretation of historical man's essence. That is why it is futile to object to Heidegger's interpretation on the basis of any prematurely "philological" grounds: if Heidegger interprets Hölderlin "out of context," he nevertheless thinks his poetry within a more rigorous "context"—that of fundamental ontology and its account of the relation between apparent and non-apparent meaning, between said and un-said, thought and un-thought—than any mere philology can come up with (because *as* mere philology it cannot think its own essence and therefore always has to interpret on the basis of an un-thought [i.e., metaphysical] interpretation of Being). Nevertheless, a question can still be asked. An oblique way to formulate it would be to ask whether Heidegger's interpretation of Hölderlin's *ungeheuer* as *nicht geheuer,* i.e., unfamiliar, and this in turn as *unheimlich* leaves anything over, a self-translating difference from itself that is not quite gotten across by changing *un-* to *nicht-*. On a purely "verbal" level—when we translate *ungeheuer* into English or French and not into German—it is clear what does not make it across: it is the monstrous and the monster, the monstrous of man and the monster that is man. (And that Hölderlin does, to some extent, mean monster is corroborated by his famous statement of "the tragic" in the "Notes to Oedipus": "The presentation of the tragic rests principally on the notion that the monstrous [*das Ungeheure*], the way in which god and man mate ["couple," *sich paart*], in which the natural force and the innermost part of man become one, boundless, in rage, is understood through the purification, by a limitless scission, of the boundless act of becoming-one.") A less oblique way to ask the question of this excess monstrosity (of translation) would be in terms of Heidegger's "law of history": that is, if in thinking the same as Hölderlin, Heidegger remembers to say it differently, to say it in its difference from itself—in short, remembers that Hölderlin has "his own" language only in dialogue with the foreign language of the Greeks—does he also remember to think the same of the Greeks and of the Greek in its internal difference from itself—in short, does he remember that the Greeks also had "their own" language only in dialogue with a foreign language? In other words, we are asking about Hölderlin's famous first letter to Böhlendorff (4 December 1801) and its interpretation of the conditions of poetry-writing for the Greeks and for us Hesperians in terms of differing relations between that which is one's own and that which is foreign, *das Eigene* and *das Fremde*, for the Greeks and for us. Heidegger not only refers to the letter and its scheme throughout the two hundred pages of his lectures—for instance in his abbreviated version of the "law of history": "that which is one's own the most distant—the path to that which is most one's own is the most difficult" [*das Eigene das Fernste—der Weg zum Eigensten der schwerste*] (179)—but also gives it a more elaborate and explicit interpretation than anywhere else in his work. In brief, the scheme runs as follows: that which is national, natural, their own [*das Eigene*] for the Greeks, what they are born to, is what Hölderlin characterizes as the "fire from heaven" and "holy pathos"; whereas that which is foreign and needs to be appropriated for the Greeks is what he characterizes as "the clarity of representation" and "Junonian sobriety." For us Hesperians, it is the reverse: our nature, what we are born with, that which is our own [*das Eigene*], is precisely "the clarity of representation" and "Junonian sobriety"; whereas that which is foreign and in need of appropriation for us is the "fire from heaven" and "holy pathos." What is natural and *das Eigene* for the Greeks is foreign ["*das Fremde*] for us; and what is foreign for the Greeks is natural and *das Eigene* for us. There is a chiasmic reversal in the relations of *das Eigene* and *das Fremde* for the Greeks and for us, and the reason is easy to see: what we are born to, what is natural, national, and proper for us is precisely that which the Greeks—whose nature was different from ours—appropriated: that is, their culture. Our nature is Greek culture. The ramifications of this reversal are far-reaching: for one thing, it means that we Hesperian artists cannot simply imitate Greek art—treat it as though it were a nature to be imitated—because that art is the response to a different nature from ours. In short—as Peter Szondi puts it—it means a wholesale rejection of Winckelmannian classicism.[7] On the other hand, it does not mean a wholesale turning away from the Greeks, for that which is one's own, says Hölderlin, as to be learned just as much as that which is foreign; and because it *is* that which is one's own—natural, national, that which we are born with—it is the most difficult to use freely and this is why we will never surpass the Greeks in the clarity of representation and Junonian sobriety that we are born with and that for them was foreign (and therefore easier to use freely). In any case, much could be said about this (and I have done so elsewhere in three essays on Hölderlin).[8] Here we are more interested in what Heidegger does— and what is done to Heidegger—when he comes to interpret this letter and its historical scheme. Although he follows the letter faithfully in his interpretation of it, Heidegger nevertheless makes a slight shift when he applies the letter's scheme of *das Eigene* and *das Fremde* ("that which is one's own" and "that which is foreign") to interpret the poem "the Ister" and the Greek determination of man's essence. In short, whereas Hölderlin's scheme maintains an internal doubleness of that which is one's own and that which is foreign, *das Eigene* and *das Fremde*, both for the Greeks and for us, Heidegger identifies Hesperia (in these lectures, simply "Germany" or the "Germans") with that which is one's own, *das Eigene*, and Greece with that which is foreign, *das Fremde*. In doing so, Heidegger not only changes Hölderlin's bipolar scheme of a relation (by inversion) of bipolar terms into a simply bipolar scheme of us (Hesperians, Germans) and the Greeks, that which is one's own and that which is foreign, *das Eigene* and *das Fremde*, that is to say, of simple terms— and thereby reduces Hölderlin's version of the relation between the Greeks and us to one of the terms of that relation. No, more important than what this shift does to Hölderlin's scheme is what it does to Hölderlin's *Greeks*. That is, whereas Heidegger is able to preserve a certain doubleness of, a certain internal difference to, us Hesperians, Germans—insofar as we are ourselves, *das Eigene*, only in dialogue with the Greeks, *das Fremde*, etc.—in identifying the Greeks with

7. Peter Szondi, "Überwindung des Klassizismus," in *Hölderlin-Studien* (Frankfurt am Main: Suhrkamp, 1967). See our reading of Szondi in "Hölderlin in France," in *Readings in Interpretation: Hölderlin, Hegel, Heidegger* (Minneapolis: The University of Minnesota Press, 1987).

8. In "Endpapers: Hölderlin's Textual History," "Hölderlin in France," "Heidegger Reading Hölderlin," all in *Readings in Interpretation*.

the simply foreign, *das Fremde*, he nevertheless is not able to pre-serve the *Greeks'* difference from themselves, their own "dialogue" between that which was their own, *das Eigene*, and that which was foreign for them, *das Fremde*. In other words, by calling the Greeks simply *fremd*, foreign, Heidegger collapses that which is their own and that which is foreign, *das Eigene* and *das Fremde*, for them. This is evident throughout his interpretation in his constant identifica-tion of the foreign, *das Fremde*, with the Greeks and the Greeks with the east and the south, the fire from heaven. In short, Heidegger—in calling the Greeks foreign, *das Fremde*, for us—quite simply reverses Hölderlin's terms and calls that which for Hölderlin is our own, *das Eigene*—the clarity of representation, Junonian sobriety, i.e., Greek culture, say—foreign, *das Fremde*. And in doing so, he also renders that which is radically foreign for us—i.e., the Greeks' nature, that which is natural and their own, *das Eigene*, for the Greeks: the fire from heaven. holy pathos—our own, that is to say, *Greek*. That this shift effaces the Greeks' internal difference to themselves becomes clearer if we identify the Greeks' *nature*, that which is their own, *das Eigene*—i.e., the fire from heaven, holy pathos: namely, as the East, the Orient, or, in some of Hölderlin's texts (for instance, *Hyperion* or the third version of the *Empedocles* drama), Egypt and the Egyptians. That is to say, the Greeks' nature, that which is their own, *das Eigene*, is somebody else's culture: the Oriental fire from heaven and holy pathos (just as our Hesperian nature, that which is our own, *das Eigene*, for us is also somebody else's culture: the Greek clarity of representation, Junonian sobriety). If it is legitimate to read Höld-erlin's scheme in this way, then what happens in Heidegger's identifi-cation of the Greeks as foreign (for us), *das Fremde*, for us—as the fire from heaven and holy pathos, as the South and the East—is his turn-ing of what is a threefold historical scheme of Orient, Greece, and Hesperia into a twofold scheme of Greece and Hesperia: in other words, Heidegger turns a scheme of us (Hesperians) and them (Greeks) and *their* them (the Orient) into a scheme of us and them, Hesperia (or "Germany") and Greece. To turn the Greeks into that which is simply *foreign* for us (when for Hölderlin it is that which is *our own*), then, means to collapse the Greeks' nature and the Greeks' culture, *das Eigene* and *das Fremde*, and thereby, quite simply, to suppress the radical difference of the nature of the Greeks: that is, to suppress the Orient, the East, Egypt, etc. This suppression of the Orient is legible throughout Heidegger's interpretation of Hölderlin

and the Greeks in his consistent reduction to a twofold scheme—
Greece and Hesperia—of what is well marked everywhere in Höl-
derlin as a threefold scheme: Orient, Greece, Hesperia. In the "Ister,"
for instance, the threefold is marked by the names of three rivers: one
Oriental (the Indus), one Greek (the Alpheus), and one Hesperian (the
Ister):

> Wir singen aber vom Indus her
> Fernangekommen und
> Vom Alpheus, lange haben
> Das Schikliche wir gesucht,
> Nicht ohne Schwingen mag
> Zum Nächsten einer greifen
> Geradezu
> Und kommen auf die andere Seite.
> Hier aber wollen wir bauen.

> But, as for us, we sing from the Indus,
> Arrived from afar, and
> From the Alpheus, long we
> Have sought what is fitting,
> Not without wings may one
> Reach out for that which is nearest
> Directly
> And get to the other side.
> But here we wish to build.

If we come *here,* to the West, to Hesperia, to the Ister—"Man nennet
aber diesen den Ister. / Schön wohnt er" [But one calls this one the
Ister. / Beautifully he dwells]—from the East and the Orient *by way
of Greece,* then what this means, at the very least, is that our origin
and source cannot simply be a matter of us and the Greeks—of the
Ister and his Greek guest (Hercules)—cannot be a simply Graeco-
German origin. Rather the "origin" is, as it were, a Graeco-Oriental
(or Graeco-Egyptian) origin, and this would offer a different way to
read the lines about the Ister's seeming to go backwards:

> Der scheinet aber fast
> Rükwärts zu gehen und
> Ich mein, er müsse kommen
> Von Osten.
> Vieles wäre
> Zu sagen davon.

> But it seems almost
> To go backwards and
> I mean, it must come
> From the East.
> Much could
> Be said about this.

That is, the Ister seems almost to go backwards not in its hesitating at the source and seeming almost to go East to West but rather in its natural itinerary, in its going from West to East—as though its historical origin were in Germany and the West and not in the East— whence (from the Indus through the Alpheus) we have historically come—and whence, historically, *it* must come: *und / Ich mein, er müsse kommen / Von Osten* [and, I mean, it *must* come from the East]. In short, rather than *going* backwards—West to East—the Ister, as truly historical, must *come* from the East (and the antithesis between *going* [*gehen*] and *coming* [*kommen*] would support such a reading). This reading of Hölderlin's historical scheme cannot help but have implications for Heidegger's "law of history"—in short-hand, again, "that which is one's own the most distant"—and the hyperbologic of not *being* at home and *coming to be* at home, *Unheimischsein* and *Heimischwerden*. In other words, that which is the furthest, the most distant, the most foreign, for us is not Greece and the Greeks—strictly speaking, i.e., Hölderlin speaking, this is our own, *das Eigene*—but rather the East and the Orient. And it is most foreign for us because we are separated from it by our *Greek nature*— our Greek metaphysics, ontology, epistemology, aesthetics, etc. If we are not at home, exiled, we are *not* not at home in relation to, or exiled from, Greece and the Greeks but rather "in relation to," and exiled from, the East, the Orient. And because the relation of nature and culture, that which is one's own and that which is foreign, *das Eigene* and *das Fremde*—i.e., the clarity of representation and Junonian sobriety on the one hand and the fire from heaven and holy pathos on the other—for the Orient was exactly the same as it is for us[9] (how else could the Oriental fire from heaven have been natural, their own,

---

9. Cf., our "Endpapers: Hölderlin's Textual History," in *Readings in Interpretation* for this scheme:

	Egypt (Orient)	Greece	Hesperia
nature		"fire from heaven," "holy pathos," . . .	
culture		"Junonian sobriety," "clarity of representation," . . .	

das Eigene, for the Greeks?), to be not at home in relation to, or exiled from, the Orient means to be not at home in relation to, or exiled from, ourselves: i.e., not the Graeco-Hesperians or Graeco-Germans but the Hespero-Orientals, Germano-Orientals. In short, we are not at home not because we are exiled *from* Greece but rather because we are exiled *by* Greece from ourselves: the Orient, the East, Egypt, etc. Again: it's not just that we are not at home, but rather that we are not at home in relation to not being at home; or, better, we are not just exiled (from Greece, say) but rather exiled *from* exile (exiled from the Greeks' exile, say), as Blanchot puts it in writing on Kafka. From such an exile (from exile), there is no return—not even a return to statements (or "laws") of history like: "Hesperia is the Orient," "We are the Orientals (or the Egyptians)," etc. For such statements would identify that which cannot be identified—that which makes all (self-) identification impossible—in the terms of any ontology, no matter how fundamental. In other words, there is a radical disjunction between us Hesperians and the Orient, and Greece *is* it. To "identify" ourselves as Orientals would amount once again to reducing that which is radically foreign for us to that which is our own, the Oriental to the Greek. It would amount to the same thing as saying "We are dead" and meaning the death of the Greeks—that which is natural and our own, a death in which we can identify ourselves. To say "Hesperia is the Orient" or "We are the Orientals" is to say "We are dead" and to mean the death of the Orient—that which is radically foreign for us, a death in which we cannot identify ourselves because it is not *our own* death (i.e., the death of the Greeks), not being dead for ourselves, but an other death: being dead for somebody else, a death without death. This would be one way to read Hölderlin's determination of man's historical essence as monstrous: the monstrosity of history, history as the monster.

POSTSCRIPT:

A perhaps more straightforward way to put this would be by way of two quotations from Paul de Man's "The Riddle of Hölderlin"—a review essay in the *New York Review of Books* that dates from 1970 and remains, for those who can read, one of the best essays on Hölderlin. The first is an explanation of the attraction of Hölderlin's scheme for critics with a utopian or apocalyptic bent: "Thus the transposition of Hölderlin's philo-Hellenism into a literal historical scheme yields an interpretation of the present that is, to some critics, reassuring; during a period of history that is part of our civilization, men could think of the gods as actual presences from which they were not separated by transcendental distances. If this was possible for a consciousness not essentially different from our own, it follows that the absence of gods, painfully experienced as everyday reality, may be only a passing dark phase between two stages of unity, one past but another still to come."[10] Although this statement does not apply to Heidegger's interpretation immediately—not without some translation to make it fit (for example, of the terms "consciousness" and of "essentially different")—it is close enough to his law of history, being not at home and coming to be at home, etc. De Man's—that is, Hölderlin's—answer is uncompromising: "True wisdom begins in the knowledge of its own historical ineffectiveness. When Hölderlin invokes the possibility of future moments of historical splendor, comparable to what Greece used to be in the past, such evocations are accompanied by the foreknowledge that people will be conscious of the achievement of these periods when they have ceased to be and have become in turn parts of the past. Nothing could be more remote from schemes that conceive of history as either apocalyptic failure or salvation." To transpose this into the terms of our reading of Hölderlin's scheme: if we as Hesperians can be the nature for an other Greece—other Greeks and other Greek gods to come after us—it is only as *dead*, as the Orient (or Egyptians): that is, as dead not for ourselves, but as dead for somebody else. The upshot would be that "Greece" and "the Greeks" is something we invent in order not to face this other death: an other death that reminds us that there never were any Greeks in the first place—and therefore no Orient or Hesperia (or Germany) in the first (or last) place either—but only a monstrous wearing away and wearing down, the ceaseless erosion of monstrous material history.[11]

10. Paul de Man, "The Riddle of Hölderlin," *The New York Review of Books* 15, no. 9 (19 November 1970): 47–52. This essay is now reprinted in: Paul de Man, *Critical Writings, 1953–1978* ed. Lindsay Waters (Minneapolis: The University of Minnesota Press, 1988).

11. Perhaps this is the direction in which Heidegger thinks in a remark of the "Letter on Humanism" (1946): "We have still hardly begun to think the mysterious relations to the East, that were put into words in Hölderlin's poetry" [*Wir haben noch kaum begonnen, die geheimnisvollen Bezüge zum Osten zu denken, die in Hölderlins Dichtung Wort geworden sind*]. Something like an "Oriental," "Egyptian," reading of Heidegger—these terms being read in a Hölderlinian sense—is Jacques Derrida on Heidegger on Trakl in his Paris seminar of spring 1985 and in the essay "Geschlecht 2: Heidegger's Hand," in *Deconstruction and Philosophy* ed. John Sallis (Chicago: University of Chicago Press, 1987). In French in Jacques Derrida, *Psyché, Inventions de l'autre* (Paris: Galilée, 1987).

E. S. BURT

Cracking the Code: The Poetical and Political Legacy of Chénier's "Antique Verse"

André Chénier left a legacy in two parts: a fragmentary, unfinished and unpublished poetic work; a set of published articles on political topics that were partially responsible for his meeting his death on the scaffold during the Terror. What kind of double legacy is this to hand down?

Because the poetic work was left unpublished, because the political works were published to such dramatic effect, the question has a peculiar immediacy. The first task of editors in preparing Chénier's manuscripts for publication has been to provide the poetic work the polish that it lacks, thereby making it inseparable from the history of its reception.[1] The political works on their side have also posed a problem. Strongly argued, passionate reflections on issues ranging from partisan spirit and the constitution, to the National Assembly and the trial of Louis XVI, the political articles are topical enough pieces of journalism to have provided a battleground for the ideological disputes over the inheritance of the French Revolution and of the Terror.[2] Critics have tended to seek to determine by their means

---

1. The unfinished state of the poems has tempted more than one critic to bring scissors or pen to bear on them. Gérard Walter reproaches Chénier's first editor, Hyacinthe Latouche, for "suppressing passages deemed 'subversive' and indecent." "Introduction," in *Oeuvres complètes*, ed. G. Walter (Paris: Gallimard, 1958), xxxv. No less a critic than Leo Spitzer rewrites a stanza of "La Jeune captive," claiming that the poet himself would have done so "had he lived longer." *Interpretationen zur Geschichte der Französischen Lyrik*, (Heidelberg: Selbstverlag des Romanischen Seminars, 1961), 103.

2. See François Furet, *Interpreting the French Revolution*, trans. Elborg Forster (Cambridge: Cambridge University Press, 1981), 3–14, for a discussion on the Revolution as the site of a conflict over national identity. Chénier's work has served as one

YFS 77, *Reading the Archive: On Texts and Institutions*, ed. E. S. Burt and Janie Vanpée, © 1990 by Yale University.

whether Chénier was guilty as charged of being an "Enemy of the people," or whether the libertarian and antipartisan sentiment he expressed in his political writings was not, on the contrary, closest to the spirit in which the Revolution was undertaken.[3] The existence of these two parts to the legacy has led to a third area of difficulty: the apparently innocuous decisions made by editors about the shape of the poetic work are suspiciously ideological; the ideological battles tend, on the other hand, to get translated into such questions as whether poetry makes a good weapon in the war of ideologies, or ought rather to exist in retreat from political questions, whether Chénier mistakenly conceived of the poet as warrior and legislator, etc.[4]

The two parts to Chénier's legacy raise a question: can they be thought of together, despite differences in formal treatment, degree of completion, status of publication, or audience addressed? Ought they to be thought separately, despite those places where the literary and the political can be made to share a common definition—as mode of action on a public, as the products of a single intention, as leading to indeterminable effects? The *Essai sur les causes et les effets de la perfection et de la décadence dans les lettres et les arts*,[5] where

---

focus in the game of "capture the flag" that gets played out in interpretations of the Revolutionary period.

3. See, for representative views, the "Introduction" to the Pléiade edition by Chénier's twentieth-century Marxist editor, Gérard Walter, op. cit., vii–xxxvi, as well as his biography, *André Chénier, son milieu et son temps* (Paris: Laffont, 1947); Francis Scarfe, *André Chénier: His Life and Work* (Oxford: Oxford University Press, 1965); Paul Dimoff, *La Vie et l'oeuvre d'André Chénier jusqu'à la Révolution française: 1762–1790* (Geneva: Droz, 1936), vol. 2, 117–73. All translations from the French are my own.

4. Jean Starobinski, in "André Chénier and the Allegory of Poetry," *Images of Romanticism: Verbal and Visual Affinities*, ed. K. Kroeber and W. Walling (New Haven: Yale University Press, 1978), 39–60. He finds Chénier to take a crucial turn away from political allegory to a Romantic poetry of the self. For Starobinski, it is this poetry of lyric expression that has a future.

5. At various moments in the *Essai*, literature is defined to harmonize with political action: "Two things, being more than others the fruit of genius and of courage, and ordinarily of both, lead most surely to true glory: these are great actions that uphold the commonweal [*la chose publique*], and good writings that enlighten it. To do well is that which may most make a man great; to speak well is not to be disdained either; and often a good book is itself a good action; and often a wise and sublime author, being the slow cause of healthy revolutions in customs and ideas, may seem to have done himself all the good that he makes others do." Walter, 622.

In other passages from the *Essai*, Chénier distinguishes literature from the political, with which it nonetheless lives in harmony, because it provides knowledge of corrup-

Chénier traces together in a fictional geneology the degeneration of literature and of republican political institutions, is the central theoretical text where the question is addressed, as the political writings are the place where it is given its most clearly pragmatic turn.[6] But it is in the unfinished epics, above all in *Hermès*, where is told the history of mankind with respect to the law, that the theoretical possibility of defining the literary and the political "so that they agree with or else exclude one another,"[7] and the practical necessity of deciding on a given occasion which definition is to be preferred, come together. It is thus in that epic that we can best discover the principles that divide, and bring together, the two sides of the legacy.

Now it is a peculiarity of Chénier's poetical legacy, named as the chief offering of *Hermès*, that it is no whole cup of poetry he hands us, but a cracked and fragmentary vessel. Why is the poetical work so fragmentary and what do its perceptible cracks have to say about the political? The question has been obscured by the assumption that Chénier embraced unproblematically the political and aesthetic models of the Greco-Roman tradition. The fragmentariness of the work has been considered exclusively in this light, without taking into account Chénier's interest in the Orient, and without considering whether his fragments might not lie outside, or border on, the ideals of the western tradition.[8] A digression into the fragmentariness of the poetical works is thus required.

---

tion in the state. For a corrupt republic, letters are a salutary reminder of antique institutions, and are far removed from the avarice and pragmatic economies governing power relations in the state (623). In tyrannies, however, he finds letters to turn frivolous and their degeneration actively to propagate the ills in the public domain (624). In this case, literature has to retreat, in the person of the poet, from the neighborhood of political action (624–25).

6. In *Avis au peuple français sur ses véritables ennemis,* for example, Chénier justifies his examination of an enemy "party" of writers by means of a claim that the Revolution is intimately bound up with writing: "All the good and evil that has been done in this revolution is owed to writings; it will perhaps be there also that we will find the source of evils that threaten us" (206). In *Réflexions sur l'esprit de parti,* previous to a critique of the chaotic ideas and bad metaphors of Burke's *Reflections on the French Revolution,* he finds one of the characteristic marks of the Revolution to be that of good writing (242).

7. Cf., Paul Valéry, "Réponse à une enquête (sur la chose littéraire et la chose pratique)," in *Oeuvres complètes* (Paris: Gallimard, 1957), vol. 2, 1148.

8. Chénier's famous lines on the birth of the poet ought to be considered in this context: ". . . a Greek, in her young springtime, / Beautiful, from the bed of a spouse nursling of France / Bore me French in the heart of Byzantium" (72). The French poet is born in, and oriented toward, a Greek East.

A peculiar set of conditions—Chénier's premature death, his disorderly method of composition,[9] and his transitional position between the neoclassicism of the late eighteenth century and the romanticism of the nineteenth—have provided critics with ample material for speculation. Many pages have been written that attempt to fill in the gaps and to produce a continuous narrative: how Chénier would have developed had he survived the events of the Terror,[10] how he would have knit together the fragments jotted down in his notebooks for publication, how he would have negotiated the transition from the didactic philosophical poems of the eighteenth century to the lyrical voice of the Romantics.[11] Common to the general run of these stories is an implicit reproach directed at the poet for having failed so signally to provide his poems with the autonomy and aesthetic perfection we expect from the miniature totality that is the work of art.

We may ask whether the work is not as it stands complete. Does Chénier pass on to us, for reasons laid down in the work, a lack of polish that he finds to be the polish of poetry?[12] The specific finish to

9. See Paul Dimoff, "Préface" in Oeuvres complètes d'André Chénier, (Paris: Delagrave, 1946), 3 vols., vii–xxv, for a discussion of the manuscripts. Chénier's writing practices contribute to the difficulty facing editors. He worked on many poems at once, noting down randomly isolated lines, long fragments, prose synopses or critical reminders to himself; he added to apparently finished poems, inserted short poems in longer poems, or developed, out of the single image of a longer poem, a shorter poem. The poems themselves comment on their composition.

10. Examples of this kind of speculation are too frequent to be enumerated. Paul Dimoff, op. cit., 432–37, provides one of the most fully developed of the fictions attempting to overcome all the disjunctions of the work and life in a story of what would have happened had Chénier been "preserved by miracle from the perils of the Revolution."

11. Did the work remain unfinished because there was a defect in Chénier's poetic conception? A whole school of Chénier criticism concentrates on his transitional position between the long didactic poems of the eighteenth century and the emerging lyric of Romanticism, to find in Chénier's incomplete recognition that the future lay with the lyric the explanation for the fragmentariness of the long narrative poems. Similarly, the brittleness of some of the Odes and Bucoliques derives, or so the theory goes, from a neoclassicism in which too much attention is paid to the respectful recycling of old clichés, and not enough to the expressive originality of the lyrical subject. See, for example, Francis Scarfe or Jean Starobinski, op. cit. Henceforth cited in the text.

12. In a passage from the Essai, Chénier talks about an epic on America projected as unfinished: "As for Mr. . . . . it is a pity that with such great talents he has not carried through so beautiful an enterprise. We would have a poem to oppose to the ancients. But, as we have heard him say several time, his design, in beginning, was not to finish this work. He was already too old and had not yet finished several writings that have

be given poetry is addressed explicitly in various places, among others, in Chénier's much celebrated and misunderstood definition of the task of poetry from *L'Invention:* (*"Sur des pensers nouveaux faisons des vers antiques"*) On new thoughts let us make antique verse (127).

The central difficulty of the line centers on its articulation of incongruous terms—"new thoughts" and "antique verses." Where we might expect a relationship of a simple contrast—old or ancient opposed to new or modern—we get a different, puzzling articulation between language and thought: the task of poets is to give us antique, that is, outdated, verse on new thoughts. *Ancient* connotes a continuity between present and past, either within a single existing being, or within a tradition, but *antique* names the no longer extant, the untimely. It marks a rupture with a continuous narrative joining present to past.

Much of the interpretative effort that has been expended on Chénier has consisted in translating articulations like this one into oppositions, and then reading Chénier's definition of the poet's task as that of overcoming the opposition by the discovery of metaphors expressive of a larger totality. Had "new thought" been opposed to "old form" then the thesis of Francis Scarfe would be correct, and the "central problem of *L'Invention* (might) be reduced to the paradox: imitate the Ancients but dare to be new and original" (94). For Scarfe, Chénier stands opposed to his age around the issue of metaphor, which the poet sees as no mere ornament or poetic vehicle for expressing the thought of Enlightenment philosophy, but rather as the sensuous form in which the imagination reveals itself. Scarfe finds evidence that Chénier is an early Romantic poet and theorist of the lyric imagination in *L'Invention*, where invention is said to be the art of knotting things together in metaphors: ". . . in the arts the in-

---

placed him in the first rank among our poets. His project was only to show by this sample what road had to be followed and to which he alone was capable of holding. He aspired to take possession of this land without conquering it, and that his flag planted on the shore should intimidate and make flee whoever might desire to approach it. He wanted the short and precious fragment that he has published to be like the painting that Apelles left imperfect and that no other hand dared take upon itself the charge of finishing" (686).

Paul Van Tieghem, "Un 'Monsieur . . . ' mystérieux: André Chénier," *Revue d'Histoire Littéraire de la France* 35 (1928): 92–98, (henceforth cited in the text) has convincingly demonstrated that the "Mr." in question is Chénier himself and the poem, his epic *L'Amérique.*

ventor is he / . . . . Who, by certain knots, unforeseen and new, / Unites objects that seemed rivals . . ." (124). That Chénier only two lines previously defines the other half of the poet's task as the critical one of separating what old metaphors have assembled, of making peaceful "rival seeds" (124) by undoing false resemblances, seems to have escaped Scarfe, who has nothing but scorn for the threads of materialism and critical thought that tie the poet to his age. Scarfe's thesis comes to grief somewhere between the Scylla of the evidence available and the Charybdis of the evidence lacking. If the same poem, *L'Invention,* where Chénier supposedly gives his theory of a poetry of lyric expression, turns out to be, as Scarfe bad-humoredly states, "a piecemeal composition which does not logically hold together" (94), one has to wonder whether the failure is not in the account of the poetic theory, rather than in the poem. Nor is it particularly convincing to be told, faced with the formulation "On new thoughts let us make antique verse," that for Chénier, originality lies "in perceiving hitherto unknown analogies and in giving them new expression" (96). Surely, had the poet meant to say the opposite of what he did say, he would have said so.

A brief article by Paul Van Tieghem, "Un 'Monsieur . . .' mystérieux: André Chénier," provides a more complex and theoretically informed understanding of the line, which it still translates into a binary opposition:

> Chénier possesses to a rare degree that faculty of splitting himself that allows one to be almost simultaneously creative artist and critic attentive to grasping in advance the effect that the work, seen in a manner from the outside, will produce when it will have been finished. The continual see-saw motion that we observe in his works between the practice and theory of his art can be explained by this. One could almost say that he always has in front of himself two pieces of paper; onto one he throws down his poetic projects, onto the other he writes the general reflections that these same projects inspire in him, he notes the reactions that the work of art makes the philosopher conceive. [96]

Van Tieghem splits off a projective, inventive writer, a Homer who does not clearly envisage the questions to which he unwittingly provides answers, from a reflective, critical writer, whose belated position with respect to the text allows the discovery of things ignored by the inventive writer. The capacity of the poet to act as reader of his

own work—to uncover its foresightedness and its shortsightedness—
turns the poet into a theorist analyzing the failures and successes of
his original project.[13]

Now Van Tieghem's direct interest here is in explaining why Chénier was haunted by the unfinished work. The critical position of the
modern involves, for Van Tieghem, a theory of the fragment. A critic
is able to see in retrospect what is missing from the legacy of the past,
and in his belated, self-conscious commentary, will seek to compensate for the failure to achieve the totalization aimed at. In the most
literal sense, this is the position of the eighteenth-century observer
who considers the monuments of the past from the perspective of a
Winckelmann or a Warburton. He has to take into account a discrepancy between the avowed aim of transmitting formally perfect entities, symbolic works of art, and the fragments or ruins that constitute the actual legacy of the past. The new thought Chénier wants
to translate into his fragments is a thought concerning the material
conditions of the production and transmission of the works of the
past.[14]

In the last analysis, of course, the critical posture of the modern
restores the symbolic model criticized. The opposition to symbolic

13. For Van Tieghem, the new thoughts are those of a critical Enlightenment
thinker, and "antique verse" can be glossed as meaning perfect formal treatment: "It is
not easy, when one is very hard to please over the quality of verse and very ambitious
about the value of ideas, to make *antique verse* on *new thoughts,* to be at once the
thinker and the artist, the Rabelais drunk with modern culture and the Ronsard in love
with antique and perfect poetry" (97). "Antique" is not, however, a synonym for formal
perfection. Nor is it certain, in Chénier's vocabulary, that both of the terms in the
formula are to be positively weighted. "New thoughts" are not to be swallowed *tel quel*
by a pleasure-seeking wine drinker. In a fragment to *Hermès,* speaking of the discovery
of the new world, Chénier evaluates discovery in two entirely contradictory ways:
"Speak at the end prophetically of the discovery of the new world. Oh destinies, hasten
to bring this great day which . . . which . . . . But . . . no, destinies, defer this fatal day,
and if possible, let it never arrive, this day which . . . which . . . etc. . . ." (415). See also
the fragment from the *Essai* quoted in note 12, where the poet plants a flag in a New
World from which all will flee.

14. There is some evidence for this position. In *Hermès,* Chénier makes it the
concern of modern science: "Science wants, not content with admiring the form and
the work, to know the material and to see the hand act" (407). The poet would be
seeking to figure the critical posture of modern science with respect to the action of the
hand on the material that "to their (Greek) eyes is yet too veiled" (125). Indeed, Chénier,
who compares the path of the poet with that of the wandering comet, and the poet with
Mercury, is perfectly capable of adopting—temporarily—the scientist's position. However, it would be a mistake to think that he confuses his alchemy with the experiments
of Newton or Descartes.

writing is a negative moment quickly subsumed by a larger resemblance to it. A newly made fragment, however self-consciously it
distances itself from a naive harmony between form and idea, necessarily reinstates a similar harmony, for the fragment then becomes
the form adequately expressing the thought of modernity; it, too,
"paints the spirit to the senses" (126), although the spirit in question,
the spirit of Enlightenment, becomes critical and materialist. One
might legitimately say of this scheme what de Man, in his article on
Benjamin "The Task of the Translator," says of Gadamer's: it is "the
scheme or concept of modernity as the over-coming of a certain
awareness or naiveté by means of a critical negation."[15] In Van
Tieghem's view, Chénier still concerns himself with "*finishing* some
little part" (98), with composing some perfect fragment exhibiting all
the autonomy and aesthetic detachment of the masterpieces of the
Greeks.

The more rigorous formulations of Nancy and Lacoue-Labarthe in
L'Absolu littéraire give the stakes of this view for literary history.
They explain that the "romantic fragment, far from bringing into play
the dispersal or bursting apart of the work, inscribes its plurality as
the exergue of the total, infinite work."[16] The fragment supplies the
critical perspective missing from classicism. But it also points forward to Romanticism by its "fundamental theme of finishing" (67)
and by its promise of future works to be written in the perspective of a
dialectic of becoming. The characteristic path of the Romantic
work—the development of consciousness as it projects itself outward
into the visible world, and then bends back onto itself to critique its
prior, naive understanding—is already implicit in the self-conscious
fragment for Nancy and Lacoue-Labarthe. They state that the "fragment . . . completes and incompletes [*achève et inachève*] at once
the dialectic of completion and incompletion [*de l'achèvement et de
l'inachèvement*]" (71). It proves an unstable form pregnant with the
promise of a Romanticism that will have fully incorporated into itself
the whole history of the development from the Greeks to the Enlightenment as a coming-into-consciousness of modernity.

At least one of Chénier's readers saw him as a Moses looking over

15. Paul de Man, "'Conclusions': Walter Benjamin's 'The Task of the Translator,'"
in *The Resistance to Theory* (Minneapolis: University of Minnesota, 1986), 76.

16. Philippe Lacoue-Labarthe and Jean-Luc Nancy, *L'Absolu littéraire: Théorie de
la littérature du romantisme allemand* (Paris: Seuil, 1978), 69. Henceforth cited in the
text.

into just such a promised land. Victor Hugo suggests that Chénier's oddly cut lines and his neoclassical brittleness of diction contain the seeds for a perfecting of poetry:

> . . . this incorrect and sometimes barbarous style, these vague and incoherent ideas, this effervescence of imagination, tumultuous dreams of a wakening talent; this mania for mutilating the sentence and, so to speak for carving it *à la Grecque;* the words derived from ancient languages employed in all the breadth of their original acceptance; these strange cuts, etc. Each of these defects of the poet is perhaps the seed of a perfecting for poetry. In any case, these defects are not at all dangerous, and it is a question of rendering justice to a man who did not enjoy his glory. Who would dare reproach his imperfections while the revolutionary axe lies still bloody in the midst of his unfinished works?"[17]

For Hugo, the fragment does indeed constitute a transitional entity. Its very failures and imperfections show a way, prove replete with a promise to Romantic poetry of an inexhaustible development.

Despite surface differences, Hugo and Van Tieghem share a common vision of how the poetic legacy works to establish a coherent historical picture. As a seed develops into a tree, so a young man with his audacious and incoherent dreams develops into a maturer, more critical thinker. As a father hands on to a son in an unbroken line the findings of the past which the son has to turn against, in order to constitute himself as an inventive father, so the works of the Moderns in the domain of poetry can be said to derive from those of the Ancients, insofar as they first criticize and then extend metaphor to cover larger narrative sequences.

Hugo notes, however, that Chénier's work was interrupted previous to his having become the promised poet of becoming. Further, he puts his finger squarely on a problem: what Chénier's unfinished texts actually offer is a translation between two languages: one, the untimely writing of "antique verse," at once barbarous, tumultuous, and mutilated, dead, obsolete; the other, the polished, living, and expressive language of French. Chénier is less interested in breathing new life into past models or in establishing his poetic filiation, than in carrying forward into modern French the features of inscription: its unnatural inversions and incisions, its sculpted stoniness, its muti-

---

17. Victor Hugo, *Littérature et philosophie mêlées,* in *Oeuvres complètes,* ed. Seebacher (Paris: Robert Laffont, 1985), vol. 12, 94.

lated, fragmentary state, etc. Hugo's understanding of Chénier's art as an art of translation between dead and living languages corresponds to what the poet himself says of it. In *Hermès*, the poet envisions that this poem will offer itself in a "new world" as an "antique writing and no longer a language" (405). The poetic legacy opens onto a new land insofar as its own language has become unusable as language. *Hermès* bequeathes to future sages "thinking lines," "powdery, half-eaten, obscure" (405) that do not claim that it is poetry's chief task to communicate spontaneous or reflected emotion. An emphatic, if puzzling, refusal of the expressive Romantic lyric distinguishes *Hermès*.

What does the translation into living language of a language of inscription have to offer? One offering is clearly knowledge of a dead aspect of language that tends to get overlooked when it is considered a means of communication. The fragmentariness of the work derives partly from Chénier's perception of a discrepancy within language between what humans mean by it and the means by which it says it, its codified, systematic and inhuman features, of the sort that a future sage who cannot understand what a writing means, could nonetheless discern. Antique verse offers knowledge of the code even as it survives the death of meaning. But the struggle to translate inscriptional features into the living language of French is also productive. It arrives in some unnamed, featureless "new land," which is its other offering. It opens onto something. Both of these offerings are hinted at by the preposition that articulates the relation between new thought and antique verse. Poetry is not new thoughts expressed *in* the form of antique verse, as the traditional topos would have it. Poetry is antique verse *on* new thoughts. Two distinct metaphors are suggested here. On a new foundation, on the underlying ground or sustaining surface of new thought is to be erected the edifice of antique verse. The new thought is (of) the condition or sustaining surface. The task is to discover or invent. The other metaphor that comes to mind is very different. Antique verse rises on new thoughts as a heap of stones is piled up to mark a grave. The new thought lies buried under rubble; a radical loss of meaning has taken place; antique verse records, stands for a lost expressive voice, and keeps on standing past its loss. The task is to warn that the code is not subject to the same laws of progress, perfectibility, becoming, as human thought.

In *Hermès*, the question of code—system of laws, collection of rules and conventions, dictionary of equivalent terms (specifically, between a natural and an arbitrary language)—also explains the conjugation of the literary with the political. Of concern to poet and to law-maker alike is the instituting of signs in a code meaningful to an interpretative community and transmissible to posterity. Potential failures of meaning, breakdowns in transmission, interest both as well. From the perspective of the active establishing of rules governing the interpretation of a code, as from the perspective of the failure of an interpretation to be handed down intact, politics and poetics lie roughly within the same domain. In the second song of *Hermès*, Chénier seeks out the common precondition for the establishing of codes and for their conservation. The condition for invention in arts, sciences, and statecraft, he says, is writing, conceived as active, primary art. The condition for conserving and progressing in them is also writing, but a writing relegated to a secondary position as the means of preservation and transmission of the other arts:

> Avant que des Etats la base fût constante,
> Avant que de pouvoir à pas mieux assurés
> Des sciences, des arts monter quelques degrés,
> Du temps et du besoin l'inévitable empire
> Dut avoir aux humains enseigné l'art d'écrire.
> D'autres arts l'ont poli; mais aux arts, le premier,
> Lui seul des vrais succès put ouvrir le sentier.
>
> [394]

> Before of States the basis was constant,
> Before being able with pace more assured,
> In the sciences, in the arts to climb several steps,
> Of time and need the inevitable empire
> Had to have taught to humans the art of writing.
> Other arts have polished it; but to arts, the first,
> It alone to true success could open the path.

So begins the dense fragment that traces the fictional development of writing in conjunction with the development of political institutions. The discovery of political institutions goes hand in hand with the seizing and fixing of the writing code. In the beginning, writing is the primary art. It is the art that opens the path for the steady progress of other arts, including that of government. Writing is active: "An eloquent hand . . . makes seen invisible and rapid thought" (394). It manifests and fixes the invisible and unstable. As the poet tells the story of how Hermes' gift of writing develops, he will show that institutions take shape at each stage by way of an increasingly complex interpretation of the writing code. Beginning with a contractual model in which writing testifies to treaties between individuals, political entities will be discovered that regulate exchanges among larger groups. Each new institution establishes itself by discerning and elaborating new patterns to which meaning is assigned; each one sheds light on sign relationships previously obscure.

Modernity, Chénier will further suggest, needs to be reminded of this because in one of the stages in the seizing of the writing system, the active capacity to make thought visible that writing has on the "page of Egypt" (394) is covered over and it gets conventionally determined as a transparent, faithful, and enduring repository for "our souls and customs" (395). The passage just quoted already foresees this reversal: at first writing opens the trail for arts, sciences, and statecraft. Later, it loses its primary status and becomes a secondary art polished by other arts; it conserves what has already been discovered, in keeping with its other function as memorandum: "An eloquent hand . . . holds . . . (main . . . tient) invisible and rapid thought" (394). The stage when writing gets irrevocably determined as window glass or shiny mirror in Chénier's fiction, is the stage during which the phonetic alphabet is discovered and writing becomes subservient to spoken language. It corresponds to the opening of the Classical era. Along with the invention of a western Greece will come the foundation of a stable state, the development of the arts and sciences, the beginning of man, and the reorientation of the world, now a Western world that has forgotten its oriental cradle, along with a North-South axis. But it has to be borne in mind that the turn that makes writing the subsidiary of other arts is not the only way that written signs work. It is, simply put, the one that has had currency in the Western tradition as it has been handed down to us.

The eloquent hand always both "holds and makes seen"; it is only by arbitrary decree that it is determined primarily as holding, secondarily as manifesting. There is something to be gained by this determination, since it enables the history of other arts to unfold as a continuous, steady, progression along a path. But at no moment does writing lose its double force. Its manifesting activity may go underground; it does not, however, lose it. The continuous history that determination of writing as secondary enables can be disrupted by its other force.

The reverse is also true. The activity of the hand making thought visible can always undergo alteration, take on the aspect of a static, holding hand. A quick look at Chénier's description of the development of hieroglyphic writing shows that the Egyptians *for us* are always nothing more than the once inventive, now unintelligible handwriting they left. However, to themselves, the Egyptians were much closer to being Greeks.[18] We have a compelling reason for reading their "antique writing," for their history shows they were unaware of how their writing was rendering itself antique; their story may unwittingly be our own:

> De là, dans l'Orient ces colonnes savantes,
> Rois, prêtres, animaux, peints en scènes vivantes,
> De la religion ténébreux monuments,
> Pour les sages futurs laborieux tourments,
> Archives de l'Etat, où les mains politiques
> Traçaient en longs tableaux les annales publiques.
> De là, dans un amas d'emblèmes capiteux,
> Pour le peuple ignorant monstres religieux,
> Des membres ennemis vont composer ensemble
> Un seul tout, étonné du noeud qui le rassemble;
> Un corps de femme au front d'un aigle enfant des airs
> Joint l'écaille et les flancs d'un habitant des mers.
> Cet art simple et grossier nous a suffi peut-être
> Tant que tous nos discours n'ont su voir ni connaître
> Que les objets présents dans la nature épars,
> Et que tout notre esprit était dans nos regards.
> Mais on vit, quand vers l'homme on apprit à descendre,
> Quand il fallut fixer, nommer, écrire, entendre,
> Du coeur, des passions les plus secrets détours,
> Les espaces du temps ou plus longs ou plus courts,
> Quel cercle étroit bornait cette antique écriture.
> Plus on y mit de soins, plus incertaine, obscure,
> Du sens confus et vague elle épaissit la nuit.
>
> [395]

> Thence, in the Orient those knowing columns,
> Kings, priests, animals, painted in living scenes,
> Of religion somber monuments,
> For future sages laborious torments,

18. This is consonant with Warburton's insight, in his *Essay on Hieroglyphs*, that the Egyptians sought to transmit a science by their hieroglyphs. We quote from the readily available French edition, *Essai sur les hiéroglyphes des Egyptiens* (Paris: Aubier Flammarion, 1977).

Archives of the State, where political hands
Traced in long pictures the public annals.
Thence, in a heap of heady emblems,
For the ignorant people religious monsters,
Enemy members will compose together
A single whole, astonished at the knot that reassembles it;
A body of woman with the forehead of an eagle child of air
Joins the scale and the flanks of an inhabitant of the sea.
This simple and crude art sufficed us perhaps
So long as all our discourses knew not how to see and know
More than the present objects in scattered nature.
But one saw, when toward man one learned to descend,
When it was necessary to fix, to name, to write, to hear,
Of the heart, the passions the most secret detours,
The spaces of time either longer or shorter,
What a narrow circle confined this antique writing.
The more pains one took with it, the more uncertain, obscure,
Of meaning confused and vague it thickened the night.

Five stages in an interpretation by a tormented future sage are sketched out around the inscriptions: in the first stage, the obelisks are considered as religious monuments, whose hieroglyphs are read as pointing toward a metaphysics; in the second, the knowing columns are called archives of the state on which a history has been written; next, they are considered as a ruin, a heap of heady emblems, from which one is chosen to explain in a meta-code the composition of the code; fourthly, the whole of the Egyptian code is compared to a living language having the power to express man's inner world; and finally, Egyptian writing is determined to be a nonlanguage, an unintelligible writing, whose law of becoming is not that of progressive enlightenment, but of becoming-more-obscure.

At each stage in the seizing of the hieroglyphs, a double movement can be discerned. On the one hand, the logic is of invention and destruction: a new institutionalization takes place that involves the ruin of an old system. The fixing and destroying work is most apparent in the first three stages of the passage, where the knowing columns are first called "monuments of religion," then "archives of the state," then, "a heap of heady emblems." By the last two stages, where the destruction of Egypt is more visible than its construction, and where the presence of the interpretative voice is paramount, the in-

stituting signs regulating the interpretation have become verbal co-
lossi like man, nature, the heart, spaces of time, or certainty and
clarity.

On the other hand, the logic that regulates the development of
each system from the inside, as a system of meaning, is that of polishing, in its twin sense of perfecting and wearing away.[19] Each new
interpretation takes into account something left out or obscure in the
earlier system. It enables a larger set of exchanges, and is addressed to
a larger group. The heads of state and religion in the first scene give
way to representative members of the polis at work, "political hands"
tracing. By the third stage, a whole mass—the people—are involved,
that soon give way to "us," men and women of the present who judge
the Egyptians as lesser versions of ourselves, and then to "one," a
pronoun large enough to include both the "us" who came after them,
and them, the third-person Egyptians. The wider audience is found at
the price of erasures: the vivid scenes of living beings—kings, priests
and animals, are effaced in the second scene to leave "long pictures."
by the third scene reference is uncertain. In the fourth and fifth
stages, past referents like the state, man, or metaphysical beings are
denied by the interpreter, who then asserts the writing to be meaningless.

The twin logic made visible in Egyptian writing knits together
writing as inventive—manifesting and destroying—and writing as
polishing—perfecting and wearing away.[20] At each stage, the doubleness of the hieroglyphs—they are both pictures and characters, as
Warburton informs us—gets stabilized by the erect columns into a
totalizing interpretation, implying a unified interpretative community around it. On closer view, however, a discrepancy or obscurity,
entailing a new interpretation shows up in the very signs—the knowing columns—that fix the code. As the passage progresses, instead of
a wider interpretative system managing to overcome the doubleness,
it keeps on migrating somewhere else and getting harder to master.
By the fifth and final stage, not only has the elucidating process led to

19. For a discussion of the law of "usure" in Warburton's discussion of the development of Egyptian writing, see Jacques Derrida, "Scribble," in William Warburton, op.
cit.

20. See Chénier's discussion of the challenge French poses to the poet at the end of
L'Invention for another twist on the same theme. French is described as having a twin
source: in the barbarous, rusty, proud, and indocile Frankish tongue; in the polished,
civilizing, seductive, easily-molded wax of Latin.

total obscurity, as night falls on the Egyptians, but the doubleness spills over into the comments of the interpretative voice itself: the same line tells us that this antique writing thickens the night *of* meaning [*elle épaissit la nuit du sens*], that is, has become unintelligible; and affirms that it thickens the night *with* meaning [*elle épaissit du sens la nuit*], that is, the folds of the curtain falling, and thus unintelligibility itself, are thick with significance.

This interplay is worth a closer look, because the features of Egyptian writing are translated into the language of the interpreter, making the story into an allegory for a French present.

The problem in the code's development lies chiefly in the signs that institute—the erect columns—and that are not regulated by the interpretative system they set up. They have to lie outside the system that holds sway at any stage in order to establish it; but because they are themselves double and are not regulated by the system they establish, they can be toppled at any point. The first stages show most clearly that the columns lie outside the system they regulate: the obelisks are first called "somber monuments," and are then picked up again and elucidated as "archives" set up in an open, public space. The move from the religious to the political code entails a disclosure, a publication of the space defined by the obelisk that was dark in the first scene. The monuments of religion are pushed over, and in their place rise the secular archives of the state.

To understand the darkness of the monuments, we have to look at the interpretative system they regulate. The monuments establish religious allegory as the way to decipher isolated picture words: the living scenes are words that mean literally, properly, the physical beings depicted, the kings, priests, and animals. Figuratively speaking, however, they mean metaphysical, otherworldly beings. A similar interpretation is at work in the accumulation of nouns and adjectives provided by the French speaker describing the columns. Each semantic unit has a proper, literal meaning but can also stand for an abstract entity—the priest for the spiritual, the king for the temporal, the animal for the physical world. Religion's monuments act to stabilize the doubleness of the hieroglyphs, their referential and their figural capacity, into a hierarchy of meanings: first the proper meanings, then the figurative one.

But what about the monuments themselves? Are they signs having a literal, proper meaning, or are they figures? As signs arbitrarily chosen to perpetuate the memory of the gods, they surely have a literal meaning, awarded to them by religion's decree. But, the monuments of instituted religion have substituted for natural signs—"the august book and sacred letters" of nature mentioned a few lines above. They do not just stand for something; they also stand in, in the absence or loss of something; they commemorate the loss of the pantheistic gods. The articulating preposition *of*, foregrounded in Chénier's line by inversion and sonorous repetition (*De là, dans l'Orient . . . . De la religion*), is undecidable in the same way. It tells us that the monuments are the property of religion, which erects them to remember the gods. But it might also be that religion belongs to the monuments, that they are monuments *to* religion, reminders of its death. If the genitive is subjective, then religion has erected the monument. If objective, religion lies buried under it. The articulating preposition that tells us which is the proper term and which the extended one is undecidable. For the Egyptians living by the monuments, interpreting the hieroglyphs on their face, the obelisks are stable, enlightening. But there is an undecidability in the instituting sign that already imperils the monuments of religion and opens out onto the secular interpretation of the next scene. Just so, the genitive repeats the gesture of stabilizing and destabilizing the property relation in Chénier's poem.

In the next stage the destabilizing sign from the first stage, the memorializing sign, is incorporated into the interpretative system and the columns move onto center stage as archives. Documentary writing, where signs serve to record, is the primary function of writing here. At this stage, writing is already alphabetic. Chénier follows Warburton who suggests that the obscurity of picture words necessitated the invention of a conventional alphabet of hieroglyphs whose letters "express words, and not things" (160). Some picturing function is still discernible, but it is less important: the long pictures in which the annals are recorded also serve as symbols of the "long-standingness" of the state, of the duration of its continuous history. A hierarchy of sign systems gives the priority to documentary writing over fictional writing.

The primary feature of the interpretative system is that writing has become conventionally determined as a secondary art. Hieroglyphs are assigned to express the inventive signs of the earlier stage; verbal deeds, like other deeds, take place and then are written down, recorded. Much could be said about the space set up: it is a public space where men are considered with respect to their job functions, their roles in the state apparatus, where arts and strategies are being practised by crafty hands. Once again, Chénier's lines translate the situation into French: a fully articulated grammar shows up in the relative clause describing the archives. One does not have to be a volitional subject to be the subject of a sentence; one does not have to perform any deed worth recording to be doing something in a sentence. In the place of meaningful subjects or deeds there is a subject-verb-object construction: "where political hands traced . . . annals." Roles, grammatical functions, have taken precedence over semantic units of meaning, much as the scribes' hands take a role in maintaining the state machinery.

But what of the archives? They establish a public space, a polis, which promises to last so long as records are kept. The archives themselves, however, are of another matter. They are material columns, and as such, are subject to a very different set of accidents than the state. They can outlast it, as the obelisks have outlasted Egypt. They can fall into rubble before the Egyptian adventure is over, as they do in the next stage. Furthermore, as material signs, in excess of the "where" that they help institute, they are eminently appropriable into other contexts. They constitute a "where" of a very different sort than the "where" of a room or a square or a city. The adverb *where* [*où*] is the undecidable feature in Chénier's translation of the problem. As an adverb introducing a relative clause, it relates hands to the place indicated by the antecedent archives. Hands trace where there are archives, that is, inside the state. But *where* can also be an adverb meaning: *there where, the place where.* The phrase would then define where the archives are: "archives of the state [are] there where political hands traced." In other words, the archives might not be opening the space within which scribes work; the scribes might be opening the archives wherever they leave material traces. The page is designated as the archive; the state as an invention masterminded by secretaries.[21]

The crafty political hands, so modestly effacing themselves as

---

21. Cf., Warburton, op. cit., 160, who explains that epistolic writing—a code at once unambiguous and, at first, secret—was made possible by the invention of an alphabet by a secretary to the King of Egypt. For Chénier, the development of the state itself, with its mechanisms, its secrets, its publicity, is indissociably linked with the alphabet.

mere recorders of deeds, and reducing writing to a skill among others, are effectively the "doers" and "rulers" at this stage. What they are doing is actively repressing something. The sign system operative allows for the marking of local losses and posits a continuity transcending them, but it actively forgets that the promised continuity depends on the survival of the material columns and traces that constitute the archive. It represses the accidents and misappropriations to which the archive is subject. The excluded materiality of writing returns to organize the next scene—in the heap of rubble and the dream emblems composed out of dismembered body parts.

Before turning to the emblem, which as stage of assembly recounted in the present tense, turns out to be the crucial one for an understanding of the lesson of the hieroglyphs for present-day institutions, a few summarizing remarks are in order. We have shown that instituting signs establish increasingly more complex systems of interpretation, with greater possibilities of exchange, at the price of some loss of expressiveness. But the columns lie outside the system they set up. They are always unsteady, are subject to another set of evaluations, of accidents, etc., and may serve to undo the very system—however long-lasting—they have erected. The instituting signs construct and undo, they fix and crack the very codes they allow us to crack. The undecidability of the signs that institute has to be distinguished from the stability that reigns within the sign system instituted, however. The latter relies on a forgetting or repression of the instability of the articulating sign. That repression can be positively or negatively evaluated depending on whether one is faced with inventing institutions or maintaining those already found.

It is not necessarily a simple matter to know what kind of period one is in, however. In 1790, in *Avis au peuple français sur ses véritables ennemis*, Chénier will state that the period the nation is traversing is one of division and intense uncertainty; it is in the "interval that there must necessarily be between the end of the past and the beginning of the future" (203). The uncertainty is over the question of whether the nation has entered into the enjoyment of rights already discovered, or whether the institutions that will establish them have yet to be grounded. In 1791, writing on the National Assembly's work on the constitution, Chénier suggests that the Revolutionary moment is over, the new edifice in which people have to learn to live in peace has already been built. He warns the Assembly against the dangers of continuing to act as if the house had not yet been constructed:

> So long as the National Assembly lasts, the attentive peoples, watching always act the hand that has destroyed everything and rebuilt everything, will remain always in suspense and seem always to foresee some new thing. One only inhabits a house with security once the workers are no longer there. [236]

In the same passage, however, he suggests that the state edifice cannot be said to be firmly grounded until people are convinced of its stability, and that the time of division and uncertainty cannot end until the constitution that will guarantee the people its rights has been written:

> Among the causes that must make us hope ardently that the National Assembly, abandoning to future legislatures all that does not require its hand, not lose an instant in finishing the constitution, and put an end to its immense work, the hope of seeing finish all these parties, which tire us and deteriorate the public spirit, does not seem to be counted among the least. . . . Then only will everyone, patriots and malcontents, be well convinced that the edifice is stable and firm. . . . Then only will it be possible for concord and peace to be reborn among us, as among our legislators. [236]

The state edifice is built and requires only maintenance and polish; the peaceful state has not yet been firmly grounded in conviction.

The uncertainty that Chénier consistently sees as characterizing the Revolution has an analogue in the third stage of Egyptian writing. When we look to what the interpreter says of the emblem and its interpretation, we discover an open question as to whether any ruling interpretation has been set up at all. A whole has not yet been composed, it is to come: "enemy parts *will compose* a single whole." But a means has also already been found to gather disparate pieces, in the "knot that reassembles" enemy parts. The knot has now to be maintained. The French commentator explains that interpreters of the emblem waver about its status in about the same way as the nation wavers over the status of the period it traverses. Among other features that suggest the stage as analogous with the uncertain 1790s, is the use of a terminology of assembly and of parts. Throughout his brief career as political journalist, the National Assembly and partisan politics were Chénier's central preoccupation.

But if the emblem is a promising place to investigate what Chénier takes to be the stage in the development of the code France
traversed during the Terror, it is also a singularly difficult place to do
so. What kind of interpretative system is established by a "heap of
heady emblems," which, at the very moment that it gives the code to
the community, already stands as a ruined, undecipherable column?
What is the code that allows the enigmatic emblem to be deciphered?

Warburton, from whose *Essay on Hieroglyphs* Chénier has been
borrowing heavily all along, provides a clue. The hieroglyph that
Chénier describes can be identified as the figure accompanying paragraph 55 of the *Essay,* which is a figure of offering. It shows a woman
with an eagle perched on her head, wearing a formfitting dress of a
criss-crossed design that is reminiscent of scales or tilework. She is
offering a platter of cups to an enframed male figure, bearing a staff
and swathed from neck to toe in a garment whose more loosely
crossed hands Warburton shows to be like those of a mummy. The
pedestal on which the male figure stands is covered with hiero-
glyphics, and there are inscriptions as well above and below the platter offered by the female figure. And Warburton explains: the hieroglyph manifests "a mixture of diverse kinds of Egyptian writing"
(219).

Chénier's translation of the hieroglyph also recapitulates and
brings into conjunction the two earlier stages of writing described in
Hermès: the word-pictures of the first stage with their religious significance, and the words-standing-for-words of the second stage, with
their political function.[22] The emblem represents the stage in which
a code as a dictionary of equivalents is being proposed that will allow
for a maximum translatability between its diverse kinds of writing. It
can be identified as a poetic composition for it talks about the sign
system and how it signifies. However, just as the instituting signs of
the earlier stages exceeded the interpretative field they set up, so does
this offering exceed the intention of maximum translatability that
informs it. Instead of providing maximum intelligibility for the diverse kinds of writing, the code starts to become fragmented and

22. For Warburton, there are four sorts of Egyptian writing: 1) the Hieroglyphic,
divided into curiological and tropic; 2) the Symbolic, divided into the tropic and the
allegorical; 3) the Epistolic; 4) the Hierogrammatic. The last sorts were alphabetical,
and stood for words, whereas the first two sorts were symbolic and stood for things (op.
cit., 136). Chénier has telescoped these four kinds into two.

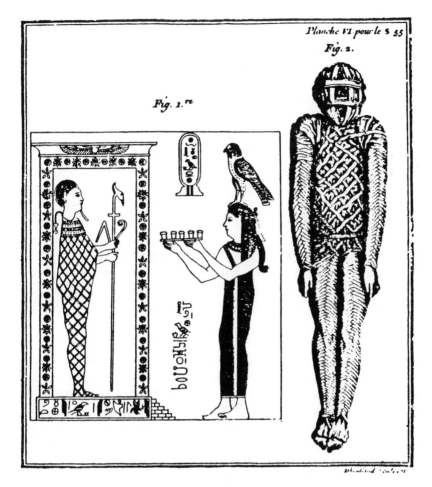

Figure 1. Sixth Illustration, for §55

FIGURE 1 is taken from the Isiac Table. It represents an offering. The mixture of diverse kinds of Egyptian writings that can be seen in it is described in §26.

FIGURE 2 represents a mummy wrapped only in its first layers of bands, for the sake of a comparison with the idol of Figure 1, which is also wrapped in bands, and a judgment of the origin of the God to whom the offering is being addressed.

With the permission of Aubier-Flammarion.

unintelligible. We register here, above all, a failure of interpreters to come to grips with the poetic emblem.

It is easy to see that the translation of the emblem assembles the diverse kinds of writing. On the one hand, are brought together body parts, figures left over from the earlier stage when living pictures of physical creatures were the literal form in which abstract meanings were expressed. There are plenty of *disjecta membra* from physical beings of different provenance here. The eagle drifts down from the air; the flanks are the flotsam of a denizen of the sea; the woman's body dwells on the earth. "Scale" suggest that we may even have a salamander, scaly creature who, according to legend, can live in fire. On the other hand, all the words that stand for other words, the grammar and alphabet of documentary writing are piled up here as well. The conventionalized parts of a language are being assembled, as can be seen in the French sentence structures which exactly repeat the earlier patterns. The first clause repeats the pattern of the monuments' description ("Thence, in the Orient. . . Thence, in a heap . . .; For future sages laborious torments. . . . For ignorant people religious monsters; Kings, priests, animals, painted. . . . A single whole, astonished . . ."). The juxtaposed second clause repeats the subject-verb-object pattern of the archives' description ("political hands traced . . . the annals; a body of a woman . . . joins the scale"). Evidence of structural work with a language voided of meaning can be found in other places as well. An alliterative chain joins in the blah blah blah of an emblem an *aMas d'EMBLEMEs, Monstres reLigieux, MEMBres ennEMis, coMPoser ENsEMBLE, rassEMBLE,* that engenders and shades off into further strings, as, for example, the fricatives joining *Femmes, Front, enFant, Flancs.* The principle is of reassembling language parts into structural patterns without considering meaning. The emblem is also put together as a grammar or an alphabet whose structures do not refer to anything outside language.

But the emblem does not just assemble the diverse kinds of writing. It tries to make them translatable, to bring them together in a larger system that allows their deciphering. As a dictionary permits the exchange of one term against another across the whole terrain of the language, whatever the derivation of the individual terms, so the emblem tries to make all of the pieces derived from its earlier stages accessible, translatable into one another. It does so by providing a bridging term that brings the enemy elements of picture words and conventional letters (or figure and grammar, in the French) into conjunction with one another: the woman's body *joins* the scale and the flanks. Now the fishes' flanks are a region of the body and can substitute for the woman's thighs by likeness. As in the earlier stage where pictures gave visible form to metaphysical being by resemblance, so do these flanks substitute for those of the woman. The scale, on the other hand, is not a body part but a covering bearing a mosaiclike motif of interlocking parts. It can represent conventionalized grammar, both because it figures a set of relationships and because it is a carapace, a covering. The scale, like the woman's dress in Warburton's figure, does not resemble the body; it substitutes for it as a conventional sign decreed to stand for another sign. The scale designates writing as a secondary art, as an artificial structure of arbitrary signs. The emblem thus asserts that a larger figure, the body of the woman, bridges the gap between the two kinds of writing signs found in the earlier stages. It brings them into relationship, opens a communicating door between religious allegory and documentary writing. The woman's body is a figure that relates all the signs in the Egyptian writing system as translatable. Whether the thighs are disclosed by way of a metaphorical transfer, or by taking off the dress of conventional written language, it is the same thing. In both cases, a single signified, the woman's body, is disclosed. The larger figure articulates the two kinds of signs as exchangeable.

But what is the status of the larger figure, the sign that carpenters the joint?

The instituting sign that offers the dictionary is just another sign in the dictionary to which the key is needed. The emblem comments on this as well. The woman's body can join scale and flanks in a very different way. When one plank joins another, when an individual joins a group, when, a little further on, a new word enrolls itself in a regiment of other words, joining does not mean "to make communicate." It means enlistment, enrollment, enumeration. The woman's body is just one more heady emblem flung onto a heap of others. The scale and the flanks and the forehead and the woman's body are so many unrelated terms. The emblem offers the code as a set of figures and conventional characters, translatable by recourse to a larger figure that says grammatical structure and figures are interchangeable because they all signify the "body of language." But it also offers the writing system as a heap of names or letters to which access has been lost. The emblem, we can say, is *self*-fragmenting.

An enigma arises as to the origin of the term, a woman's body, that bridges and does not bridge the gap between the two systems. The problem can be stated as follows. Does the larger figure that makes all signs translatable emerge, by chance, in the midst of a list of diverse kinds of writing? Or, is a figure decreed in order to allow translation, which then turns out to have already been altered, added to the list as just another piece of language? Have instituted signs, letters, become inventive? Are instituting signs getting altered into conventional signs? The crossing of terms shows that the emblem takes as its problem the undecidability of writing. It is suspended over the question of whether writing manifests itself as an active force capable of producing meaning independent of human intention, or is always altering its active force by maintaining iterable terms. Because Chénier has been attributing agency to the *hand* writing, rather than to human will, it is clear that the poem envisages the problem from the perspective of the laws of a *text* and not of expressive language.

The problem can be understood in visual terms, by reference to a mosaic, one of the etymological meanings of emblem. Structurally speaking, a mosaic is a network of tiles joined, as the planks in a floor, by blank spaces or articulating intervals. On the face of the tiles appears a figure, a picture delineated without concern for the design of the ground. The mosaic is somewhat like an anamorphic painting, in which a picture appears at the expense another. But it is unlike anamorphic painting in that one picture of a mosaic is most often a representational painting of a human scene, whereas the other is a geometric design. Furthermore, one never can quite erase the visible cracks running through the figure in a mosaic, nor quite forget about the parts of the human figure in examining the design. The other pattern is always interfering. One can crack one code, say that of the figure, only by forgetting about the crackwork of the tiles, say that of the structure of enumeration. But, as in a mosaic, there is too much evidence of the other code's activity to be sure about the prevailing pattern. It is impossible to say whether the emblem is constructed as an alphabet, from which a figure emerges by accident to gather all the terms, or is constructed as a figure, which is then added to the signs it is meant to translate as one more undecipherable piece.

The French interpreter comments upon how the poetic emblem was received by its audience. The people who interpret the "heap of heady emblems" dwell in ignorance. In trying to understand the double aspect of the code offered by the emblem, one inevitably misunderstands it. The decisive move is the interpretation of the emblem in terms of interpretation, that is, in the attempt to understand where the suspension of meaning by listing comes from and what it means. People understand the irresolvable conflict over the emblem's origin as the expression of the essence of some divine author. The doubleness of the emblem is read as the representation of a hybrid god, a monstrous being ruling over the different elements. The various parts are made the moments of a mythic narrative of transformations (from the belly or flank of a fish, to the eagle, child of air, to the woman's body, to the dead scale of the mummy's bands) by which the god's essence as creator is revealed. The self-fragmenting fable about the emblem's undecidable origin is understood as a literal narrative revealing the nature of a divinity. The emblem is a figure for language, and it poses an open question about the way one of its terms joins others; the figure is taken as the proper, literal meaning of some monstrous creative force manifesting itself.

In a fragment attached to *Hermès*, Chénier comments on the propensity of people to misinterpret the emblems and apologues of its sages:

> Most fables were without a doubt the emblems and the apologues of sages. . . . It is thus that were made such and such dogmas, such and such Gods . . . mysteries . . . initiations. The people took as proper meaning what was said figuratively. . . . Origin of religious follies. [411–12]

And later:

> This mania of believing that the Gods had their eye on all their little disputes, and that on the most frivolous occasions a miracle would come to violate the laws of nature. [413]

People decide that some divine author reveals itself in this undecidable text. The emblem does not know whether it originates in meaning or in enumeration. But it seems to be impossible, when one tries to understand it, not to decide that the suspension of meaning is the visible form of a thought.

Now within the ignorant people, there are actually two divergent sacrifices being made to the monstrous divinity. On the one hand, there is a sacrifice, discussed by Chénier in a political text called *Les Autels de la peur*, of thought to belief (358). Thought tells us that we cannot tell whether someone means the figure to emerge, or whether it just emerges out of the spewing up of the words in the language.

Belief tells us that the emblem means to tell us this. That is super-
stitious nonsense. It cannot be that some single author controls the
effect of what is stated to be an uncontrollable machine.

On the other hand, another group of people, working within the
same interpretative framework, but inflecting it differently, sees a
chance to chase after private interests and pleasures. Among the signs
indicating this group are the terms ascribing human feeling to the
empty verbal entity of the emblem: "heady," "astonished." This
group can be said to make another kind of sacrifice to the God, which
Chénier also names in *Les Autels de la peur*—the sacrifice of conscience, the moral faculty of judging action (358). There are initiates
into the mysteries of the God, knowledgeable people who understand
that the larger figure may have been produced by an accident of structure. They treat the machine producing meaning as machine, having
nothing to do with human bodies or wills. Language is just language;
one can play with it, exploit it for the power it provides.

The emblem asserts that texts always undecidably refer to the
world and to language, undecidably offer a sage's understanding and
offer things no sage could mean. But this group grasps the emblem as
meaning "just language producing more language effects." They forget that the emblem provides only *one* figure from a heap for the way
that the hand writing may *always* be working. The story shows that
the grasp of the writing system is indissociable from the progress of
institutions, as well as of the arts and sciences. To claim that this is
just this language working to proliferate extra meaning is to deny that
the machinery might be operative in those places which were of most
concern for Chénier in writing the history of Hermès' gift, namely, in
politics, religion, arts, and sciences. It is also a literalization to understand the figure for the monstrous text as just language play, since the
play by now involves institutions, legal and religious codes, etc. Chénier translates the technical manipulation of the textual machine
into the prepositions of the emblem.

The prepositions do not merely relate semantic units into larger
units of meaning; they also disarticulate and rearticulate them. Take
the *de* which relates astonishment and knot as a subjective attitude
toward an object of perception ("a single whole, astonished at the
knot . . ."). Besides functioning to relate parts, the *de* makes the line
into a self-reflexive commentary on the potential of knotting prepositions to produce wholes out of unrelated parts. It can also relate these
semantic units in a very different way on which it provides a very

different commentary, however. It can make the "single whole" into the object of an action for which the knot is the agent, thereby entirely changing the meaning of the adjective "astonished" to cracking or splitting (one of the significations of *étonner*): the phrase would then read: "a single whole, cracked by the knot."[23] The preposition turns the sentence into a metacommentary on the capacity of knotting prepositions to fragment into parts the wholes that it assembles. A whole surprised at the knot that makes it a whole trembles by the selfsame knot. Or take another example among the many that could be found: the *au* that joins a woman's body, a forehead and an eagle. The preposition gives us at least two separate figures: the woman's body *with* the forehead of an eagle; the woman's body *on* the forehead of an eagle. To this could be added another relation: because "au front" is the place of conflict between two enemy members, it can be read as a battle line, a front, the interval or line where a conflict over interpretations is joined.

The prepositions and joining intervals of the emblem are hyperactive. They seem to be producing and destroying meaningful structures. They seem to be acting to try to undo the figure, to point to its enumerative ground. But in fact, the hyperactivity is really a simulation of production and destruction: it looks like someone is offering further knowledge of the systematicity of the text, when in fact all we get is accumulated instances of how one can make purely relational, grammatical terms mean. The group of technicians just offers more parts to the monstrous divinity of which it can proleptically make sense. Prepositions are not pre-positional to meaning in the emblem; they do not undo the anthropomorphism whereby both grammar and figure are translated into meaning. They simply provide added instances of how meaning can be made of functional, grammatical relations; they simulate, as a technical operation simulates, the operation of the understanding. Nothing is happening here; nothing is getting destroyed, nothing is getting established. We are just watching busy hands simulating the work of construction and destruction

---

23. *Etonner*, besides meaning "to cause a violent moral commotion by admiration or fear" also has a more literal meaning in French. It can mean "to produce a violent commotion, a trembling" of the sort that sometimes rocks Californian buildings. By the nineteenth century, it will have taken on the very technical meaning of "cracking something," (*étonner un diamant*). The *Petit Robert* provides as synonyms *fêler*, *lézarder*: to crack, to split. The lizard is not a salamander at all. It is a fissure, an interval produced within an apparently seamless surface.

in order to enjoy the power to make sense of everything that anthropomorphism offers.[24] Drunken interpreters with stupefied faculties are more clued in about the artifice of writing, and the power
signs provide for making and undoing systems, but they are senseless
to the danger clearly indicated by all the disarticulated body parts
lying about. When the sage gives us the emblem as an allegory of
textual undecidability, he does not give a religious code to live and
make sense by, but a code to die by—in thought or in conscience.

Understanding textual allegory as a "negative theology," or as free
play with a linguistic machine is to misunderstand it. That is how the
dead Egyptians understood the emblem; they knelt at the foot of what
Chénier calls a "murderous idol" (396).

The problem spills over into the meta-text of the French interpreter as well, despite the comfortable distance of several thousand years
from the text on which he comments. The body, the forehead, the
scale, and the flank, are joined by "heady" to form the larger figure of
a "heady . . . body." Juxtaposition, abusive coupling, produces the
larger figure here and makes the Egyptian text communicate with the
French meta-text. The Frenchman is commenting on the emblem,
but his commentary adds a new part of which the emblem makes
sense. We cannot say he means to do this, since what he tells us is that
the textual machine can produce meaning out of random juxtaposi-
tions. We cannot say, however, that he does not mean this, since he
also tells us that this machine can always be made to spin by any
skilled technician with a grip on the mechanism. The beheading of
the French interpreter, who starts to get confused with the dead Egyptians, is also figured by the text.

The text gets stuck in a machinelike mode when we try to interpret its inhuman conflict in mythico-religious terms, as pointing
to divine intention. It just keeps on spitting up new parts that join to
make larger figures, and that join in the list of mutilated parts. So long

24. For example, in trying to determine what "child of the airs" modifies, one is
faced with a dizzying number of possibilities: does it modify the eagle alone? Does it
modify the woman's body with (or on) the forehead of an eagle, or at war with the eagle
over territory at the front? Does it modify any *thing* at all, or, deserted child (*enfant
désert*), dropped here to complete the line, does it only have the air of being a modifier?
It might be a commentary on the poetic imagination, "child of airy fancy," or a commentary on the need for an artifice to fill out the rhyme, the "child of a musical air."
"Child of (multiple) airs," it surely also reunites all these possibilities. "Desert child,"
it comments on its sterility and emptiness. A confusion of tongues can be heard in the
very modifier that strikes the most satisfyingly harmonizing of notes.

as one persists in thinking the inhuman way that texts engender meaning by random juxtaposition in terms of a negative theology or as the mere play of the signifier, one is stuck in this mode.

Chénier analyses the Terror as an epoch when people were making like the Egyptians, that is, translating into meaningful human terms the undecidability of texts. The period was characterized by an attempt to come to grips with a textual problem that its only managed to literalize. The French commentary hints at who is identifying itself with the monstrous god: the people, in whose name the Revolution was undertaken. "People" is a collective term for disparate members related by proximity; it is also a term that collects into a single whole, a body subjected to a single set of laws, a singular will. To understand "people" as a body, we have to forget about disparate peoples and understand its enemy members as members of a collective body to which they are subject. The freedom of each individual member, however, depends upon each having the possibility of appropriating, in private, for their own interests, the machinery of the state. This is fairly straightforward *Social Contract*, and is a figure for the textual problem of a collective term. The Terror takes the figure literally: individual people keep getting sacrificed so that the will of the people as a whole can reappear, and individual people keep appropriating the mechanisms of power the concept "will of the people" provides.[25] Chénier does not offer this textual allegory because he sits

25. The point could be supported by the analysis of various political articles, among which the aforementioned *Les Autels de la peur, Avis au peuple français sur ses véritables ennemis,* and *Réflexions sur l'esprit de parti. De la cause des désordres qui troublent la France et arrêtent l'établissement de la liberté* states the problem to be one of misinterpretation. By an anthropomorphism with distinctly religious overtones, the people (defined as a public space or legal system of relations), are viewed as a *body:* "This Society of (Jacobins) has produced an infinity of others: towns, boroughs, villages, are full of them. Almost all obey the orders of the mother-Society, and entertain with her a very active correspondence. She is a body in Paris, and she is the head of a vaster body spread over France. It is thus that the Church of Rome *planted the faith* and governed the world by congregations of monks. . . .

A simple ambiguity was enough for everything. The constitution being founded on the eternal truth, *the sovereignty of the people,* all that had to be done was to persuade the forums *(tribunes)* of clubs that they are *the people"* (273–74). A finger is placed on a similar anthropomorphism humanizing the inhuman in the poems. The "warlike" (187) *Iambes* in particular are illuminating of the mechanical aspect masked by the appeal to the "body of the people." For example, in "Voûtes du Panthéon, quel mort . . ." the personified guillotine weeps, seeks consolation and justice, tries to save France by calling its vassals to it by name. The machinery of decapitation is greased by the personification. In the name of "humanity," of patriotism, etc., it starts to decapi-

at the feet of the God Language and ignores "real" people, or because he takes pleasure in mere formal play. He offers it because texts always do offer such allegories, and because their misunderstanding in religious terms has consequences for "real" people.

The only way to get the machine unstuck, since the anthropomorphism is a step that cannot be undone by interpretation, is to recall the enumerative possibility that is the ground for the figure. In the tale from *Hermès*, it is by enumeration of the unintelligible emblems, rather than by the attempt to understand them, that people topple the monstrous god and new discoveries are made: "Quelque peuple à la fin par le travail instruit / Compte combien de mot l'héréditaire usage / A transmis jusqu'à lui pour former un langage." [Some people at last by work instructed / Counts how many words hereditary usage / Has transmitted to it to form a language.] Enumeration also turns out to be the key to the political allegory with which the fragment ends.

> Le passé du présent est l'arbitre et le père,
> Le conduit par la main, l'encourage, l'éclaire.
> Les aïeux, les enfants, les arrières-neveux,
> Tous sont du même temps, ils ont les mêmes voeux.
> La patrie au milieu des embûches, des traîtres,
> Remonte en sa mémoire, a recours aux ancêtres,
> Cherche ce qu'ils feraient en un danger pareil,
> Et des siècles vieillis assemble le conseil.
>
> [396]

> The past of the present is the arbiter and father,
> Conducts it by the hand, encourages it, enlightens it.
> Forefathers, children, grand-nephews,
> All are of the same time, they have the same wishes.
> The fatherland in the midst of ambushes, of traitors,
> Goes back in its memory, has recourse to ancestors,
> Seeks what they would do in like danger,
> And of the centuries grown old assembles the counsel.

---

tate those who once made it function. Nor ought one to think that Chénier sees in the vengeance of the axe turned against its wielders a "just" solution. The guillotine is impartial. It does not stop calling roll. Whoever wields it in the name of justice becomes subject to its justice: "You will save France. / For your arms la Montagne . . . / Le Gendre . . . / Collot d'Herbois . . . / More than one Robespierre, and Danton / Thuriot, and Chabot; at last the whole band; / And club, commune, tribunal; / *But who can count them?* I recommend them to you. / You will call the roll" (188).

Take just one of the sententious statements that regulates the fatherland as it collects itself into a political unit: "The past of the present is the arbiter and father" [*Le passé du présent est l'arbitre et le père*]. This commonplace works as a true-false statement that assembles into one counsel, one piece of advice and one representative group, three distinct interpretations of the relation between present and past as a father-son relationship. 1) The past is the arbiter and father of the present, that is, it invented the model that the present imitates. This is the way that French classicism understood Greece. 2) The past *of the present* is arbiter and father, that is, the past invented by, belonging to, the present, fathers. The French interpretation of Latinity as the inversion and satirizing of the Greek model is also represented. 3) The past of the present, by way of the ambiguous genitive, might also be the pastness that possesses the present, that makes it unintelligible to itself, that lives on in it, that obsesses it, that it cannot master. An Egyptian is also included on the counsel, as the forefather of the disjunction between action and meaning potentially repeated in the present. These are three interpretations of a single true-false statement, three ancestors to a counsel.

But a fourth, and very different, translation can be found. The line actively asserts: the past is the arbiter and father, from the present, for the time being [*Du présent, le passé est l'arbitre et le père.*] Other assemblies are possible, the true-false statement being simply the way the present has decided to understand the relation. An exchange among sons of the advice given by Greek, Roman, and Egyptian ancestors is just the rule by which, for the present, things are to be interpreted.

The rule thus shows a disjunction between the conserving true-false statement that governs interpretation within the counsel, and the inventive, active writing which imposes the code on the present. The rule regulates the disjunction: for there to be a present, for the fatherland to appear, one has to forget about the arbitrariness of the inventive fiction. On the other hand, as a willful fiction, the rule enrolls itself on the list as an already-past rule that can be subverted by a critique recalling its fictional origins. The decree, "Let the past be arbiter, for the present" signs up as one in a series of other arbitrary rules.

Chénier's politics are not a party politics, however closely a passage like this one might seem to associate him with the constitutionalism of the moderate Feuillants. He is explaining that, for there to be a political space, and not a religious one, a violent imposition of a fiction has to take place and be forgotten. But he is also explaining that that fiction can always be shown to be a repressive fiction, an arbitrary and violent decision about an undecidable relation, and as such, can be subverted by any text that recalls writing's materiality. The political emerges by way of undecidability, be it as a strategy for making use of undecidability to impose an interpretative law, or as a critique that recalls undecidability to topple worn-out fictions. The poet separates himself from the scribes of the second stage of Egyptian writing, the political hands who hid the violence of the fiction regulating the state. He, unlike the scribes, has written his rule on the list of falling idols. Chénier, the political thinker, concerned with peace inside the house, tells us that, for the fatherland to be convinced of its stability, it has to forget about the violence of the rule. But Chénier, the poet, is critical of the arbitrariness of such laws. The fiction of humane familial relations drawing together pious sons in the fatherland is a mask for a machinery anything but humane. The political thinker is at his most revolutionary in his poems.

Two distinct reasons, both of which touch upon the political, emerge to explain why Chénier did not publish his fragmentary poetry. He may have wanted to cordon off the dangerous productivity of textual allegories. His understanding that people tend to read poetic language in mytho-religious terms, romantically, as translating formal structures and figures into single totalities expressive of a divine artist's intention could very well be one reason for what amounts to an act of self-censorship. But there is another, and perhaps more compelling reason. An invisible hand offers us poetry by a posthumous author; the "thinking lines" of "antique verse" never do appear as the lyric songs of a human author, but always as the legacy of writing itself. They cannot be thought as expressive, lyrical language; they are always thinking along the lines of the political.

KEVIN NEWMARK

Beneath the Lace: Mallarmé, the State, and the Foundation of Letters

> Les robes de ces solennités mondaines, c'est la fantaisie même, aventurée parfois, hardie et presque future, qui se fait jour à travers des habitudes anciennes. Qui regarde, y voit, mêlés au satin, des symptômes dont se révèle déjà le secret, sous la gaze, sous le tulle ou sous les dentelles.
>
> —La Dernière mode

Looked at through the prismatic lens of its critical reception, it seems that there is something new to be seen in Mallarmé studies these days. The conventional hemline of literary interpretation that for the first half or so of this century did such a good job at keeping a delicately aesthetic and hermetic *oeuvre* away from the prying gaze of coarser and more public questions like history, ideology, and politics seems now to be inching its way up, threatening to reveal in the process secrets of a potentially embarrassing and even scandalous nature.[1] The scandal here, though, lies in the revelation that what passes for the shockingly new and indecent has been there all along, only in the mode of a symptomatic denial and cover-up. In Mallarmé's case, we do not have to wait for a history of reception to register a

---

1. See, among other recent treatments of Mallarmé, Lucienne Frappier-Mazur, "Narcisse travesti: poétique et idéologie dans *La Dernière Mode* de Mallarmé," *French Forum*, January (1986); Barbara Johnson, "Erasing Panama: Mallarmé and the Text of History," *A World of Difference* (Baltimore: Johns Hopkins University Press, 1987); Vincent Kaufmann, "De l'interlocution à l'adresse: la réception selon Mallarmé," *Poétique* (April 1981); Jean-Luc Steinmetz, "Mallarmé, l'Histoire," *Centre International d'Etudes Poétiques* 165 (January–March, 1985). The scene of intrusion, which is also potentially a defilement and defloration, is obliquely noted by Gardner Davies in his *mise à jour* of the critical bibliography: "the winds of Freudianism, structuralism, deconstructionism and other methodologies which it is sometimes difficult to identify clearly have swept across the vulnerable field of literary criticism, all of them originating in other disciplines." See, "Divagations on Mallarmé Research," *French Studies* (January, 1986), 4.

YFS 77, *Reading the Archive: On Texts and Institutions*, ed. E. S. Burt and Janie Vanpée, © 1990 by Yale University.

threat to formal autonomy from some sort of textual outside, for the threat was never outside of the (hypothetically) self-enclosed structures of his texts to begin with. For instance, it would hardly have been necessary in 1899 for Arthur Symons to attach a "subtle veil" to Mallarmé's writing to shield it from the desires and disturbances of what he calls the outside world, if it were not already possible to glimpse, on the inside of the text and etched in negative as it were, something like the symptoms of social and critical upheavals. Such a secret "future," already neatly referred to and anticipated by Mallarmé himself in *La Dernière mode,* will finally break through the surface in a much cruder form in the journalistic celebration of "Le Camarade Mallarmé," as he was baptized in *L'Humanité* following the events of May, '68.[2] Rather than a linear itinerary of purely empirical events, the history of Mallarmé reception between Symons's celebration of *l'art pour l'art* and J. P. Faye's, inversion of this well-known aesthetic slogan into a kind of *l'art pour tous,* is a balanced dialectic of concealment and disclosure in which each of the successive stages in the interpretation of a textual enigma helps to bring into relief whatever was only implicitly available or recognized in the other. And while it would be irresponsibly naive to ignore the very different ideological implications at stake in such positions, in the long run they function side by side within the same closed system of clearly demarcated distinctions and choices.

Factional pressures and rhetoric aside, reducing Mallarmé to the polarity of formalism and reference, a private *poésie pure* and a public *journalisme engagé,* and seeking to privilege one pole over the other by means of a history of reception might be the least historical gesture conceivable, since it repeats in a preconscious and therefore uncritical mode a set of unresolved tensions whose irresolution Mallarmé himself identified as one of the principal conditions of a truly historical consciousness. For although he never questions the pragmatic necessity of approaching language as thought it were susceptible of division into the textually self-reflexive and the historically referential, the neat separation of language into its constitutive elements remains theoretically problematic within Mallarmé's writing. We should approach with caution the practically effective but the-

2. See Arthur Symonds *The Symbolist Movement in Literature* (New York: E. P. Dutton and Co., inc., 1919); J. P. Faye "Le Camarade 'Mallarmé'" and "Mise au point"; Philippe Sollers "'Camarade' et Camarade" in *L'Humanité,* 12 September 1919 and 10 October 1969).

oretically questionable attempt to describe, separate, and ultimately choose between the inextricably intertwined components of language, which appears in certain prose texts as the "desire" of an entire generation in "crisis." That attempt shows up in "L'Après-Midi d'un Faune" as a tragic "crime" that will eventually undo the possibility of knowing with certainty the difference between formalism and reference, fiction and history.[3]

Certain texts, not very distant in time and concern from "Crise de vers," go so far as to suggest the inevitability of a collapse of the distinction between history and fiction, and as a consequence end up by making the one seem wholly dependent for its existence on the other. Thus, near the conclusion of "Sauvegarde," a short text about the place of institutions within the State and in particular about the place of *l'Académie* within France, Mallarmé proposes for consideration the following opinion: "Whereas social relations and their changing measurement strictly or loosely calculated, in view of governing, are a fiction, which is itself dependent on *belles-lettres*—because of their enigmatic or poetic principle—the duty of maintaining the book becomes imperative in an absolute sense" (420).[4] In effect, the proposition that social relationships and their determination are a fiction, and its corollary that fiction is a branch of the linguistic structures of texts, lead ultimately to Mallarmé's oft-repeated and much ridiculed affirmation that, "the whole world exists only to end up in a book" (378). In other words, for Mallarmé, *il n'y a pas de hors-texte*. But Mallarmé's yoking of the social to the fictional/textual in this way cannot legitimately be used as an exclusionary (or inclusionary) principle to deduce a kind of absolute *inside* of the text, in the way, for example, that the simple opposition at work between *l'art pour l'art* (Symons) and *l'art pour tous* (Faye) could be shown to function. For to go on to say, as Mallarmé does, that the calculation of changing social relationships,

3. See "Crise de vers": "An undeniable desire of my time is to separate, in view of different assignments, the double status of the word, on the one hand raw or immediate, on the other essential." Stéphane Mallarmé, *Oeuvres Complètes*, ed. Henri Mondor and G. Jean-Aubry (Paris: Gallimard, Bibliothèque de la Pléiade, 1945), 368. All further references will be to this edition. In "L'Après-Midi d'un Faune," rather than face up to the undecidable question of fiction/history that results from the crime of having "divided the dishevelled tuft . . . that the gods kept so tightly tangled," the faun ultimately chooses to hide from this negative knowledge in a self-imposed numbness and forgetfulness. (52–53)

4. "Sauvegarde" was itself first published in a topically journalistic, or *"brut"* context as one of the ten monthly contributions, *Variations sur un Sujet*, that Mallarmé made to the popular *Revue Blanche* during 1895.

or History in its broadest sense, is a function of the poetic principle of writing, is to warn against any facile assumptions with respect to what these textual principles might consist in, as well as what they leave out. Precisely because the poetic principle founding history and fiction remains indeterminately "mysterious" and problematic, the task of *l'Académie*, which relates to deciphering the link between language and action ("Letters" and "diverse activity"), becomes crucial in a sense that is as historical and social as it is "literary."

"Sauvegarde," as its title suggests, is a text about protection and preservation. In the hyperbolic and ironic vocabulary of crisis he is fond of using, Mallarmé describes a situation in which the entire nation of France, the organization of the State itself, is posed on the brink of disaster because writing is being threatened spiritually by treasonous forces: "the Poet calls upon literary Supremacy to lift up a kind of (protective) wing when writing is threatened by high treason or a *coup d'état*, in this case, spiritual" (420).[5] Writing is associated here with that quality of mind capable of founding a State through the establishment of "the link of Letters that changes diverse activities into official pomp." It needs the protection of a State institution, the Academy, against the nullity and mindlessness of factional commotion to which books are always open: "Intellectual (book)bindings . . . open to the gratitude as well as to the jeers of whoever, throwing himself madly about, for or against, it's all the same, assumes the status of a stage actor, doubly sham" (420). What makes such factional commotion a mindless sham is not its concrete objectives and the means it employs to realize them, but rather its inability or refusal to face up to its own relation to the book and to account for its own allegorical, fictional dimension. The danger is that the activity that is in fact the product of an unknown and impersonal poetic principle will be mistaken by ideologues for an autonomous and self-conscious actor or force: "Imagine a government so poorly informed as to mistake itself for the allegory from which it comes" (419). When this happens, the State loses all legitimacy by merely reproducing and even mythologizing the involuntary, mechanical aspect of its

---

5. Mallarmé's use of the term "spirituel" is not without its ambivalences. Here, for instance, it would be difficult to determine whether the threat is to spirit and writing, or whether it is the spiritual aspect of the *coup d'état* that is so threatening for writing. On the question of spirit, politics, and writing, see Jacques Derrida, *De l'esprit* (Paris: Gallilée, 1987).

operation, rather than interrupting it by adopting a critical stance toward it.

Fortunately, both for such a government and its uninformed representatives, the State is provided with a safeguard, *l'Académie*, the highest and most civilized institution of all, since its sole responsibility is to writing: "The highest institution . . . the Academy . . . its aim . . . the bond of Letters . . . everything ends up with or comes back to writing. . . . Our foundation . . . was aware, stepped aside" (417, 418). At times of crisis, that is whenever writing is being threatened, and as Mallarmé makes clear, this is always and everywhere possible, the poet or writer appeals to the institution of the Academy. But *L'Académie* is not just the highest among many institutions. It is also the institution that becomes the highest by stepping aside, by *removing* itself from the classificatory system of all other institutions. "The highest institution . . . the Academy," cannot be considered an institution like any other: "its aim, the bond of Letters, makes it totally unique. . . . Our foundation . . . was aware, stepped aside" (417). Paradoxically, it is in cutting itself off from other institutions that the Academy can resist the State's tendency to ossify into mere institutionalization: "I picture to myself, occupying, like a sanctuary, the center of the comprehensive hemicycle, where it consents to sit only occasionally—while that elite functions on regular votes, the Academy, which would cut itself off [*se retrancherait*] or keep itself back for some special or rare act, who knows which" (417).[6] Describing the physical appearance of one of France's most massive buildings, L'Institut, Mallarmé suggests the difference the Academy can make by reinflecting that fixed space toward the question of writing. At the center of the comprehensive hemicycle, where the semicircular and horizontal curve of the Institut de France is completed and surmounted vertically by its hemispherical dome, there is the occasional "act" operated by *l'Académie*, rare, special,

6. This exclusionary status can be taken to refer to the fact that the regular Thursday meetings, or *séances ordinaires*, of the Academy do not take place "sous la coupole" but down the hall in another room. But Mallarmé makes the concept of the Academy depend on its capacity to "cut itself off" on behalf of writing, rather than on the empirical existence of *l'Académie française*. We must distinguish between two possible referents that are not necessarily always compatible: the empirical one that can be found *Quai de Conti* and the one that can only be found or founded by reading and writing. The same proviso would apply to every term in Mallarmé's text, including reading and writing.

undetermined. Whatever this act is, it is prepared for only when the Academy manages to "cut itself off" or "keep itself back" from the regularized, architectural mass of other institutions.

The cut is also a kind of military maneuver, then, the French verb *se retrancher* suggesting the protective measures that the Academy must take to *entrench* itself against the rigidly conventional programs and sessions of the very Institute of France in which the Academy is housed, for instance, since such partisan institutions can continue to function without making the question of the Book the occasion of their existence.[7] Thanks to *l'Académie* and the strategic operation of the cut, though, the Book remains open. Because spirit, along with "its mark, books," is always open to the mindlessness of sham factions, the Academy, the protective wing of letters, must always be ready to move aside, to dig down and make the cut from such treasons in order to act on them effectively. The fact that the Academy operates *within* an institutional form it serves to disrupt— "The Academy, occupying the *center* of the comprehensive hemicycle"—also means that its defensive power of entrenchment is simultaneously an offensive act operated on the inside of what it cuts itself off from. The "wing" of the Academy is a sword as well as a shield. It serves to open and to protect the space of writing, of a dash, for instance, that separate *l'Académie* from all the other, nonlinguistic, geometrical and architectural institutions.

"The highest institution . . . the Academy.

This dithyramb, why, in the form of a cupola—" (416) "*Sous la Coupole*" (Beneath the dome), is a figure that refers to *l'Académie française* by way of the architectural solidity of *l'Institut de France*, a state run building at the center of which the Academy occasionally sits. Why does the Academy appear in such a form, such a figure? To ask this question, at least in the way that Mallarmé does in "Sauvegarde," is to reopen the question of the Book. It is to cut through the architectural dust of *l'Institut*, the Institution in general

---

7. The empirical fact that the Academy has since the time of the Convention become one of five sections comprising the *Institut de France* changes nothing here. Regardless of the empirical status of an "institution" like the Academy, what will continue to distinguish it in a radical way from all other institutions, as well as from the concept of the institution itself, is the nature of its *possibility*: that is, the possibility of the book as the question of writing *as* writing prior to and after all other questions: "To wipe away the dust, of masterpieces, except by calling them to mind, remains an idle act. . . . Intellectual (book)bindings should end up by being notoriously so" (418, 419).

as well as of L'Institut de France, by reminding us—"wiping the dust off masterpieces . . . by bringing them to mind"—that *l'Académie* is itself nothing but a book of dithyrambs, that is, a book composed of poetic praises to the Book. An institution of the book to the book, *l'Académie* is thus always under the cupola of the Institute as well as already outside of it, being the one institution whose task is to question how the state and its institutions are made possible by the book. To ask why the Academy appears in the form of a state building is one way of making a cut from the actual palace, one way of inscribing a trench or a dash that asks about writing and its relation to the state, as well as about the figures and diacritical marks that compose them. The cut and the sword are in addition a pen: when they inscribe these questions they also help accomplish the task of the Academy *as* book; that is, the perpetuation of writing as well as of the "social relations" that are founded by it.

But the reference to continuity, transmission, and posterity implicit here seems to lead to an inevitable misunderstanding in another direction, according to Mallarmé. The Academy, "this dithyramb," is not just a book in an immediate and unproblematic way. The Academy does not just occupy a building; it is also a select society made up of a prescribed number (forty) of living men (and now women), whose sole function is to speak for and to administer the rights and obligations of the Book. And the actual membership of the *Académie française* has a nasty habit of confusing the "eternal" nature of the writing it holds in trust and represents with its own human and social stature: "All the harm can be traced back to this quiproquo: one would like them to be immortal, whereas it is in fact the works" (418). Mallarmé is undoubtedly poking fun in this article at the French practice of referring to members of *l'Académie* as "les immortels," an epithet that has not failed to take on a cynically humorous connotation given that holders of the "forty-first chair," that is, those never admitted to the Academy, include the likes of Descartes, Pascal, Rousseau, Diderot, Baudelaire, and Mallarmé himself. But in a more radical sense the task of preserving the book with the Academy's official seal—"*A l'immortalité*"—results simultaneously in a kind of death sentence pronounced on *any* given subject. It is not just because of the vagaries of the selection process that many academicians have failed to achieve immortality; it is also that in order to enter the immortal Academy in the first place they must be forgotten *as* individuals. Their names will refer henceforward *only* to the Academy, that is, to writing and to the book. For as long as they exercise their legitimate powers as trustees of the Book's perpetuity, academicians are not themselves to be considered as living human subjects, but are to be viewed only "from the perspective of eternity, abstract, general, vague, outside any familiarity" (419). Consequently, the book is also a tombstone: "That murmur, rather, that brings to the attention of the elect walled-up in the after life . . . the funeral slab of the dictionary . . ." (418). The discussions that take place in the Academy not only make its members attentive to the dictionary, the reviewing and revising of which, of course, is one of its principal tasks. The dictionary they revise also signifies their nonexistence as expressive subjects, their immurement behind the tombstone of its "scattered words" (418). They tend to a book in which they read of their own encrypted death and preservation as caretakers of the book.

From the question of *l'Académie française*, "Sauvegarde" leads along a circuitous itinerary that passes by way of the State, the Institution, Writing and the Subject, before it eventually winds up by predicating all possible social relations, that is, History in general, on the survival and transmission of the Book. But what kind of economy of gain and loss is this, anyway? The fact that the preservation of this kind of writing, as overseen by *l'Académie*, can be achieved only at the price of the living subject—"This Hall . . . . What business do the living have here?" (418)—should give us pause. For it is one thing to say that social relationships are a "fiction" that must be recognized as such. It is quite another to suggest, however, that once this fiction and the book have been saved from sham factionalization, no room will remain in the social and institutional context for any living subject. In "Sauvegarde" itself, the mortal space of the Academy is survived only by a collection of "specters," "shadows," and those who "have no head to fall." How could such disembodied heroes inherit and perpetuate the writing of the book, and just what sort of social and historical force could they be expected to exert? Questions like these, which eventually threaten to cut open the complicated but otherwise comprehensive and comprehensible logic of "Sauvegarde," become especially acute in those texts where the problematic status, or "death," of the lyrical subject is itself the poetic principle as well as the theme. For this reason, considerable help can be gained by pursuing them in the highly conventionalized and self-reflexive form of a Mallarmean sonnet.

Une Dentelle s'abolit
Dans le doute du Jeu suprême
A n'entr'ouvrir comme un blasphème
Qu'absence éternelle de lit.

Cet unanime blanc conflit
D'une guirlande avec la même,
Enfui contre la vitre blême
Flotte plus qu'il n'ensevelit.

Mais, chez qui du rêve se dore
Tristement dort une mandore
Au creux néant musicien

Telle que vers quelque fenêtre
Selon nul ventre que le sien,
Filial on aurait pu naître.

The last in a series of three sonnets published in 1887 and grouped around the general theme of absence, negativity, and death, "Une Dentelle"[8] is considered not only to be the most difficult and beautiful of the triptych, but also the one that progresses out of a situation of almost total despair toward a state of qualified redemption for the poetic subject. The question, just as in "Sauvegarde," is the means of transmitting intellectual legacies and thereby securing a kind of immortality. The real motivation for the text on *l'Académie*, it turns out, is Mallarmé's own project for the administration of a national "fonds littéraire," an institutional means of overseeing "a treasure [fund, or foundation] left by the classics to their posterity" (418–19). It is a similar concern that orients the triptych, where the main theme becomes the challenge and responsibility that devolves on every poet to preserve "the immortal breath" or poetic spirit which he inherits from the language of his predecessors. It matters little whether one chooses to identify the poetic legator referred to metaleptically in the first sonnet—"The ancient chamber of the heir"—as Baudelaire, Vil-

---

8. *Oeuvres Complètes*, 74. "A lace abolishes itself / In the doubt of the supreme Game / To half-open like a blasphemy / Only an eternal absence of bed. / This unanimous white conflict / Of a garland with the same, / Fled against the pale pane / Floats more than it buries. / But in the dream-gilded one / Sadly sleeps a mandolin / With hollow musical nothingness / Such that towards some window / According to no belly but its own, / Filial one could have been born." Translated by Robert Greer Cohn: *Toward the Poems of Mallarmé* (Berkeley and Los Angeles: University of California Press, 1980), 209–14.

liers, or even an earlier version of Mallarmé himself, since in any case it is the continuity of a lineage that is the problem. What is at stake ultimately, named in the last line of "Une Dentelle" as a hypothetical "filiation," is the philosophical concept of History, considered here as the minimal possibility of a *future:* for where there is no possibility of extending past experience into some kind of future, history must remain an empty concept, devoid of any sense whatsoever. The question the sonnet addresses, and which is inherited and passed on from one text to another in Mallarmé's entire *oeuvre,* is whether a historic consciousness is possible beyond something like the death of the poetic subject. We should stipulate that the interruption at issue is something *like* death, that is, closer to a figural "death" than an empirical death. It is this figural death Mallarmé has in mind when he describes himself after his metaphysical crisis of the sixties as "perfectly dead," and it is with an interrogation into the figural status of death that the poem "Une Dentelle" is concerned.

Whereas in "Sauvegarde" the negativity inherent in the preservation of the book is first met by way of the ironic reference to the unfounded pretensions of stodgy academicians, in the sonnet it becomes the very origin of poetry. In order for the poem to begin, something has to be destroyed, eliminated, or at least suspended. Not only has the title of the poem become a blank, but "Une Dentelle" itself, which by default is the title as well as the incipit of the text, is dying here, in the process of being abolished. But can we be immediately sure just what this "lace" is? To judge by the commentaries the opening has elicited, the threat to wholeness implied in the verb "s'abolit," which in the context points to an effacement, pulling away or tearing of the lace, has contaminated not just the artisanal fabric used to adorn windows, beds, and other items, but the intelligibility of the reading process as well, since it seems impossible to ascertain whether "dentelle" should be read as a curtain, a membrane, a self, or a text. Edmund Wilson, a perspicacious if not overly thorough reader of Mallarmé, suggests in *Axel's Castle* a possible reason for the frustration (or elation) of all subsequent readers of this kind of poetry. He refers to figures like the lace as "metaphors detached from their subjects," whose result is that "one has to guess what the images are being applied to."[9] For Wilson, such metaphors are a sign of the "confusion," even the "insanity" of symbolist poetics, which tears figures

---

9. Edmund Wilson, *Axel's Castle* (New York: W. W. Norton and Co., 1959), 21. All further references to this work will appear in the text.

from their referents and then fuses them back together willy-nilly without any regard for their natural order. But rather than following Wilson as he guesses about the kind of referent the metaphors have been reattached to, we ought first to follow out Mallarmé's thematization of the abolition, detachment, or tear that befalls the figure of the lace in the movement of the poem. Before we ask what the figure of the lace refers to, we must take into account the possibility that it is first of all the capacity of figure to refer unproblematically that is being abolished or torn in Mallarmé. It may be that "une dentelle" is not just a figure among others that refers to something else, but also the proper name for the text by Mallarmé, "Une Dentelle," in which poetic language undoes its own pretension ("s'abolit") to provide a stable ground for the relation of figure to referent.[10]

What is dying in this sonnet is the received idea of the status of metaphoric language within poetry, "la dentelle" being one of the tradition's commonest figures for poetic textuality, passed on to Mallarmé by Nerval, among other predecessors. But then what tradition is being preserved and inherited in the place of that idea? Is Mallarmé's poem abolishing the poetic tradition it inherits instead of preserving it as it ought to? Is it rather inheriting this tradition insofar as it manages to preserve poetry *as* the tearing of figure away from determined reference? And what would it mean to preserve and transmit language as the site of a kind of figural cut or tear; that is, a cut that, because it is only figural with respect to the actual lace, can become a literal cut in our ability to determine the crucial link between figure and referent? One definition of symbolism as it is articulated in this exemplary symbolist text would thus be: the literary inheritance and interrogation of a genetic and metaphoric transmission of poetic language. What dies in order to be critically examined is the unproblematical link between a metaphor and its subject or object, or between a text and its eventual reading and understanding. The "fallen trophies" mentioned in the first sonnet of the triptych also name symbolism as a collection of lifeless *tropes*, that is, texts that narrate the "fall" and detachment of metaphors from their subjects, among which can be included the common metaphor of symbolism itself as the historical period that links the corpus of romanticism to our own twentieth century.

10. For a cogent and meticulous reading of the way the poem refers constantly to the uncertain status of its own power to refer, see Hans-Jost Frey, "Zweifel und Fiktion," in *Studien über das Reden der Dichter* (Munich: Wilhelm Fink Verlag), 1986, 46–50.

The linguistic negativity, fall, or death, which becomes an issue in the lace of the first line, is then localized in the second line of "Une Dentelle" by the reference to a curious form of "doubt": "une dentelle s'abolit dans le *doute.*" But in this poem, writing is *both* the lace *and* the doubt. It is first the "lace" that contains the implicit question of the relation of figure to referent, and then the "doubt" that becomes the site where this question is made explicit in the destructive act of a tear. Writing is both figure and the place in which the figure is undone, the self-obliterating relation between the lace and the doubt. It is here, where the interrogation or "doubt" about what writing does to itself as figure or "lace" is carried to its extreme, that the lyric poem radicalizes the journalistic report of "Sauvegarde." In "Sauvegarde" the threat to writing that is being parried by an institution like *l'Académie* is considered as coming to and acting on writing from without. But in "Une Dentelle" it is the doubt that is produced in writing itself that calls into question the survival of what the poem was written to perpetuate. Mallarmé's triptych thus wonders how far it is possible to preserve and transmit the originary tear or cut that determines the social and fictional fabric of language. Who or what is left to inherit when something like the institution of writing, "that fold or somber *lace,* which contains the infinite" (370), tears itself open in the very act of its genesis and retransmission?

The same problem is posed to dramatic effect in another text about literary heritage, *La Musique et les lettres,* again, in the vocabulary of crises: "Storm, luminous cleansing; and in upheavals, due wholly to (the) generation, recent, the act of writing scrutinized itself to its very foundation . . . to the point, I would say, of wanting to know if there is any place left for writing" (645). The meaning of the formulation depends on how one reads what Mallarmé refers to as the *cause* of these stormy upheavals, "la génération, récente." Is the cause the act of generation, production in its most recent manifestation, or is it merely the latest group of contemporaneous individuals who share a given attribute? Mallarmé's phrase can be read to mean either that critical self-scrutiny is a characteristic of the turbulent new generation of (symbolist) writers, or that writing is itself the initiatory storm in which the phenomenon of generation as critical production takes place. Indeed, it must be read in both ways at once, since what distinguishes the recent generation of writers Mallarmé is talking about is their capacity to bring about, or *generate*, the question of how writing is produced. What is odd here, though, is that the condition of possibility of the "generation" of writing is simul-

taneously unsettled by its own critical examination and is thus
threatened by extinction at the moment of its inception. Again, who
or what is left for writing after writing generates itself by putting
itself into question? The question is asked once more and answered
later in the same essay. After the storm, after the explosion, Mallarmé
asks, "What is the point?" to which he answers, "A game" (647). So
too, in "Une Dentelle," the mutually exclusive relationship of the
"lace" and the "doubt" becomes the pivotal space in which a certain
kind of game is played out: "le Jeu suprême."

The game, though, is enigmatic. On the one hand, it plays for
"supreme" stakes, life and death. On the other hand, as mere game or
play, it risks going nowhere, remaining only diversion and diversion-
ary. The question, "What is the point?" can just as easily be read as a
display of frustration as a genuine inquiry. And the way this question
is worked out in "Une Dentelle" is by developing a tension we have
already seen implicit in the term "generation," for although the sonnet ends with a reference to birth or genesis, this birth seems destined
to remain only a hypothetical game, "Filial on aurait pu naître." The
term "generation," of course, as well as corollary terms like "conception" and "birth," establishes a metaphorical system in which intelligible activities of the mind, like poetry-making, are understood by
analogy to empirical sciences like biology. The question at this point
is not whether this figural system is legitimate, for this is the only
system available to us for "conceiving" of thought, but rather whether there are elements within the system itself that disrupt it beyond
recognition. In other words, is anything introduced by the "conception" that cannot be reassimilated to the literal (biological) and figurative (intelligible) meanings of birth, but that would serve instead to
"detach" the genetic figure from their intended respective meanings
of creativity and "production"? This question determines the way
commentators have reacted to an erotic dimension of the poem, implicit in the "game" of line 2 and the "bed" of line 4. The fact that this
bed is named as "eternally absent" is most often taken by the critics
as confirmation of the successful passage in the poem from the literal, sensuous locale of an erotic game to an ethereal "conception" of
poetry's supreme play.[11]

11. An interpretation made plausible by reading Mallarmé's own question as a
statement of principles: "What good would be the marvel of transposing a natural fact
["le lit," for instance] into its near vibratory disappearance according to the play of the
letter [le jeu de la parole], though, if it were not in order to derive from it, without the
nuisance of a near or concrete reminder, the pure notion" (368).

The paraphrastic commentary of the sonnet given by one of its English translators provides a good example of this sort of interpretation:

> A pair of lace curtains is blown by a breeze, wreathing around each other like lovers. There is no bed, or rather, there is an eternal absence of bed, but you can't stop two amorous curtains, not in a Mallarméan huddle, you can't! The supreme game probably refers to poetry. Now, the sestet: Here broods the dreamy poet, with his *mandore*, his instrument for making poetry, sorrowfully, in a silence that is empty. Now then, he seems to be thinking, if I could only impregnate, fertilize by parthenogenesis, as it were, myself, I could conceive, beget, sire and mother, a son of my own, a poem. Line 12 seems to mean that if he alone could do what the curtains are doing by the pane, the pane meaning also the source of light and creation, why, then he would be self-sufficient and happy.[12]

Aside from the immediate satisfaction or disappointment at having an elusively hermetic sonnet translated into such an easily comprehensible, because utterly banal, domestic scene, we should not remain oblivious to the somewhat more interesting vacillation that takes place in this passage around the game's erotic and poetic valences. The stark transition in the paraphrase from the bedroom curtains' unstoppable "amorous huddle" and the commentator's enthusiastically ejaculative, "you can't!", to the flat assertion, "the supreme game probably refers to poetry," is so wholly unprepared that one cannot help wondering why the reader does not bring the two references together. Why keep the erotic and the poetic "conception" apart unless, and perhaps in the face of some unnamed threat, it is in order to avoid identifying the initial suggestiveness of the "supreme Game" simultaneously with both poetic and amorous activity? Just as with the lace earlier, it is not possible to order the levels of meaning in the figure (in this case, poetic first, erotic second) without ignoring what the poem is doing with the figure's capacity to mean. The "Jeu" may not just be a figure that refers to both a poetic and an erotic meaning, but an actual contest, "Jeu," between two heterogeneous models of poetic language, each of which threatens to interrupt the meaning of the other.

MacIntyre's hesitation in this regard thus becomes paradigmatic

---

12. C. F. MacIntyre, *Stéphane Mallarmé: Selected Poems* (Berkeley: University of California Press, 1957), 158.

for any interpretation of the text. It traces out and then elides a threat specific to the poem's intelligibility, since by bringing the game of the solitary poet into contact with the playful huddling of amorous curtains the reading necessarily opens the door, or at least a window, to all sorts of fantastic shapes and figures; in short, to the "blasphème" that is mentioned in line 3, and that would function as a decisive lack of reverence with respect to the poem's entire program of conception.[13] For once the erotic component of the "game" in line 2 becomes apparent it then threatens to extend itself uncontrollably throughout the text and distract us from ever coming back to and understanding the poem's supposed lesson about the creative potential of poetic writing. Rather than providing a vehicle for meaning that leads directly from literal conception to poetic birth, the erotic aspect of the game may actually deflect the reading from its intended destination and take it in a completely different direction. And without the caution of a transcendental foundation or guarantor of sense, like God and its correlates light and poetry, presupposed rather than logically deduced here, this is always possible. Sex in this text, though, is not just a figure for an empirical act that diverts our attention temporarily from the serious business of poetry, since as we have seen with MacIntyre, it is always possible within this system to reunite biological productivity with poetic creativity through the metaphorical figure of conception. Sex is also the figure for what in poetic language considered as a "Jeu" between two different figural models contests the figure's own capacity to provide a meaningful link or union between biological and intelligible conception. There is always something a bit kinky about this kind of sex since, by inflecting, tearing, or perforating a state of balance and equilibrium within a unified figural system, it actually serves to reopen the question of figure and referent rather than closing it off.

In this poem, for instance, where does MacIntyre get the idea that the game is composed of a "pair" of two *different* curtains in the first

---

13. Emilie Noulet, one of Mallarmé's earliest serious readers, counsels against falling into such an impious "trap": in order to make sense of the poem the reader must resist the erotic temptation here and refer the "Jeu" uniquely to "God, generator of light and life." See, *Vingt Poèmes de Stéphane Mallarmé* (Geneva: Librairie Droz, 1967), 158. R. G. Cohn performs a similar interpretative gesture by tracing all figural registers back to the originary and procreative "light of the sun" (208–09). Leo Bersani does not see what difference such a question would make, and suggests we be satisfied to remain "in the intervals between such alternatives." See, Leo Bersani, *The Death of Stéphane Mallarmé* (Cambridge: Cambridge University Press, 1982), 71.

place? "*Une* Dentelle s'abolit," in the opening stanza, and the second stanza explicitly says, "Cet *unanime* blanc conflit / D'*une* guirlande avec *la même*." The erotic "huddle" has only *one* player; for this game the number one merely relates to itself specularly in order to constitute itself as a desirable "pair." "Conception," literal or meta-phorical, never has to become an issue, here. The opening scene, a kind of voyeuristic looking in through the lace curtain on the bed-room window—perhaps even onto Hérodiade's absent but imagined and violently desired bed—can become as graphic or pornographic as one wishes, but one has at least to recognize that the treatment of the erotic remains far from being a hymn to the marriage bed, with its attendant connotations of legitimacy and progeny. Allowing the "one" in "*Une* dentelle" and "*unanime* blanc conflit" to carry the weight of the lopsidedly erotic figure points up the "onanisme" or onanistic aspect of the game. What remains difficult to determine is whether there is more than one solitary player involved in the onanis-tic scene, a provocative alternative that "floats" between the lines juxtaposing "blanc *con*flit" to "*con*tre la *vit*re blême." In any case, it is not possible to take this game as a synthesizing figure for what we ordinarily understand to be poetic conception, generation, or creativity. What is ill-conceived and illegitimate in following the erotic game turns out to be the free play of the signifier. And this game exceeds the conventional metaphorical pattern of biological and po-etic conception of meaning by focusing attention on detached letters whose arbitrary power to signify cannot be reduced to a binary model of physical entities and conceptual ideas.

The game, then, is double, and duplicitously double at that. On the one hand, it is the articulation of the double aspect of "concep-tion" into the figural passage from natural genesis to poetic creativity. According to a classical conception of metaphor, an activity of the mind manifests itself by analogical reference to the empirical world, poetic production using genetic reproduction ("le lit") to make itself more concrete for understanding, though in such a way as to differ-entiate itself from the merely empirical in which it appears ("absence de lit"). On the other hand, the game is also that supplementary aspect of the figure, erotic elements that do not necessarily contrib-ute to reproduction, or the free play of the signifier, for instance, that get out of hand and threaten to subvert or pervert the projected "con-ception" into an absolute loss of misconception and insignificance. Something in the game's own promise of a passage, transmission, or legacy from natural to poetic understanding threatens to stand in the way and block access to the very thing that it promises. This is the risk without which the game could hardly be called supreme.

It is this element of risk that affects the "doubt" in such a way that it must now be understood not only to touch upon the figure of the lace given in line 1, but also the outcome of the supreme game referred to in line 2. In terms of the temporal thematics of transmission and legacy in the sonnet as well as in "Sauvegarde," the doubt always relates to a historical "past" as well as to a kind of undisclosed "future": the writing that interrogates the legitimacy of any received "figure" also leaves open to question the outcome for history of putting this interrogation into play. Mallarmé poses the same question with regard to the possibility of a future for his friendship with the dead Villiers: "Do we know what it means to write? . . . this senseless *game* of *writing* consists in undertaking, by virtue of a *doubt,* the task of recreating everything in order to verify that *one is* where one ought to be (since, allow me to express this apprehension, there remains an *uncertainty*)" (481, emphasis added). In the same essay, Mallarmé says of himself what he says elsewhere of the Academy; "whoever writes cuts himself off," *se retranche,* and what he cuts himself off from is everything, "integrally," Mallarmé adds. Through the operation of "doubt" the writer removes himself from all that is presumed natural, all that is previously instituted, in order to "recreate" it. That the operation of the cut is related to a past as well as to a future is made clear in the essay on Villiers where "doubt" plays over the natural and instituted world already given, but is also, in "uncertainty," a form of doubt concerning the world of the subject left in the wake of this questioning. In the more compressed framework of "Une Dentelle," the double instability and uncertainty of writing is brought out effectively by the self-splitting syntax in line 2, the locus of the "doute *du* Jeu suprême." Here the grammar, the rules of the game, contribute to produce a structure that is simultaneously retrospective and proleptic, a kind of writing that interrogates the past it has inherited, "a lace," in order to open up an unpredictable future. For, grammatically speaking, the genitive link between the doubt and the game, "le doute *du* Jeu," can be either subjective and retrospective—the doubt belongs to and is controlled by the game of writing, "the Supreme game's doubt abolishes a lace"— or objective and proleptic—the status and outcome of writing is what is cast into doubt, "a lace is rent in the doubt about the Supreme game."

What Mallarmé calls writing, the "recreation" of an uncertain future thanks to a process of "doubt" with respect to the past, is historical, not in the same sense that empirical events are historical, but in the sense that, by instituting a "cut" into the past that subjects all of its figures to doubt, writing is the condition of possibility for history conceived as a future that is opened by critical thought. "Le doute du Jeu suprême," is philosophical in nature and Cartesian in structure; it is a formalized activity of methodical doubt that reflects on everything, including itself as game, and as such it is the first step in any genuinely dialectical development of the mind. Georges Poulet is very close to the truth when, in speaking of Mallarmé's procedure, he says, "It is the act of negation through which one constitutes one's existence and thought. The Mallarmean operation is thus comparable to 'the internal operation of Descartes'. It is *ultra-Cartesian.*"[14] Poulet, of course, is commenting on *Igitur* and the narrative struggle it recounts with a philosophical heritage that ends in a form of mental suicide, but it holds for the sonnet that the nature of doubt is such that it must inevitably turn back on itself to become the doubt *about* the future of writing and thought itself. What makes Mallarmé's procedure "ultra" Cartesian in Poulet's terms, moreover, is the supreme risk it takes by putting its own rules into doubt, and once the connection with philosophical suicide has been made, it becomes impossible not to read the "Jeu" as also containing the first person pronoun, *je* or *cogito.* The Cartesion certitude of its own doubt remains sheltered from the most radical threat as long it leaves intact the form structure of the "Jeu," which unconditionally links the (doubting) consciousness to a subject. Mallarmé's concept of writing, on the other hand, asks whether this relation between consciousness and self is not perhaps a mere game. Writing, for Mallarmé, is a form of reflexive negativity so immense that after allowing all else to be put into doubt, it allows for doubting the game's grammar, the formal conditions of the self *as* doubt. That amounts to doubting doubt, to doubting the game and fabric of thought into oblivion, and to opening out onto the doubtful future of one's "own" situation: "where one ought to be . . . remains an uncertainty."

This doubt would be a truly "hyperbolic" or supreme doubt. And it can be said to operate in Mallarmé's text wherever the technical aspects of the grammar or syntax, which make the meaning possible,

---

14. Georges Poulet, *Etudes sur le temps humain 2: La Distance intérieure* (Paris: Editions du Rocher, 1952), 333.

are in themselves insufficient to determine the meaning of the poem's figures. Whether the "Jeu" refers to a philosophically serious operation of reflection (the thinking subject) or to an empirical version of self-reflection devoid of any higher meaning (represented thematically by an act of the not-so-philosophical body), the grammatical ambiguity of the "du" casts into doubt the autonomy of the subject referred to. It is not just that the "Jeu suprême" can refer, as any number of critics have noted, to *both* poetic and erotic "creativity." As we have seen, *creativity* is a loaded term that gives the game away in advance. For it subjects both dimensions of the text to a specular figure of aesthetic *and* philosophical meaning as a metaphorical model of conception and birth. Rather, in being *able* to "recreate" nongenetically, that is, from a linguistic model whose logic is no longer merely physical nor yet wholly intelligible, the "creativity" specific to both thought and the natural world, the free play in writing *necessarily* unsettles the ability of its own grammar to determine fully a reference to either. Once we notice how the uncertain grammar affects the subjective/objective status of the all-important game, "Jeu," it is difficult not to ask whether the real conflict, rather than being between the empirical and the thinking subject, is not between the subject as meaning (objectively empirical or subjectively thoughtful) and the subject as writing (the meaningless free play of the *je* as it is constituted in the purely formal rules of the "Jeu"). By making it impossible to decide on how to read the grammatical status of the genitive, Mallarmé's writing runs the risk of producing an absolutely empty, insane figure—"this senseless game (jeu) of writing."

The most effective way of parrying the threat posed by writing's hyperbolic doubt is by treating the radical openness of its outcome as though it could itself be conceived, known, and represented in advance. This would amount to anticipating it as a moment within a larger cognitive process, a moment that, for all intents and purposes, would have already taken place rather than remained to come. In order to state with any assurance that the text is "about" writing, for example, it is logically necessary to presuppose a discursive perspective or vantage point *beyond* the moment of definitional uncertainty, from which writing could become the subject of the question. "Nothing will have taken place but the place," is the way *Un Coup de dés* will have dealt with and resolved in advance the same dilemma of writing's supreme risk by anticipating a minimal place of coherent enunciation as the final result of a kind of worst case scenario for thought. When all else fails, one can always try to succeed in telling the story of the failure itself, "if only to disperse the empty act" (*Coup de dés*, 475).[15] In the essay on Villiers, as a means to shelter the writing subject from the risk of falling prey to an unthinkable "duperie bordering on suicide," Mallarmé makes reference to a mode of writing that would recuperate writing's open-ended risk. In order to pass beyond the constitutive doubt that makes it possible in the first place, writing attempts to recreate and transmit in advance the knowledge of the open-endedness of its own operation. It does so as *theater:* "One by one, each one of our conceits, to bring them forth, in their anteriority and to see" (481). Writing is capable not only of creation and production, it is also capable of bringing anything into being as though it had already taken place and could be viewed as *anteriority.* By treating the doubt of writing as though it too could be made visible, by bringing forth a sequential representation that would include even that which abolishes sequence, writing would attempt to hide from its own dubious future.

In "Une Dentelle" this is the perspective adopted in the theatrical representation of writing as a play or a game organized around the poles of light and dark, the sun and the night, knowledge and nonknowledge. Writing, "that spot of ink related to the sublime night" (481), may be what threatens to blacken or "abolish" the everyday world of minds and bodies, but it still plays itself out, at least at the beginning of the poem, on a visual, theatrical, and intelligible stage presided over by the light of a rising and setting sun of cognition. The curtain goes up— "une dentelle s'abolit"—to reveal a scene that is accessible to the eye of the spectator through the picture window of the theater. What the spectator gets to see in "Une Dentelle" is no ordinary play, however; it is rather the dawning light of philosophical reflection as it is made manifest in Mallarmé's concept of writing. Reperforming what he calls elsewhere, "the internal operation for instance of Descartes . . . joining theater and philosophy" ("Crayonné au théâtre," 319), Mallarmé's sonnet attempts to represent the philosophical dilemma of recreating the whole world through the unpredictable play of writing. The main character here, writing, acts out for all to see the play of doubt as it

15. That the "acte vide" would in this way be reduced to a mere moment that could be recuperated by narrating it retrospectively, or, on the contrary, that such a "dispersion" would serve only to disseminate the void of the act along every point of the textual line, remains to be established by a more detailed reading of the text.

grapples with and contests the world as we know it, including the natural light of the sun as well as the cognitive stability of all those philosophical concepts, like conception and birth, that use the solar system as a model. The Mallermean theater, in other words, through its own step-by-step representation of writing as though it were a character in a play that could be staged retrospectively, seeks to overcome the radical destruction of determinate and determinable representation that is involved in writing.

In writing conceived of as theater, even the destruction of sequence and intelligibility is susceptible of being anticipated and represented sequentially, "one by one," in a visible and proleptically intelligible order. In a first step of reading the sonnet, the thought that moves out to meet and transform the world through writing seems to destroy all solid entities in order to produce an intelligible figure of itself as the "absence éternelle de lit." In a second, more radical move in the same process, the negativity of the thought can be turned back on its own figures to ask whether the thinking subject is not a mere formal game, produced blasphemously by the free play of writing and devoid of any further meaning. The resulting inability to decide on the status of thought can be represented as a stalemated agon between the single-minded introspection that deprives itself of the warmth of the bed and the onanistically self-indulgent play that single-handedly reduces the poem to pure eroticism. This "blanc conflit" is then depicted sequentially in the theater as the alternating movements of a floating curtain. In so doing, however, the representation cannot avoid putting into play an aspect of figuration that necessarily enacts or recreates the undecidable openness of its own status as representation. It does so by marking the place of sequential articulation in the poem, the linking genitive in "le doute *du* Jeu suprême," as being itself undecidable by means of any sequential logic, or grammar, and thus prepares the way for the undoing of the semantic determination of a thinking (and feeling) subject in the play of the key word "*Jeu.*" For, unlike the floating of a curtain, whose movements can be brought to light one by one, the crucial relation between writing as figure and writing as the destruction of figure cannot be reduced to a linear sequence. The priority of the "doute" over the "Jeu," as well as the relation between the self as self-conscious doubt and the self as formal game, is made *simultaneously* necessary and impossible to decipher in the writing out, rather than the representation, of the poem.

As a consequence, the figure of the bed, glimmering eternally in the half-light of the first stanza's conflict between consciousness and sensuality, becomes infinitely more blasphemous when it contests both orders of experience by shading into the uncertain status of the three letters "l-i-t" that return to haunt the rhyming words of the second stanza, "conflit" and "n'ensevelit." These letters, in fact, can tell us a great deal about what Mallarmé's "doute du Jeu suprême" does to both the world of sensuous reality and the movement of thought. The wholly graphic, textual nature of the problematic "bed" that is inscribed in certain syllables of the second stanza suggests that writing neither preserves the world naturally, as a simple perception, nor does away with it conceptually through the sheer annihilating power of the mind, but rather, that it operates otherwise, through the "play" of letters, *l, i, t*, for instance, that are neither merely empirical nor conceptual, and suggestive of both at once. As typographical markings, these letters interrupt, disrupt, and keep at a certain distance both the natural, given order of things, as well as the logical transformation of this order into a systematic form of thought. The linguistic disruption is never allowed to become a total destruction and erasure of what it puts aside, since it also *marks* the interruption it enacts and in so doing reserves a certain space, a blank, for that world and its transformation into thought, however distanced, deflected, or indirect it may be.

The nature and outcome of the ensuing linguistic relationship between the mind and the world now becomes the focus of the poem's unresolved question. Because it is written rather than perceived or thought, the "eternal absence of bed" cannot be negated as easily as the natural world or the thinking subject, not without leaving a trace or remainder of its letters. Thus, Mallarmé merely points toward its disappearance in the highly qualified, blinking movement of the French verb "entrouvrir." "Entrouvrir" means "to half-open," and in this poem the figure of the lacework opens only enough to leave a space for an empirical world that cannot ever be done dying or disappearing and for a world of conceptual thought that remains unconditionally deferred or postponed. It is neither opening nor closing, but a kind of written, typographical suspension of both that hovers *between*, or *entre*. It never quite becomes the space of a fully defined and therefore *closed* opening, *ouverture*, much as the hovering apostrophe in "entr'ouvrir" marks the place of the abolished letter "e" in the French verb "entr(e)ouvrir." And this mark of the figure's erasure actually *addresses,* apostrophizes, or summons the very bed which the theatrical scene describes as eternally absent: the question of the "bed" and the entire figural world contained within it returns to haunt the second stanza by way of its written trace in words like "con*flit*" and "enseve*lit.*" For this same reason, we should be careful not to restrict the "blanc conflit" between meaning and nonmeaning to itself meaning only a uselessly meaningless or sterile form of playful activity in the text. It ought rather to be read here as a supplementary figure for the as-yet-blank or white spaces that are opened by and between the play of the letters, and in which the undecidable question of the poem's ultimate status and thus of its transmission and literary legacy, is suspended rather than merely destroyed, "ce conflit . . . flotte plus qu'il n'ensevelit."[16]

The fact that the poem doesn't end there, however, reveals how the pressure to move outside this intolerable suspension or blank of the future works in turn to suspend its undecidability at the very moment it is named as such. For everything that holds for the quatrains seems to change in the tercets, where the immanent possibility of change is signaled by the conjunctive "Mais," a pivotal term that opposes what follows to what precedes. By treating the undecidability of the quatrains as though it were a preliminary negativity that could itself eventually be negated, the oppositional logic of the "Mais" programs a reading of the tercets that would stress by contrast their positivity. The tercets seem to balance out the indecision of the quatrains through the introduction of a symmetrical set of opposing forces, valorized positively. The absent bed in the first stanza appears in the tercets as a present sleeping mandola, for instance. Linked to the bed because it is "sleeping," the dormant instrument is however able to fill the room with the promise of sexual reproduction that was originally missing or stymied. For the mandola is pregnant, its pear-shaped form is a protruding belly that suggests the hypothetical birth that will result "Selon nul *ventre* que le sien." The formal balance that is achieved by bringing the two opposed thematic moments of the sonnet together into a negative/positive synthesis, a sexual union eventually capable of giving birth to its own "Aufhebung," [*sublation*] is as perfect and aesthetically satisfying a version of the dialectical

16. For a comprehensive reading of the non-negative, suspensive character of the mark, the remark, the opening, the veil, the blank between the letters, and the supplement, Mallarmé's "writing in white," see Jacques Derrida's "La Double séance" in *La Dissémination* (Paris: Editions du Seuil, 1972).

process one can hope for in "symbolist" poetry. Thus, the "*ne pas être*" of the opening absence is filtered across the "*mais*" of the first tercet before it is picked up again in the "*fenêtre*" of line 12, and finally reechoed and sublated in the poem's final word, "*naître*." In the poem's most daring gesture, the conflictual lack of union, or *mariage blanc* of the quatrains is later overturned in the coming together under the same familial roof—*chez qui*—of the negative maternal instrument (*la mandore au creux néant*) with the paternal and personalized dreamer (*celui qui du rêve se dore*) in lines 9 and 10.

It is clear that in the movement from the quatrains to the tercets a new mode of poetic language is invoked: from poetry conceived as the critical reception and breakdown of a mimetic model of language that can be figured as *theater*, the sonnet moves toward a more positive conception of poetry as *music*.[17] Music, in this poem at least, seems able to pass beyond the problematization of writing and representation, beyond the undecidable impasse of a negative epistemology to the celebration of a liberating and positive form of art. On the thematic level, this move is represented by the replacement of the activity of philosophical "doubt" in the quatrains by that of an aesthetically creative "dream" in the tercets. The implication is that by substituting a poetry of autonomous dream for one of universal doubt, the power of language as voice and melody would somehow be able to replace and compensate for the undecidable outcome of poetic language as the critical reflection on its own statements and cognitions. The question at this point would be whether the aesthetic compensation for the suspension of philosophical self-knowledge would not itself constitute something like the "dream" of philosophy. For if it were possible to bypass the inconclusiveness of the question of language as figural representation and cognition in favor of a model of language as pure illusion, as a form of sonorous and verbal play that recognizes and rejoices in its fictional nature, then it would be possible by the same token to reintroduce the concept of philosophical certainty and truth, albeit in a negative mode, on the far side of its problematization.

Before deciding whether Mallarmé's writing does conform to this

17. Mallarmé's concept of music is not straightforward. It never appears except in a relationship to other modes of discourse, juxtaposed sometimes to theater, as in "Richard Wagner, rêverie d'un poète français," sometimes to poetry, as in "La Musique et les lettres." It is always organized around a discussion of meaning, subjectivity, history, and politics.

model, it is necessary to look more closely at the way poetry as music actually functions in the tercets. One of the most obvious places to locate an aesthetic of music is where the poetic and sonorous resources of the words break in on, supplement, or replace their representational value. This occurs throughout the poem, as we have seen in the reappearance of the epistemologically unreliable figure of the "bed" in words like "conflit" and enseve*lit*," but it is not recognized and celebrated as a positive value until language as music and dream is thematized at the end of the poem. Thus, in line 12, the very word that designates theatrical representation, *fenêtre*, breaks open and allows its individual sonorous elements to announce the birth of music that occurs in the poem's last word, "naître." The word "naître" not only *refers* to any and all extralinguistic acts of birth, physiological as well as intelligible, it also actualizes a purely intralinguistic "birth" by bringing into being a new *rhyme*, "fenêtre/naître." Beyond the critical failure to demarcate and control the limits, the birth and death as it were, of theatrical, representational language and cognition in the first part of the sonnet, there is in the tercets the musical and fictional, or nonreferential, conception and transmission of poetic language.

Of course, before it performs this promised birth in the ultimate word of the sonnet, "naître," the self-enclosed space of poetic music or rhyme is already introduced into the poem by way of the sleepy "mandore" in the first tercet:

> Mais, chez qui du rêve se *dore*
> Triste*ment dort* une *mandore*

There is nothing new in pointing out the musical self-reference at play in these lines. Almost forty years ago Emilie Noulet demonstrated the possibility of creating the fiction of a musical score or partition here by cutting into the words: thus, "triste" can be read as the tonal indication on which the dream-music should be played, the following repetition, "*ment dort, mandore,*" referring only to itself as the "murmured refrain or recitative (*mélopée*) of an ancient instrument." (*Vingt poèmes*, 162). This double internal rhyme performs a kind of symbolic or symbolist "marriage" that also signals the birth of music. On the typographic level, the lines join, unite, or marry detached elements from different word families, "*Mais*," "*dorer*," "*tristement*" and "*dormir*" to produce the aesthetic emblem of music in the final word "mandore," while on the sonorous level they actualize a musical refrain by playing on the sounds "dore ment dort mandore." The tercets seem to confirm that beyond the breakdown of a philosophical theater of reflection on language as figure and knowledge there remains the possibility of a new "symbolist" and musical reawakening. Once the instability of the referential link between the figure and the world of natural experience has been shuffled into the background, the potential of awakening the intralinguistic links between *signifiants* (the sounded letters of words) and *signifiés* ("sound" as the ultimate meaning of the letters *m-a-n-d-o-r-e*) can become a source of endless aesthetic satisfaction and creativity. Technical resources of language like rhyme seem to allow for the production and transmission of effects of adequation in the way that sounds of words (*ment dort mandore*) correspond to their meaning (the aesthetic play of music). The work thus envisages its possible transmission at the moment it declares its fictional status to be at the furthest remove from anything outside of itself.

It is also at this point that the possibility of a reconvergence of an aesthetic of music with an epistemology of narrative can be glimpsed. For if the positivity of an aesthetic of music can be conceived as the negation, as a fiction, of empirical reference and cognition, rather than as their further problematization, then it follows that this negativity can be inscribed in its turn as a temporary stage within a larger continuum. The alternating structure of opposing moments points toward a future synthesis of both negative and positive elements, a reintegration of the self-conscious choice for a nonrepresentational music in Mallarmé's "symbolism" within a larger historical scheme that could itself lay claim to cognitive dimensions unquestionably rooted in referential and representational models. This is the principal aim and interest of recent attempts at reading nonmimetic poetic texts by way of an aesthetics of reception, and the avowed project of a critic and historian like H. R. Jauss. Jauss set himself the task of showing how a history of a text's transmission and understanding is capable of reducing the distance between the formal autonomy of a work and its referential context. By treating the nonreferentiality of poetic language as though it could be located negatively in a sequence of historical reception—at the end of one model ("une Dentelle s'abolit") and the beginning of a new one ("dort une mandore")—Jauss is able to trace a genetic process that can overcome the dissolution of literature's reference to the empirical world in the aesthetic movement that stretches from Nietzsche to Apollinaire and beyond, and in which Mallarmé's work would occupy a central place. Speaking from the retrospective standpoint that recognizes the past necessity of this negative moment while denying it any further validity, he can say with absolute assurance, "In the aesthetic processes of deconstruction and reconstruction, the subject can proceed beyond the loss of its Cartesian self-sufficiency to new forms, and aesthetic experience can compensate for the supposedly irremediable loss of the world."[18] In terms of Mallarmé's sonnet, this would mean that the poet simply replaces all the epistemological uncertainties of representational language with the deliberately determined but wholly independent features of pure semiotics, "au creux néant musicien."

Jauss's interpretation, which recognizes to some extent the text's disruption of the mimetic model of narrative, is able nonetheless to maintain narrative coherence and intelligibility by reconstruing poetic production as a progressive and self-conscious *negation,* or "hollow nothingness," of representation rather than its undecidable problematization. Can it be said, however, that the program of opposing or negating the problematics of an epistemology of representation, which begins in Mallarmé's sonnet with the"Mais" of line 9, is carried through to the end of the poem by a coherent and unilateral aesthetic of music? Does the poetic lyre, or "mandore," remain aesthetically intact until such time as its autonomous song would be negated and broken in on by a historical outside whose status remains safe from such questions? The answer depends on how successful the figure of music, the mandola, is in eliminating from its aesthetic dream the doubt that impinges on the figure of the lace at the beginning of the text. The dream, as we have seen, is the adequation of poetic effects with poetic meaning, the use of poetic language to create the illusion of a play of voice and sound in rhymes that refer only to themselves as music. As mere sound that means no meaning other than its own music, poetic rhyme states itself to be a self-referential fiction, or dream, that knows its hypothetical nature. So long as it is recognized for the fiction it is, poetic music is harmless. And in this spirit, despite what the commentators have suggested, the last line of the sonnet, "Filial on aurait pu naître," should be read

---

18. H. R. Jauss, "1912: Threshold to an Epoch," *Yale French Studies 74,* (Spring 1988) 60–61. All further references will appear in the text.

as a positive affirmation of the resolutely unrealized, or fictive nature of the poet's "birth." For it is by his recognizing that the birth can only be one that always "could have been" but never was, that the musical poet of the tercets demonstrates superiority over the doubtful "Jeu" of the quatrains.

The aesthetic dream of the pure fiction, moreover, provides the means for reconsidering how the guardians of the "Book" mentioned in "Sauvegarde" could become the unwitting agents of historical and social activity. To the extent that the members of L'*Académie* choose to see themselves as fictional subjects operating within the ivory tower of aesthetics, so the story would go, they merely aestheticize reality rather than cutting themselves off from the partisan activities of the marketplace, thereby restricting themselves to playing a negative historical role within it. By turning history into a play of aesthetics, symbolist poets like Mallarmé seem to prepare and then fall prey to an inevitable collision with those aspects of empirical existence that eventually resist aesthetification, like abolitions of rights and faculties that are no longer purely figural.

But the fact that the model for language in "Sauvegarde" turns out to be the mundane dictionary rather than the sonorous dream of a musical elite should give pause, for it serves to reopen the question of poetry as music and rhyme. Could it be that rhyme, nonreferential music, is itself a fiction of sorts, a strategy used to deflect attention away from the prosaic role that rhyme might actually play in the everyday world of the dictionary? If we turn for help to the dictionary itself, we find first of all that rhyme is defined there as a "correspondence of terminal sounds of words or of lines of verse." The definition is too pragmatic to be of help to us; it begs the question of poetry's relation to music by presupposing the "dream" of bringing together aesthetic "sounds" and meaningful "words" rather than accounting for it. It proves more helpful, however, to ask about "rhythm," the poetic principle of regulated patterns, to which rhyme, as a pattern of *sounds*, is conceptually and etymologically tributary. Emile Benveniste in his essay, "La Notion de 'rythme' dans son expression linguistique," argues that the term "rhythm," contrary to common knowledge, cannot be understood by tracing its filiation to the Greek root "rheô," which names the "flowing" movement of rivers, and so cannot be presumed without further analysis to link, by way of an analogy or poetic metaphor, a phenomenal category (the repetitive motion of flowing water) with a principle of signification (the marked regularity of poetic and semantic units).[19] According to Benveniste, the phenomenal reference to the visibility of ocean waves in the case of "rhythm," and by extension the more recent reference to the perception of sound patterns in the case of "rhyme," was imposed or grafted onto a more fundamental use, which, since Plato, has been subdued and all but forgotten in favor of the later genealogy. "Rhythm," at its origin, names the concept of "form" or "figure" at its most elementary level, before there could have been anything like a "metaphor" linking the sensuous with the intelligible. Rhythm is "form" as it is assigned at a particular moment not to a preexisting entity, but to differential relations that, prior to an act of configuration, have neither phenomenal nor conceptual identity, "the form of that which has no organic consistency," states Benveniste (333).

As such, "rhythm" names the moment of an originary figuration. It is a linguistic act by which a "formal" set of relations is instituted in such a way that it can be repeated according to a preordained pattern susceptible to being recognized in its repetition. For this reason, the examples cited by Aristotle as well as by Benveniste most often refer to the disposition, arrangement, or the patterns instituted in the letters of the alphabet, the most distinctive example conceivable of a fixed, iterable, and nonorganic "form." Rhythm is neither visible like the waves of the ocean nor audible like the chirping of birds. Benveniste says in conclusion: "Nothing could be less 'natural' than this notion" (335) which as "rhythm" and "rhyme" is the mechanical reproduction of a material inscription or trace devoid of any immediate and direct relationship to the world we think we see and hear and understand. The preordained aspect of this mechanical pattern, or "rhyme," makes its operation like the grammar of a language separated from its semantic function, or like what Mallarmé refers to in "Sauvegarde" as "a branch, the nude syntax of a sentence" (418). Rhyme loses its poetic and musical aura in Mallarmé when "belles-lettres" are stripped of their aesthetic integrity and become like the "scattered words" of the dictionary. For the dictionary is not just the place where words, units of more or less stable meaning, can be found strewn about like flowers, but also and especially the place where words, as meaning, can be seen to scatter and dissolve into the subsemantic elements of their letters, which are then ordered, patterned,

19. Emile Benveniste, "La Notion du 'rythme' dans son expression linguistique," in *Problèmes de linguistique générale 1* (Paris: Gallimard, 1966) 327–35. All further references will appear in the text.

and rhymed mechanically, like an empty grammar or a nude syntax, from *a* to *z*.[20]

The implications for our reading are considerable. If the link between rhyme and music is not naturally musical like the sounds of the voice, but is rather grammatical and inscriptional like the letters of the alphabet, then it cannot be said that the musical model of language proposed in the tercets of "Une Dentelle" is any different from the undecidable inscription that operates in the quatrains. Instead, vocalized language is an unwarranted representation of the system of voiceless inscription or notation that was there all along, though hidden, sleeping, in the "belles-lettres" of the "mandore." It would therefore not be any more exempt from the kind of questioning that occurs around the torn figure of the lace. Nor would it be possible to subscribe to a reading, which, like that of Jauss, relies implicitly on polar models to reduce poetic effects like rhyme to an aesthetic phenomenon in order to promise historical coherence and understanding on the far side of their problematization. On the contrary, by writing out the attempt to move away from the situation of doubt inscribed in the quatrains to the self-enclosed dream of aesthetics in the tercets, Mallarmé's text anticipates its aesthetic reception in order to warn against it. But what evidence is there that Mallarmé's text does not share the dream of rhyme as a simple metaphorical correspondence between sounds (aesthetics) and words (meaning)? At what point, to use the terms of "Sauvegarde," does the poem state that the link between language and the empirical world is "fictive," though in such a way that it does not automatically fall prey to this as an aesthetic fiction and so does not prevent itself from occurring in a different mode?

These questions, with their insistence on inaugurating a difference within a signifying system of relationships already in place, bring us back to the problem of literary heritage. It is now clear that whatever can be born in this poem must be born out of the womb or *ventre* of music, "Selon nul ventre que le sien." As we have seen, this music is

20. Two remarkable examples of this effect in Mallarmé are "Le Sonnet en yx," where the inexistent "ptyx" is needed for its letters to fill out the rhyme scheme, and "Le Démon de l'analogie," where the nongenetic, mechanical production of meaning from the dispersal of letters becomes the source of the allegorical narrative. The most apodictic statement of this can be found in "La Musique et les lettres": "A man who has retained a piety for the twenty-four letters . . . as well as a sense for their symmetries . . . possesses a doctrine as well as a country . . . our fund and foundation, that legacy, spelling" (646).

language as rhyme, language as the repetition of an arbitrary act of form-giving to what has neither determinate meaning nor sensuous form, like the nude letters of the alphabet. The "form" of letters is not determined metaphorically as a sonorous or visible manifestation of an inner content, the way the human voice and body can be taken to be the mere forms of an inner mind or soul. The letters of the alphabet by themselves cover nothing and mean nothing. They are a "creux néant" whose only "form" is the legibility they acquire by means of a conventional system of markings in which each one differs from all the others, constituting ultimately that "total rhythm, which would be the poem silenced, in the blanks" (367). However, as the reading also disclosed, rhyme immediately produces an aesthetic version of this blank birth that serves as a shelter from the knowledge of its constitutive dependence on the unpredictable play of the letter. It does so by representing itself as a negative moment within a natural genealogy linking meaning to phenomenal categories by way of a determined relation to sound. Rhyme as music recovers the certainty of sound by negating itself as semiotic representation and by presupposing a direct relationship to empirical reality. But the poem has shown that the assumption of an immediate relation to the empirical world is a fiction that has forgotten its fictional nature. Such fictions, or ideologies, attempt to parry the more radical fiction of rhyme as letters, which fiction is the a priori act of having instituted any relationship whatsoever between the nude syntax of the alphabet and either sound or meaning. When Mallarmé says that social relations, society, and by implication the state, are a "fiction," he does not mean that they are not real, far from it. Rather, he means that society is always based on some sort of minimal linguistic operation of form-giving or "rhyme" prior to any determination of binary oppositions. Therefore, the irreducibly poetic element in the production of a society or state must remain "mysterious," must fall outside the reach of an analysis derived solely from the opposition between the phenomenal and the intelligible since that logic is a result of the very forces it would analyze.

The surprise in "Une Dentelle" is what happens when "music" actually makes its appearance in the tercets. For the locus of its birth, the "ventre," not only follows a self-deluding aesthetic program through its reference to the purely phenomenal space of the mandola's sound box. This space, thanks to its visible similarity to a woman's pregnant belly, also manages to reintroduce the theatricality of a traditional "son et lumière" spectacle by infusing the end of the poem with a golden hue: "se dore une mandore." In addition, though, the term "ventre" occurs as and gives birth to an unpredictable and impersonal effect by way of its letters. And the *letters* of the word "ventre," rather than the sound or shape of the musical instrument it refers to, reinscribe an earlier moment of the poem. This is the moment of writing's undecidable doubt and half-opening in the quatrains: "A *n'entr'*ouvrir / *n*ul *ventre*." The word "ventre" can thus be said to reintroduce the problematic rhythm of the quatrains, the silent rhythm that dislocates the aesthetic program of a purely sonorous rhyme. For "entr'ouvrir," it will be recalled, is the place in the quatrains where writing is not resolved into the symmetrical polarities and specular valorizations of the sensuous ("le lit" as eros) and the intelligible ("le lit" as concept). Rather it results in a typographical suspension, the apostrophe of "entr'ouvrir." The apostrophe stands for language's power of figuration, its power to call forth and relate in their dialectical opposition a phenomenal and intelligible "world." But language produces this figure by instituting diacritical marks or letters (*l-i-t*, for instance), which can themselves never be reduced to mere figures, since the text they write out is neither simply present nor absent, neither subjective nor objective. Far from negating the critical question of figuration by substituting for it the dream space of poetic solipsism or subjectivity, the reinscription of the rhyming letters (*entr'*) in the womb of the tercets' music (*ventre*) shows that the aesthetic dream, whether valorized negatively or positively, is always blind (or deaf) to effects of the letter which remain beyond its own power to explain or elude.

We cannot dismiss (or celebrate) the poem for embracing an aesthetic and subjective program that it takes such pains to interrogate and interrupt.[21] The kind of birth "Une Dentelle" alludes to must be understood on a different, linguistic model, if it is to take place at all. It could be prepared only by first going back to the fiction of a determinate relation between letters and sound and meaning rather than

21. The poem itself always knows how to read an aesthetics of subjectivity, and at the very moment the rhyme wakes up the sleeping letters in poetry's belly, it puts the subjective figure of the poet (or the inattentive reader) back to sleep by showing how the music here has nothing to do with subjective self-indulgence or stoicism. Whether it is the artist lost in a dream-world of self-sufficiency or the critic who thinks he can observe with impunity and then redeem such a dreaming artist, the golden sound of the aesthetic instrument is the same from the anaesthetic point of view of the letters: the play of letters is forever poised above the lullaby of subjectivity in which new rhymes spell out the threat implicit in "ment dort une mandore" / "m'endort une mandore."

by blindly turning away from it. Such a birth, by returning to the wholly arbitrary and mechanical power of rhyme to cut into the semantic unity of music's "womb" (*ventre*), could only occur by somehow waking to repeat—that is, in a mode that defies absolute difference as well as mere identity—the originary and open-ended act of figuration instituted by the letter. Such a waking is entrusted to specters who are also readers, those men and women of the Academy who safeguard the dictionary and the rhythm of its letters by overseeing the detached metaphors already scattered there as well as the unheard-of combinations to come. To the extent that they cut themselves off from a mere dream of autonomous meaning by watching over the unpredictable play of language, they reproduce its original possibility, though in such a way that its meaning remains undecidable, a legacy to a pure future. "Filial on aurait pu naître" must thus be read not only to mean that one could have been born but wasn't, but also that one might have been born without yet knowing it.

Contributors

KATHRYN ASCHHEIM is Lecturer in French at Yale University.

E. S. BURT, Associate Professor of French at the University of California, Irvine, is the author of a forthcoming book on Rousseau's autobiographies.

PAUL DE MAN was Sterling Professor in Comparative Literature and French at Yale University until his death in 1983. *Critical Writings* is the most recent of his posthumous publications.

JACQUES DERRIDA is Directeur d'Etudes at the Ecole des Hautes Etudes en Sciences Sociales (Paris) and also teaches at the University of California, Irvine. Coordinator of the mission charged with the founding of the Collège International de Philosophie, he was elected its director from 1983 to 1984. Two volumes of his writings on institutions are forthcoming.

DEBORAH ESCH teaches English at the University of Toronto and is the author of *Senses of the Past* (forthcoming University of Minnesota Press). She is coeditor with Thomas Keenan of two collections of essays on politics and institutions by Jacques Derrida, *Institutions of Philosophy* (forthcoming Harvard University Press) and *Negotiations* (forthcoming University of Minnesota Press).

ALICE YAEGER KAPLAN teaches at Duke University. She is the author of *Reproductions of Banality: Fascism, Literature and French Intellectual Life* and of *Relevé des sources et citations dans "Bagatelles pour un massacre."*

THOMAS KEENAN teaches English at Princeton University and is working on a book entitled *Fables of Responsibility*. He is coeditor of Paul de Man's *Wartime Journalism* (University of Nebraska Press) and *Responses* (University of Nebraska Press).

276

RICHARD KLEIN teaches French literature at Cornell University. He is the author of several essays on Nuclear Criticism.

PATRIZIA LOMBARDO is Associate Professor of French and Director of Cultural Studies at the University of Pittsburgh. She is the author of *Edgar Poe et la modernité: Breton, Barthes, Derrida, Blanchot* and *The Three Paradoxes of Roland Barthes*. She is completing a monograph on Taine.

KEVIN NEWMARK teaches at Yale University. He has recently completed *Beyond Symbolism: History and Figuration in Nerval, Mallarmé, Proust, Gide, Blanchot,* and *de Man,* and is currently working on the concept of irony from Schlegel to Benjamin.

THOMAS PEPPER, a doctoral candidate in Comparative Literature at Yale University, is completing a dissertation on Derrida, de Man, and Blanchot as readers of Heidegger.

BARBARA SPACKMAN is Associate Professor of Comparative Literature and Italian at the University of California, Irvine. She is the author of *Decadent Genealogies: The Rhetoric of Sickness from Baudelaire to D'Annunzio.*

JANIE VANPÉE is Assistant Professor of French at Smith College. She has published on Greuze and Rousseau.

ANDRZEJ WARMINSKI teaches Comparative Literature at the University of California, Irvine. He is the author of *Readings in Interpretation: Hölderlin, Hegel, Heidegger.*

SAMUEL WEBER is Professor of English and Comparative Literature at the University of California, Los Angeles. His most recent book is *Institution and Interpretation.*

The following issues are available through **Yale University Press,** Customer Service Department, 92A Yale Station, New Haven, CT 06520.

63 The Pedagogical Imperative:
   Teaching as a Literary Genre
   (1982) **$14.95**
64 Montaigne: Essays in Reading
   (1983) **$14.95**
65 The Language of Difference:
   Writing in QUEBEC(ois)
   (1983) **$14.95**
66 The Anxiety of Anticipation
   (1984) **$14.95**
67 Concepts of Closure
   (1984) **$14.95**
68 Sartre after Sartre
   (1985) **$14.95**

69 The Lesson of Paul de Man
   (1985) **$14.95**
70 Images of Power:
   Medieval History/Discourse/
   Literature
   (1986) **$14.95**
71 Men/Women of Letters:
   Correspondence
   (1986) **$14.95**
72 Simone de Beauvoir:
   Witness to a Century
   (1987) **$14.95**
73 Everyday Life
   (1987) **$14.95**

74 Phantom Proxies
   (1988) **$14.95**
75 The Politics of Tradition:
   Placing Women in French
   Literature
   (1988) **$14.95**
   Special Issue: After the
   Age of Suspicion: The
   French Novel Today
   (1989) **$14.95**
76 Autour de Racine:
   Studies in Intertextuality
   (1989) **$14.95**
77 Reading the Archive: On
   Texts and Institutions
   (1990) **$14.95**

Special subscription rates are available on a calendar year basis (2 issues per year):

Individual subscriptions **$22.00**   Institutional subscriptions **$25.90**

- -

ORDER FORM   Yale University Press, 92A Yale Station, New Haven, CT 06520

Please enter my subscription for the calendar year
☐ **1989 (Special Issue and No. 76)**   ☐ **1990 (Nos. 77 and 78)**   ☐ **1991 (Nos. 79 and 80)**

I would like to purchase the following individual issues:

_____

_____

For individual issues, please add postage and handling:
Single issue, United States   **$1.50**   Single issue, foreign countries   **$2.00**
Each additional issue   **$.50**   Each additional issue   **$1.00**
Connecticut residents please add sales tax of 7½%.

Payment of $ _____ is enclosed (including sales tax if applicable).

Mastercard no. _____

4-digit bank no. _____ Expiration date _____

VISA no. _____ Expiration date _____

Signature _____

SHIP TO: _____

_____

_____

- -

See the next page for ordering issues 1–59 and 61–62. **Yale French Studies** is also available through Xerox University Microfilms, 300 North Zeeb Road, Ann Arbor, MI 48106.

The following issues are still available through the **Yale French Studies** Office, 2504A Yale Station, New Haven, CT 06520.

19/20 Contemporary Art $3.50
   23 Humor $3.50
   33 Shakespeare $3.50
   35 Sade $3.50
   38 The Classical Line $3.50
   39 Literature and
          Revolution $3.50
   40 Literature and Society:
          18th Century $3.50
   41 Game, Play, Literature
          $5.00
   42 Zola $5.00

   43 The Child's Part $5.00
   44 Paul Valéry $5.00
   45 Language as Action $5.00
   46 From Stage to Street $3.50
   47 Image & Symbol in the
          Renaissance $3.50
   49 Science, Language, & the
          Perspective Mind $3.50
   50 Intoxication and
          Literature $3.50
   53 African Literature $3.50
   54 Mallarmé $5.00

   57 Locus: Space, Landscape,
          Decor $6.00
   58 In Memory of Jacques
          Ehrmann $6.00
   59 Rethinking History $6.00
   60 Cinema/Sound $6.00
   61 Toward a Theory of
          Description $6.00
   62 Feminist Readings: French Texts/
          American Contexts $6.00

Add for postage & handling

Single issue, United States $1.00
Each additional issue $.50

Single issue, foreign countries $1.50
Each additional issue $.75

- -

YALE FRENCH STUDIES, 2504A Yale Station, New Haven, Connecticut 06520

A check made payable to YFS is enclosed. Please send me the following issue(s):

Issue no.	Title	Price
_____	_____	_____
_____	_____	_____
_____	_____	_____
	Postage & handling	_____
	Total	_____

Name _____

Number/Street _____

City _____ State _____ Zip _____

The following issues are now available through Kraus Reprint Company, Route 100, Millwood, N.Y. 10546.

  1 Critical Bibliography of
       Existentialism
  2 Modern Poets
  3 Criticism & Creation
  4 Literature & Ideas
  5 The Modern Theatre
  6 France and World Literature
  7 André Gide
  8 What's Novel in the Novel
  9 Symbolism
 10 French-American Literature
       Relationships

 11 Eros, Variations...
 12 God & the Writer
 13 Romanticism Revisited
 14 Motley: Today's French Theater
 15 Social & Political France
 16 Foray through Existentialism
 17 The Art of the Cinema
 18 Passion & the Intellect, or
       Malraux
 21 Poetry Since the Liberation
 22 French Education
 24 Midnight Novelists

 25 Albert Camus
 26 The Myth of Napoleon
 27 Women Writers
 28 Rousseau
 29 The New Dramatists
 30 Sartre
 31 Surrealism
 32 Paris in Literature
 34 Proust
 48 French Freud
 51 Approaches to Medieval
       Romance
 52 Graphesis

36/37 Structuralism has been reprinted by Doubleday as an Anchor Book.
55/56 Literature and Psychoanalysis has been reprinted by Johns Hopkins University Press, and can be ordered through Customer Service, Johns Hopkins University Press, Baltimore, MD 21218.